MIDWEST MARVELS

MIDWEST MARVELS

Roadside Attractions across Iowa,
Minnesota, the Dakotas, and Wisconsin

Eric Dregni

University of Minnesota Press
Minneapolis • London

Published by the University of Minnesota Press
111 Third Avenue South, Suite 290
Minneapolis, MN 55401-2520
http://www.upress.umn.edu

Composition by Wilsted & Taylor Publishing Services

Library of Congress Cataloging-in-Publication Data

Dregni, Eric, 1968–
    Midwest marvels : roadside attractions across Iowa, Minnesota, the Dakotas, and Wisconsin /
    Eric Dregni.
        p.   cm.
    Includes bibliographical references.
    ISBN-13: 978-0-8166-4290-8 (pbk. : alk. paper)
    ISBN-10: 0-8166-4290-7 (pbk. : alk. paper)
    1. Middle West—Description and travel. 2. Middle West—History, Local. 3. Roadside
architecture—Middle West. 4. Historic sites—Middle West. 5. Curiosities and wonders—
Middle West. 6. Automobile travel—Middle West. I. Title.
    F355.D74 2006
    977—dc22

                                                                                2006010386

Printed in the United States of America on acid-free paper.

The University of Minnesota is an equal-opportunity educator and employer.

12 11 10 09 08 07 06   10 9 8 7 6 5 4 3 2 1

CONTENTS

MINNESOTA

NORTH DAKOTA

SOUTH DAKOTA

WISCONSIN

AUTHOR'S NOTE

After weeks of criss-crossing the Upper Midwest in search of sites, I have discovered some of the best. But these attractions change: sculptures burn (as in the case of Frazee's turkey) or are dumped in a landfill (as with Xanadu: Foam House of Tomorrow at the Wisconsin Dells), or another "World's Largest" is surpassed. Keep me informed about changes, recommendations, or missed roadside attractions—there are many more fish statues out there!

Eric Dregni
P. O. Box 6381
Minneapolis, MN 55406
ericdregni@yahoo.com

PREFACE

With my stomach in the sand and the sun beating down, I'm peering up through my camera lens at an enormous fiberglass sculpture to get the absolute best angle. A man looks down at me and asks, "What are you doing? Why do you want a picture of this old thing?"

I sit up, brush the dirt off my shirt, and explain that this is the very important "World's Largest" such-and-such. I've driven for hours to see this statue up close. "See, I'm writing a book on unusual sites around the Midwest," I say, as if that explains everything.

"Well, you've certainly picked a weird one. I drive by this darn thing every day, and I could never figure out why they put it here." Then he tells me about a crazy guy in town who collects a "bunch of junk." With this tip, I'm off on my next adventure.

It's not easy convincing a passenger in my car to drive an extra day in scorching South Dakota heat to follow up on a vague rumor about a mini museum of outhouses. Or driving four extra hours in extreme allergy country to see a big cob of corn mounted on the roof of a rest stop. Finding an undiscovered oddity, however, makes my heart beat with excitement as I pray that my camera won't jam.

The tips might be excruciatingly vague: "Just turn off on exit 491, you won't regret it." What's there to see? "Trust me," is the response, leading me immediately not to. Or the advice about a not-to-be-missed site is, "Oh, there's just a bunch of characters. You'll have a blast."

This book is the result of these countless hours searching for the biggest, the smallest, the oddest, the most mysterious, and the one and only. The folks who have created these marvels are not normal, thank God. They have followed their passion, whether it's wrapping twine, stacking cans, or sipping vinegar. Locals may scorn them as kooks, crazies, or even "satanic pornographers." In spite of it all, they have persevered, and often they aren't appreciated until after death. These are the people who add character to our towns; these are the people who make living in the Midwest worth it.

ACKNOWLEDGMENTS

To David Arnott, for scoping out the B-52 Stratofortress; Sigrid Arnott, for convincing me about the runestone; Capo Dregni (traveling companion extraordinaire), Ma Dregni, John Dregni, and Michael Dregni; Hans Eisenbeis, for telling me about the underwear stash; Ruthann Godollei; Mary Healy; Scott "Starfire" Lunt; Piccola Katy, for putting up with Iowa and everything else; Megan Mullally; Todd Orjala; Dennis Pernu, for the latest on the hockey stick; Carmen Regner and Jackie Starbird, for the skinny on the fat Roman warrior; Kaia Svien, for info on the admiral; Margaret Tehven, for leading me to what we thought was an incorruptible; Mark Vesley; Andrea Vinje, for NoDak sites; John and Nick of the Stardüsters, for the soundtrack to Düluth; and Chris Welsch, for leading me to the grottoes.

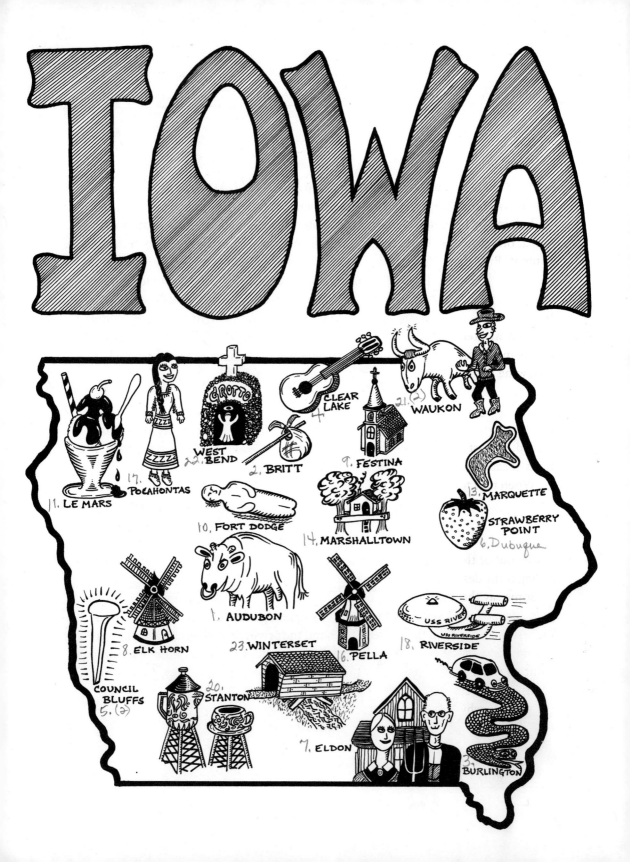

IOWA

11. LE MARS

17. POCAHONTAS

22. WEST BEND

2. BRITT

4. CLEAR LAKE

21.(2) WAUKON

9. FESTINA

13. MARQUETTE

STRAWBERRY POINT

6. Dubuque

10. FORT DODGE

14. MARSHALLTOWN

1. AUDUBON

8. ELK HORN

23. WINTERSET

16. PELLA

18. RIVERSIDE

USS RIVER
USS RIVERSIDE

COUNCIL BLUFFS
5. (2)

20. STANTON

7. ELDON

3. BURLINGTON

IOWA

"Is this heaven?" Ray Liotta asked in the 1989 film *Field of Dreams*.

"No, it's Iowa," responded Kevin Costner.

Judging by the beautiful farms in a state where 90 percent of the land is cultivated, one would assume that this is indeed some sort of paradise where all are content. But this wouldn't explain why a thirty-foot-tall talking bull was erected in Audubon or why a square block in West Bend is covered with cement arches and chilling caves plastered with semiprecious stones. Perhaps Iowans believe that heaven can be improved upon.

Even in prehistoric Iowa, the early Woodland Indians added their improvements in the form of enormous effigy mounds of spirit birds that measured 212 feet, wing tip to tip.

When European settlers took over the land, they had visions of utopia. The "Community of True Inspiration" dreamed of perfect communal living with no capitalistic personal property in their Amana Colonies. When the ideal was discarded, at least the colonies enhanced their slice of heaven by serving hearty portions of sauerkraut and Wiener schnitzel.

When new towns formed in Iowa, inventions followed. The Fenelon Place Elevator was built in Dubuque by J. K. Graves, who was tired of walking uphill. The Squirrel Cage Jail in Council Bluffs was constructed so wardens could relax and watch the inmates spin by. Snake Alley in Burlington was created to avoid going a mile out of the way to climb a bluff. Necessity may breed invention, but just as strong is the desire to relax and enjoy life.

Some say there's something in the water, but perhaps there's something in the pigs. Maybe Iowa's status as the country's largest pork producer translates to the highest literacy rate in the United States and the privilege of kingmaker status during the Iowa caucuses. This pork-fueled get-up-and-go inspired little Stanton to paint its water tower like a coffee pot and Riverside to proclaim itself the future birthplace of a starship captain.

After all, why lollygag in a perfect paradise when there are so many strange sites to see?

1

Push the button and Albert the Bull pronounces, "I am about nine times the size of a normal Hereford, and authentic right down to my toenails. . . . Please drive carefully!"

Albert the Bull
World's Largest Anatomically Correct Bull

As a "monument to the beef industry," the citizens of Audubon created a cow. Broken windmills were salvaged and bent into the shape of a bull towering thirty feet tall and stretching fifteen feet wide at the horns. This steel frame was covered with coats of concrete and gallons of brown and white paint.

While most bulls are castrated to turn them into steers with the leftovers fueling Rocky Mountain prairie oyster banquets, Audubon's bovine was left with his cement testicles intact to become the World's Largest Anatomically Correct Bull.

Push a button at the base and hear Albert lecture on the finer points of the local beef biz and boast about his stint in Tinseltown: "I went to Hollywood and can be seen in the film *Beethoven's Third*. I have been featured in several national magazines including *Home & Away* and *Midwest Living*. I was even a question on *Jeopardy*."

The forty-five-ton bull assumed the name of the president of the local Audubon State Bank, Albert Kruse, who dreamed up Operation T-Bone. This weeklong beef promotion loaded up trains with fifty carloads of cattle and nearly as many Audubon ranchers. Destination: Chicago stockyards to sell their steers.

That party has since been shortened to a one-day event with nearly everyone in town decked out in Western garb. There's no word yet if Audubon has been able to convince local-boy-made-good C. W. McCall, the musician who penned the seventies' smash trucking hit "Convoy," to come back to wax poetic about Operation T-Bone. The town hasn't waited around for this CB-talking hero to return their calls, however, and has mass-produced little statuettes of the big bull to promote the pride of Audubon.

Albert, the blue-eyed bovine, has stood as a monument to the beef industry since 1963. The mere vision of this "perfect Hereford bull" encourages hungry passersby to crave beef and hopefully stop in Audubon for a juicy steak supper after saying grace and giving thanks to the cow.

→ *World's Largest Anatomically Correct Bull,* Albert the Bull Campground and Park, Stadium Drive and East Division. From I-80, take exit 60 north onto Highway 71 for sixteen miles. Albert is on the right (east) side of the road just before downtown.

While in the Area

Just ten miles south of Albert the Bull lies a historical curiosity dating back more than a century and a half. As soon as the call to defend the Union was heard in the north, a farmer in Exira rested his plow against a little oak, packed his grip, and enlisted that very day—or at least that's how the story goes. The war that killed more Americans than any other also took the life of this loyal Iowan. The sapling that supported his plow, however, grew tall and eventually enveloped the large metal blade. This accidental Civil War monument is more moving than any plaque or statue as the oak ages and continues to swallow the metal blade into its bark. The Plow-in-the-Tree is one mile south of Exira in the five-acre Oak Park on the west side of Highway 71.

BRITT

Hobo Museum
Wanderers Welcome!

Open the door of the Hobo Museum and prepare to be confronted with "Hi! I'm a former Britt Hobo Queen! I'm just going out for a bit, but our lovely young guide here will give you a great tour of our Hobo Museum." On the day I visited, the former Hobo Queen then walked out onto Main Street and into the humid heat wave sweeping the state.

Who was that? They call her Squirrelly Shirley; she won the crown a few years ago and is very proud of it, rightly so.

The people of Britt, Iowa, don't view the hobo lifestyle as any reason to be ashamed. In fact, the wandering life of hopping freights coast to coast is glorified once a year with Hobo Day, an occasion on which nearly everyone in town dresses down.

According to a caption that accompanies early photographs in the Hobo Museum, the first National Hobo Convention gathered here in 1900 "upon the invitation of several Britt businessmen. . . . What began with a homeless soldier and a hoe became a special brotherhood of travelers." Originally, most of the townspeople weren't quite so thrilled about having a bunch of tramps converge on their little Iowa town, so the convention was put on indefinite hiatus. Then when the Great Depression teamed up with the Dust Bowl, thousands more were flung out onto the streets. Partly as a political statement to help the down-on-their-luck, Britt revived the National Hobo Convention in 1933 to say *No, thank you, Herbert Hoover.* Hundreds of hoboes hopped off the freight cars and converged on Main Street. They've been coming back every year since.

Amid the carnival atmosphere, residents of Britt dress as vagabonds and hang out with real ones in the "Hobo Jungle," complete with an old railroad boxcar in the town park. Free mulligan stew is cooked up for anyone who pops by. Back in

5

Thanks to the Hobo Museum, the Chief Theater has survived and provides a home for this collection of rovers' treasures.

Connecticut Slim probably never looked as dapper as
this department store mannequin with the jaunty tilted
Borsalino and ironed attire.

1934, Scoopshovel Scottie made such good hobo stew that he was crowned King of
the Hoboes.

Another member of the hobo royalty, Hi-way Johnny Weaver, even penned a
published song about his love of the hobo capital, entitled "On Britt's Old Main
Street." This and other ballads of life on the road are sung late into the night every
year during the National Hobo Convention, held the second week of August.

Along with welcoming these vagabonds, Britt set up a museum in the beautiful
old Chief Theater that attempts to dispel misconceptions about freight hoppers.

An August 23, 1900, front-page article from the snooty *Minneapolis Journal* carries a cartoon denigrating hoboes; a card in the museum next to the image criticizes the artist, who "thinking he was clever brought public hate toward men who were just getting by." A hobo is described as not "a vagrant or a tramp"—even though the dictionary lists them as synonyms—"but is defined as someone who is willing to work to pay his or her keep, but continues to travel."

Inside the museum, learn about famous hoboes such as Hardrock Kid, Fry Pan Jack, Mountain Dew, and Connecticut Slim, who is portrayed as a slick department store mannequin with pressed garb. Near the dolled-up dummy is a typed proclamation that the newly dubbed King—and probably Queen—must read aloud to pledge allegiance to the hoboes' code of conduct: "King's Pledge: I, the King of the Hoboes, solemnly pledge that I will uphold the constitution of the weary Willies of the Road. . . . I, furthermore, promise not to throw bricks through windows." Or perhaps the credo of the museum is summed up by a little patch for sale at the counter: "Hoboz Are People Too."

➜ *Hobo Museum,* 51 Main Avenue, (641) 843-9104. From I-35, take exit 194 onto Highway 18 going west (toward Clear Lake). Drive about twenty-six miles and turn left (south) into town on Main Avenue (Highway 111). Look for the marquee of the old Chief Theater downtown on the east side of Main. Open May through August. Closed weekends.

Snake Alley

"Crookedest Street in the World"

The steep hills along the Mississippi posed a problem for city planners of river towns, especially for Iowa's first capital, Burlington. Wealthy inhabitants of the mansions high on the hill had to weave down roads far out of their way to get downtown.

Three men of German heritage—a city engineer, a paving contractor, and an

Twisty Snake Alley used an experimental technique of tilted cobblestones so that horses' hooves could get better traction up the steep hill.

architect—didn't let the fifty-eight-foot drop of Heritage Hill bar their way into town. In 1894, this Teutonic team sculpted a shortcut street from downtown that winds up a near cliff with five half curves and two quarter curves until it finally reaches the precipice. The trio incorporated Old World knowledge about how to build on a hill; as the sign at the site proclaims, it's "reminiscent of vineyard paths in France and Germany and reflects the city's ethnic heritage."

Nicknamed "Snake Alley," this winding road was an experimental street design at the time, with bricks tilted nearly flat to allow better footing for horses trotting on the incline. Its designers galloped horses up the hill in "test drives" to see if the steeds made it without being winded. Once cars came to town, dealers zoomed up and down the street to show off their horseless carriages and terrify prospective buyers in the passenger seat.

Ripley's Believe It or Not dubbed Snake Alley the "Crookedest Street in the World," which, of course, put this Iowa landmark in the running with San Francisco's famous Lombard Street. Snake Alley, however, is a working road, so residents needn't fend off tourists to zip up the 275 feet of street to their homes on the hill.

→ *Snake Alley,* Sixth Street between Columbia and Washington, (800) 82RIVER. From I-34, take the North Main Street exit (the closest one to the Mississippi). Go south of the interstate on Main for two blocks. Turn right (west) on Columbia Street and drive up the hill for four blocks. Snake Alley is on the left (south) winding down the hill as a continuation of North Sixth Street.

Surf Ballroom
The Day the Music Died

Rock 'n' roll seemed doomed in the late 1950s. Pat Boone in his white bucks and Frankie Avalon with his disarming smile watered down this new music form to be white-bread sugary-sweet pop music sapped of rebellion to which even adults could slowly tap their toes. Disgrace struck when Jerry Lee Lewis married his thirteen-year-old cousin in 1958, the same year Elvis Presley was drafted into the army and shipped to Germany, where he met fourteen-year-old Priscilla Beaulieu.

The Surf Ballroom has undergone many facelifts, from its big-band heyday in the 1920s with Glenn Miller to the Buddy Holly rockabilly décor of the late 1950s.

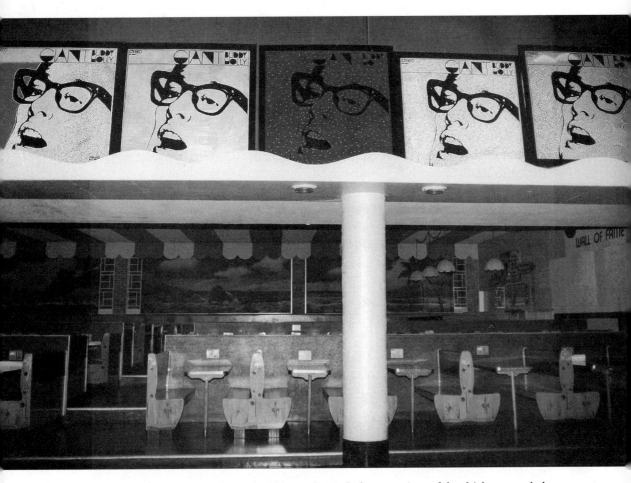

Buddy Holly has been immortalized in Andy Warholesque prints of the thick-spectacled minstrel who died in an Iowa field.

Then three musicians, Buddy Holly, Ritchie Valens, and J. P. "The Big Bopper" Richardson, brought back the beat and the danger. At just twenty-two years old, Charles Hardin Holley, a.k.a. Buddy Holly, led the bunch with his hits "That'll Be the Day" and "Peggy Sue." Having performed as a country musician earlier in the fifties, Holly incorporated the heavy beat of rock 'n' roll to become the new reigning king while Elvis was busy soldiering.

Together with Valens and Richardson, Holly and his band, the Crickets, stopped for a gig on February 2, 1959, at the Surf Ballroom in Iowa. This venue once hosted the likes of Les Brown, Glenn Miller, and Lawrence Welk but now was turned upside down by these young upstarts. After the show, the three musicians boarded a little puddle jumper to fly to their next gig. The plane crashed into a cornfield in northern Iowa, and rock 'n' roll was changed forever.

A couple of years later, four unknown British musicians formed a band inspired by Buddy Holly. In paying homage to the dead rocker from Lubbock, Texas, these young Brits changed their name from "The Quarrymen" to another insect name in honor of the Crickets. "The Beetles" was originally suggested by Stuart Sutcliffe (the "fifth Beatle"), but John Lennon added an "a," claiming he'd received a vision of a man atop a flaming pie who presented the name to them. In 1958, while still the Quarrymen (without Ringo), the band recorded Buddy Holly's "That'll Be the Day," which is now a valuable collector's item. Taking Holly's lead, the Beatles reinvigorated rock 'n' roll and led the "British Invasion" of the United States with their moptops in their eyes and Rickenbacker guitars wailing.

Another homage to that day in Iowa came in 1971. Don McLean penned his eight-and-a-half-minute song, "American Pie," about the "Father, Son, and Holy Ghost" (Holly, Valens, and Richardson) and immortalized the "day the music died" in the chorus of this oft-analyzed song. In 2000, Madonna remade this number one hit but omitted many of its verses, perhaps reasoning that no modern pop song can be so long with her audience's dwindling patience.

Today, the Surf Ballroom retains the classic wooden booths and pineapple motif of the 1950s décor of the last concert. In the ballroom, portraits of Buddy Holly in silk-screened colors à la Andy Warhol hang high opposite the stage. Old black-and-white glossies are framed on the walls at the entrance, including past performers from the Four Seasons to Pat Benatar. Upcoming revival concerts when I stopped by included Michael McDonald, Ted Nugent, and Alice Cooper.

To commemorate the second of February 1959, mourners meet at the crash site six miles off the road outside of town. Others congregate in the Surf for the "Winter Dance Party," held every Groundhog's Day in honor of these great musicians, and figure out all the hidden references in "American Pie."

→ *Surf Ballroom and Café,* 460 North Shore Drive, (515) 357-6151. From I-35, take exit 194 onto Highway 18 going west toward Clear Lake. After one and a half miles, turn left onto Buddy Holly Place for a quarter mile and then right onto North Shore Drive. The ballroom is on the right (northeast) side of the road.

5. COUNCIL BLUFFS

World's Largest Golden Spike
The Eastern Terminus

On May 10, 1869, two steam engines, the Jupiter and No. 119, stood face-to-face on the same line of track on Promontory Summit, Utah. Leland Stanford, president of the Central Pacific, and Thomas Durant, president of the Union Pacific, placed a cast-gold railroad spike to hold the last section of track, and the country was united. Immediately following the ceremony, the precious spike was removed, and soon swindlers were selling knock-off golden spikes as the real McCoy.

The spike on display at the Golden Spike National Historic Site where east met west is a fake. The real spike was allegedly kept by Leland Stanford and ended up at the school named in his honor in Palo Alto, California. With all this speculation of authenticity, Council Bluffs stepped forward with a larger-than-life replica towering fifty-six feet into the air—but slightly more yellow than gold. Apart from the size, the only obvious flaw is the missing motto on the original spike: "May God continue the unity of our Country as this Railroad unites the two great Oceans of the world."

Iowa may seem irrelevant to connecting the coasts by rail, but Council Bluffs was the last stop of the railroad going west before the Civil War. When President Abraham Lincoln signed the Pacific Railroad Act in 1862, plans were set in motion for Union Pacific to begin construction across the river in Omaha, Nebraska. This line continued west to meet the Central Pacific, which started in Sacramento, California.

In 1939, Hollywood bankrolled an epic film entitled *Union Pacific* and, as part of the PR blitz, erected the spike in Council Bluffs. Originally, the monument was covered entirely with glittery gold leaf to honor Council Bluffs and local boy Grenville Dodge, who was key in helping build the railway.

North Platte, Nebraska, wanted a piece of the publicity and laid out blueprints

Shaped like the Washington Monument, the oversized golden spike of Council Bluffs was used as a movie promotion for the epic *Union Pacific*.

to erect a fifteen-story Golden Spike Tower in the shape of the famous nail. So far, however, the plans for this skyscraper on the plains are still just a dream.

Today, Council Bluffs's spike is definitely on the wrong side of the tracks from wealthy downtown. A pair of dirty socks lies lost at the foot of the statue as freight trains rumble by. A shirtless man walks his dog over from the Golden Spike Mobile Home Park and looks the other way while his German Shepherd mix lifts its leg and lets loose on the statue—an explanation for the yellow-tinged hue? In spite of the location away from the city center, a plaque affixed to the base recalls the heady days of the railroad boom when Council Bluffs was the "Eastern Terminus of the Union Pacific Railroad fixed by Abraham Lincoln."

→ *Golden Spike*, Ninth Avenue and 21st Street, (800) 228-6878. From I-29, take exit 53A east onto Ninth Avenue. Drive about one and a half miles, and the spike is on the right (south) side of the road across from a trailer park.

Squirrel Cage Jail
Gentle Efficiency of Total Surveillance

Prisons were something of a novelty in the 1800s. Penal colonies had been set up for madmen and the diseased, but not often for criminals. Painful punishment in public was being replaced by incarceration, but usually that was just a temporary solution until the trial. In this new country where liberty was the most precious gift, to do without one's freedom was a terrible punishment. As opposed to dungeons where criminals rotted away, modern prisons were meant to rehabilitate criminals.

Many people didn't understand the logic behind these jails. How would putting someone in jail help make them a better person? Wouldn't all the criminals make huge crime rings in prison? Many didn't believe that taking away someone's freedom would teach them how to be a free man. Besides, why should they get a bed and three square meals a day while many honest poor people were struggling just to make ends meet?

In his utopian vision in the 1830s, Jeremy Bentham designed his "Panopticon," putting all prison cells in a large semicircle under constant surveillance by a single guard in a sort of godlike central position. Disturbingly, Bentham also envisioned this Big Brother model for factories, hospitals, schools, and insane asylums. Inside the Panopticon prisons, a strict schedule was followed and the tiniest violation of the rules led to harsh punishment.

Michel Foucault wrote about the Panopticon, with its "gentle efficiency of total surveillance," as a transformation from public torture: "The prison, that darkest region in the apparatus of justice, is the place where the power to punish, which no longer dares manifest itself openly, silently organizes a field of objectivity in which punishment will be able to function openly as treatment."

Two men from Indiana took Bentham's Panopticon one step further in 1881. A three-story cylindrical jail was built with ten pie-shaped cells on each level that

From the outside, the "squirrel cage jail" looks like any old brick building. On the inside, mechanical gears slowly spun the three-story cylindrical jail with ten pie-shaped cells (so the keeper could stay put).

faced outward. This enormous lazy Susan would be slowly spun by the keeper, who could stay put and watch the criminals' every action. From the outside, the Historic Pottawattamie County Jail seems to be just another brick Victorian mansion, but a peek through the dusty windows reveals the decrepit iron machinery that used to creak and squeak as it swirled.

Only three such prisons still exist in the country, and Council Bluffs dubbed theirs the "Squirrel Cage Jail," perhaps a nod to their status as the "Black Squirrel Capital." The jail's design allowed only one prisoner per floor to exit at a time.

When the levers and gears rusted up, the criminals either were stuck in the firetrap or could waltz away. Incredibly, this bizarre mechanical contraption from 1885 was kept in use until fire codes shut it down in 1969.

At the modern lockdown prison next door with video monitors filming every nook and cranny, the jailers claim to be unaware of this historic anomaly. Luckily, the Pottawattamie County Historical Society saved it from the wrecking ball and was able to place it on the National Register of Historic Places in 1972.

→ *Squirrel Cage Jail,* 226 Pearl Street, (712) 323-2509. From I-29/I-80, take exit 3 north on Highway 192 (South Expressway Street) for about two miles to downtown. The Squirrel Cage is between the library and the new courthouse, one block west of Main Street on Pearl Street, which is one-way going south. Turn into the alley and park next to the museum. Open Wednesday through Saturday.

Fenelon Place Elevator
World's Shortest, Steepest Railroad

J. K. Graves despised trudging up the steep, winding road from downtown Dubuque to his home on the hill. Dreaming of a home-cooked meal for lunch, Graves was unsatisfied with the fare fried up at the town cafés. His only option was to huff and puff in his pinstripe suit from his banking job up the hill to his house rather than slowly supping and napping during his lunch break.

On a steamer voyage to Europe, Graves was inspired by the cable cars that sped up the mountains. Perhaps while riding the funicular up the hill above the Bay of Naples and hearing the operatic strains of "Funiculi, Funicula," Graves resolved to bring a little bit of Europe to Iowa. In 1882, the banker devised a homespun elevator that chugged 296 feet nearly vertically up the 189-foot drop. Now he could dine in style and avoid paying for heartburn at the greasy spoons on Main Street.

Seeing Graves zoom skyward to his house, a neighbor begged to use the lift as well to avoid plodding up the muddy paths. Soon the World's Shortest, Steepest Railway became a public funicular for a penny fee. Thanks to a listing on the National Register of Historic Places and Dubuque pride, the Fenelon Place Elevator has survived the ravages of time, with only minor renovations to ensure the cables won't snap on the way to lunch.

➜ *Fenelon Place Elevator (or Fourth Street Elevator)*, 512 Fenelon Place, (319) 582-6496. Dubuque is in eastern Iowa along the Mississippi River across from the Wisconsin-Illinois border. From Highway 61/151, turn west on Fourth Street in town. Drive four blocks to Bluff Street, turn left, and go one block to Third Street. At the end of the block turn right on Summit and then right again on Fenelon Place.

Pull the cord to ring the bell; a buzzer sounds and the angled trolley jumps to life. The ancient cables tug the car to the top as the ballast (the other car) descends into the valley. The Fenelon Place Elevator and its lookout offer the best views of Dubuque and into three states.

While in the Area

To make nearly perfectly round pellets for rifle bullets during the Civil War, molten lead was dropped off the top of the Old Shot Tower (on East Fourth Street Extension next to Highway 61 at Hill Street along the river). During the 141-foot free fall, the liquid metal clung together in a sphere and then fizzled into a solid when it splashed into the waters of the Mississippi below. Visitors can still tour this crude weapons factory and enjoy the fantastic view of the river from the lookout.

Driving an hour and a half west of Dubuque on Highway 52 will reveal Strawberry Point's pride. Perched atop a pole outside City Hall stands a freshly painted fiberglass strawberry. Local legend tells of wounded Union soldiers returning from the Civil War resting in these fields and feasting on wild strawberries. The plump berries resuscitated the weary warriors and inspired the founding of the town. During my visit, a man outside City Hall looked up with pride at the enormous fruit and exclaimed, "The strawberry doesn't rotate except for in a high wind. I'll bet it puts on quite a show!"

Facing page: The World's Largest Strawberry has fallen only once from its pole above City Hall.

American Gothic House
Grant Wood's Muse

Many critics thought Grant Wood was mocking rural folk who farmed the fields of Iowa when he painted a stoic man with a pitchfork and his plain-Jane daughter standing stubbornly in front of a little white house with a Gothic second-story window. Others recognized it as a gentle tease of the rugged farmers whom Wood depicted in his "regionalist" style.

Wood painted what he knew. One day he sketched this little house in Eldon, but the two people he originally drew didn't fit his vision for his now-classic painting. In their place, he called up his dentist, B. H. McBeeby, and convinced his own kid sister, Nan, to model along with him.

McBeeby's stern expression, along with the Gothic farmhouse, somehow embody the strong religious values and work ethic of the Midwest. While Wood's work may have had hints of parody to it, *American Gothic* has prompted countless spoofs, many of which have been collected by Nan in the Davenport Museum of Art. The original painting hangs in the Art Institute of Chicago.

The 1881 farmhouse still stands in Eldon. Having had a stint as a candy store, the American Gothic House recently has been restored by the State Historical Society of Iowa. The inside, however, has been deemed too fragile for groups of tourists to go trouncing through to see what was behind that famous window.

➤ *American Gothic House,* 301 American Gothic Street, (319) 335-3916 or (515) 281-6412. Eldon is in southeast Iowa. From Highway 34, take Highway 16 south into town. Highway 16 becomes Elm Street (Main Street); take it past downtown. Follow the signs, which lead left (north) on Eldon Street for two blocks, then right on Caster Street, then left on Finney Street and four blocks to Burton and American Gothic Street.

Once a candy and novelty store, the American Gothic House was preserved for posterity when it was added to the National Register of Historic Places in 1974.

Danish Windmill
Moving Monuments Overseas

While driving through the Iowa flatlands west of Des Moines, a quixotic vision of an enormous Old World windmill appears above the cornfields. Another look around reveals an entire town with a Danish feel, with red-and-white flags draped from every pole. Along with Kimballtown just to the north, Elk Horn is the largest settlement of Danish descendants residing outside a city in the United States.

To honor this heritage, Norre Snede, a local Danish American, dreamed of finding an old windmill in Denmark and shipping it to the middle of Iowa. To offset a farm crisis during the 1970s, Snede envisioned turning little Elk Horn into a tourist destination. Even though many people in town thought he had a screw loose, he persisted and found an old mill built in 1848 in Jutland and insisted on bringing it overseas. A town meeting was convened, and thirty thousand dollars was raised to transport the mill piece by piece thousands of miles from its home.

When the parts arrived in Elk Horn, the ocean salt was wiped off the beams and the windmill was rebuilt with sails reaching thirty feet in each direction from the axle. More than three times the original money raised was spent to complete the project, but in 1976 the only authentic Danish windmill in the United States was open for business.

After Elk Horn imported its mill, the Danes halted further exports of their national treasures. "We made them see how important these windmills are, so now they're fixing them up again in Denmark," says Peggy Hansen at Hansen's Kro Danish bed and breakfast.

→ *Danish Windmill and Museum,* 4038 Main Street, (712) 764-7472. From I-80, take exit 54 north onto Highway 173. After about six miles, the windmill will be on the left (west) side when coming into the town of Elk Horn.

Disassembled in Denmark and shipped over the Atlantic, one of Jutland's windmills found a new home in rural Iowa. The sixty-six-foot wingspan now rises above the cornfields and is visible for miles around.

While in the Area

"Eat a Danish in Elk Horn" could be the town slogan. Jacquelyn's Danish Bakery and Kaffe Hus (4234 Main Street, [712] 764-3100) serves up *kringle, rullepølse,* and *kransakage,* or you can dine at the Danish Inn next to the windmill (4116 Main Street, [712] 764-4251) for something besides just *smørrebrød* (sandwiches).

In either of these eateries, you'll be quizzed on whether you've given a proper amount of time to the Bedstemor's House (2105 College Street, [712] 764-6082), also known as "Grandmother's House," and to the Danish Immigrant Museum

Far from her home in Copenhagen, a little mermaid replica lounges on a stone and keeps her scales wet in a Kimballtown fountain.

(2212 Washington Street, [712] 764-7001 or [800] 759-9192), whose Morning Star Chapel is a contender for the World's Smallest Church.

Continue north on Main Street (Highway 173) for a few miles to Kimballtown. Two years after the windmill was reassembled in Elk Horn, this sister Danish town erected a replica of Copenhagen's "Little Mermaid," based on the Hans Christian Andersen tale. Located in Mermaid Park (310 North Main Street) next to the Mermaid Gift Shop, this little bronze statue gazes sadly at the splashing fountain, "a very long way from her home in the sea," according to the town brochure. At least she can avoid the annual vandalism inflicted on the original mermaid sitting on a stone and peering at the Baltic Sea. Luckily, the city of Copenhagen made duplicates of the statue for quick replacement and to keep the legions of photo-taking tourists happy.

St. Anthony of Padua Chapel
World's Smallest Church

It's a slippery slope deciding what can be considered the World's Smallest Church. Must it be consecrated? Is it enough if a single priest can squeeze inside? Can it be a church for dolls? How many churches can you fit on the head of pin?

Tiny Festina didn't bother with these arguments for its bucolic St. Anthony of Padua Chapel from 1886. After all, this was the site of the first Catholic mission north of Dubuque, which was built of logs in 1849—and actually seems quite a bit smaller than the actual church.

The quaint church made of wood and stone was built because of a vow. Johann Gaertner had been drafted into Napoleon's army to fight with the French in the bloody Russian campaign. Johann's mother vowed that if her son ever returned from the carnage alive, she'd build a chapel for the Virgin Mary.

In September 1812, Napoleon Bonaparte and his army entered Moscow. The town was set ablaze, possibly by Russians trying to slow the French advance. The occupation lasted thirty-five days, after which Napoleon retreated to avoid the harsh Russian winter. About half a million of his 600,000 strong army either deserted, died, or were taken prisoner. Johann Gaertner was one of the lucky ones who made it out of Moscow with his life.

Johann's mother would have to wait until her son also survived the debacle of Waterloo in 1815 before he would return home. She didn't live to realize her promise, however, and the task fell to Johann's son and daughter-in-law to fulfill.

In 1886, the tiny twelve-by-sixteen-foot chapel was completed. Rather than dedicating it to the Virgin Mary, they named it after Saint Anthony of Padua—patron of lost articles (Johann?), sterility, animals, and amputees. Stars dot the ceiling and the altar has a statue of Saint Anthony and Saint Francis. Four mini pews fill the space inside and are more like love seats than the usual heavy oak benches.

The "World's Smallest Church" was named for Saint Anthony of Padua, the martyr who could neutralize poisoned food and convince a fasting horse in Rimini to eat after showing it the sacrament. Every year a festival is held at the church on this saint's day (not one stomachache has ever been reported).

Every year on June 13, hundreds converge on the little chapel to indulge in the feast day of Saint Anthony—even though as a Franciscan monk Anthony had taken a vow of poverty. Few people can fit into the chapel at a time, but others can pay their respects to the huge boulder that marks Johann Gaertner's tomb and marvel at a grave marker cross that has been swallowed by an enormous tree.

Although this may not be the absolute smallest church in the world, it boasts a great story. Smaller replicas of the smallest Iowan church can be seen at both the House of Clocks in Waukon and Bily Clocks in Spillville.

→ *St. Anthony of Padua Chapel.* Festina is in northeast Iowa. From Decorah, go south on Highway 52 for eleven miles to Calmar. Turn south on Highway 150 into Festina. Follow the signs from town onto the dirt roads that lead about a mile out of town. The church is on your left after crossing a small bridge over the Turkey River.

While in the Area

Sixteen miles north of little Festina off Highway 52 is Norway's "western home," the Vesterheim Norwegian-American Museum (523 West Water Street, Decorah [563] 382-9681). As the largest museum in the country dedicated to a single immigrant group, the Vesterheim sprawls through sixteen buildings and includes an entire wooden ship, the *Trade Wind,* stuffed inside the three-story main complex.

While the actual museum is popular, the excellent Norwegian restaurant next door—with "I LOVE NORWAY" stickers glued on all the napkin holders—is always full. In spite of the ubiquitous Norskie brouhaha, brochures mysteriously claim "IT'S AN ALL AMERICAN TALE," perhaps in polite deference to their newfound land. Local businesses on the main street may raise the Stars and Stripes near their large Norwegian flags (it's all red, white, and blue, anyway), but Viking Realtors, Viking State Bank, and others let it be known they haven't forgotten their roots.

FORT DODGE

Cardiff Giant
Authentic Imitation of the Fake

"There were giants in the earth in those days," declares the Bible in Genesis 6:4. Reverend Turk of Ackley, Iowa, took these words as literal truth, but cigar maker George Hull of upstate New York would have none of it. Turk insisted that every word in the Bible was fact, so if the good book said giants walked there, so it was. Hull, an avowed atheist, continued arguing that this was a bunch of hogwash, but to little avail.

Instead, Hull decided to test the gullibility of these stubborn Christians. He contracted a sculptor from Chicago to carve Hull's image in a twelve-foot chunk of gypsum quarried from Fort Dodge. Hull had the piece buried for a while, careful to avoid the pit Michelangelo had fallen into when the Italian artist tried to pass off a sleeping cherub sculpture as an ancient relic in 1496. Cardinal Riario of San Giorgio bought that story, but he later discovered the ruse and demanded his money back.

Hull went a step further than Michelangelo did to age his artifact. Sulfuric acid was splashed on the gypsum, and wooden mallets and steel knitting needles were used to hack "pores" into the skin of the seven-thousand-pound giant. Only later would Hull admit that he should have inserted hair for added authenticity.

While his neighbor was on holiday, Hull snuck onto his land in Cardiff, New York, and put the giant in the earth. A year later, in 1869, workers dug a well on the neighbors' property and discovered the "Cardiff Giant."

Hull took over the archaeological dig from his neighbor and hoisted a tent above the burial site as curious onlookers paid fifty cents a pop to sneak a look-see. While many scholars denounced the find as fraud, Christians hailed the discovery with cries of "The Scriptures are fulfilled" and "Lot's Wife?" and, of course, references to the giants in the earth from Genesis.

A group of doctors declared the giant to be proof of "petrification," the result of

Above: Fort Dodge's Fort Museum Frontier Village has a replica stockade to protect the replica Cardiff Giant secured inside its walls.
Facing page: "Petrifactionists" claimed that this stone figure was an actual American mummy, while others took it as biblical proof of "giants in the earth" from Genesis. This replica of the imitation Cardiff Giant was quarried from Fort Dodge gypsum just like the original fake. *Photograph courtesy of the Fort Museum Frontier Village.*

mummification. A Native American Onondaga woman from the area speculated that this was a giant Indian prophet who had warned of the white man's coming and that this medicine man would rise again.

Doctor John Boynton from nearby Syracuse guessed the giant dated back only three hundred years to the Jesuit missionaries who had originally settled in the area. Perhaps the priests, he speculated, wanted to impress the Native Americans with their God.

A graduate student from Yale Divinity School, Alexander McWhorte, wrote an article saying that this "American Goliath" was a winged angel or "cherubim" type of Phoenician idol. Thus, ancient sailors from the Middle East had settled in upstate New York with this icon. He noted the folded wings over the Cardiff Giant's body—leading to speculation by others that Icarus had been found. Even Ralph Waldo Emerson announced that the Cardiff Giant was "beyond his depth, very wonderful and undoubtedly ancient," according to Curtis D. MacDougall's book *Hoaxes*.

Meanwhile, Hull was basking in glory and richer for it. The statue had cost him $2,600 to have sculpted, and he sold it to some businessmen in Syracuse for $37,500, a tidy sum in those days.

Phineas T. Barnum watched the fame of the giant grow along with his envy. Barnum allegedly offered sixty thousand dollars for three months' rent of the giant, but the businessmen refused. P. T. Barnum instead built a plaster mock-up and drew even bigger crowds with his famous boisterous promotions.

The Syracuse businessmen tried to sue Barnum, but a judge threw out the case because the authenticity of the giant was called into question. An attorney from Fort Dodge, Galusha Parsons, recognized the gypsum of the giant from Iowa and remembered that a huge slab had been shipped out the year before. Neighbors in Cardiff then recalled a mysterious wagon arriving with an enormous express-mail box about the same time.

Still, people came for a peek to see what the fuss was about. When Barnum was showing his plaster fake at New York's Wood's Museum, the businessmen brought the "real" giant to the Big Apple, but the game was up. Finally, Hull confessed to the whole hoax.

Barnum's copy is on display at Marvin's Marvelous Mechanical Museum in Farmington Hills, Michigan. Another fake Cardiff Giant has somehow turned up at the Circus World Museum in Baraboo, Wisconsin.

Hull's original giant was relegated to be a sideshow act at carnivals and eventually ended up in private ownership in Des Moines. The New York Historical Association convinced the Iowa owners to sell it back to New York state for thirty thousand dollars—nearly the same amount that Hull had sold it for more than fifty years before—and it can be visited at the Farmer's Museum in Cooperstown for the hefty fee of nine dollars a pop.

The source of the mysterious giant, Fort Dodge, has recreated its own giant out of authentic Iowan gypsum. All the fanfare around the hoax and the unusual material for the sculpture put the spotlight on Iowa and its valuable mineral deposits. In 1871, two years after the Cardiff Giant was "discovered," a huge gypsum mill was opened in Fort Dodge that became one of Iowa's most important mineral producers.

→ *Cardiff Giant,* Fort Museum Frontier Village, South Kenyon and Museum Road, (515) 573-4231. Fort Dodge is in central Iowa, about one and a half hours northwest of Des Moines. From Highway 169, turn east onto Business Highway 20 (South Kenyon Road) and go one block after the first stoplight. Turn left (north) onto Museum Road, and the fort is on the left (southwest) side.

The Museum of Ice Cream

Never on a Sundae

The exact origin of ice cream is unknown, but many countries claim it as their own invention. In 200 B.C., Mongolians mixed cream, ice, and rocks, supposedly to aid digestion, but can this be considered ice cream? When Marco Polo returned from China in 1295, he possibly brought recipes for an offshoot of this bizarre concoction to the markets of Venice. But then, centuries before, the Italian peninsula had already experienced Nero Caesar demanding that runners venture into the mountains outside of Rome and return with ice for special decadent desserts. In the Florence of the Medici, *fior di latte* (the flower of milk) appeared as a precursor to *gelato* and is the classic flavor still available today in the *gelaterie* across the Italian boot.

A frozen delicacy became a royal treat when King Charles I was served "crème ice" by his French cook. The English exported the recipe for this luxury to the colonies, where George Washington supposedly declared his "inalienable right" to ice cream. The first president ran up a hefty two-hundred-dollar tab for it in 1790. According to the Museum of Ice Cream, Washington "declared his political independence" by producing his own ice cream in pewter buckets at home in Mount Vernon.

In 1874 the ice cream soda was invented, but some Midwestern towns passed laws banning these decadent desserts on the Sabbath. In 1890, soda jerks invented a special sodaless soda to be consumed only on Sundays and called it a "sundae" with a different spelling to poke fun at the purists.

The legend behind ice cream cones stems to the 1904 World's Fair in St. Louis.

Facing page: One of the stories about the origin of the ice cream cone credits vendor Ernest Hamwi, who ran out of paper cups and used a rolled-up waffle to serve his gelato. Blue Bunny keeps Hamwi's invention alive and the town of Le Mars happy during Ice Cream Days in July.

The Blue Bunny milk truck is forever parked in front of the Museum of Ice Cream.
The name Blue Bunny derives from a contest to name the new ice cream: the young
son of a journalist took a fancy to a blue Easter bunny he saw in a shop window.

A vendor ran out of paper cups to serve ice cream, so the quick-witted salesman
rolled up a waffle and declared them "ice cream cornucopias."

Ice cream bars didn't appear until 1921 when a man in Youngstown, Pennsyl-
vania, left his lemonade on the windowsill with a spoon in it. After a chilly night,
he lifted the icy treat out and went into business. Or at least that's how the story
goes.

All these facts and more are revealed at the Ice Cream Capital of the World, which just happens to be the home of Wells' Blue Bunny Ice Cream. Not surprisingly, most of the history in the museum focuses on the Wells family's struggle when they moved from Chicago to found Wellsburg, South Dakota. When times were tough on the prairie in 1911, they tried to move back to the big city. They barely made it across the Missouri River, and they settled in Le Mars when they knew they wouldn't make it all the way to Illinois. The situation went from bad to worse when they raised pigs that all died from cholera.

The Wells family struck gold, however, with their Blue Bunny Ice Cream, which rapidly swept across the state. Soon, Clarabelle the Clown toured Iowa to promote Blue Bunny and its Howdy Doody bars.

Today, Le Mars produces more ice cream than any other town in the world, and it has the world's only interactive museum of ice cream to boot. When you finish with the tour, enjoy old-style ice cream treats at the gorgeous soda fountain with its tin ceiling, tile floor, marble countertops, and wooden booths. Blue Bunny even built a playland with ice cream cone–motif tubes for kids to climb through to work off their sugar high.

→ *Ice Cream Capital of the World Visitors Center and Museum,* 1 Blue Bunny Drive Southwest, (712) 546-4090. From Sioux City, go northeast on Highway 75 for twenty-three miles. The museum is on the north side of town at the northeast corner of the intersection of Highways 75 and 3. Open year-round.

While in the Area

What is the fruit of years of prayer and gathering of tithes? A thirty-foot-tall steel Blessed Virgin Mary statue was erected after years of prayer on Trinity Heights in Sioux City (twenty-three miles southwest of Le Mars on Highway 75, turn off on Floyd Boulevard and then right on Thirty-third Street just before Sioux Tools, [712] 239-8670).

After years of gathering for prayers—and alleged miracles—on the mount before they even owned it, these devout Christians acquired the land through more miraculous happenings. Once the BVM went up, two other attractions were required for a true trinity. Thanks to even more donations, another metal relic was raised. A steely thirty-three-foot-tall Jesus Christ shines above a little pathway where every bench, rock, tree, and shrub has a dedication engraved in brass for credit in heaven. (Unclaimed objects can be claimed for a small fee and now are labeled either "This plaque available" or "Reserved.")

The final spoke of the trinity began after Jerry Traufler from Le Mars had a vision during his pilgrimage to Arkansas. Inspired to carve the Last Supper, Traufler risked heresy to avoid plagiarizing daVinci's 2D version in Milan by having friends and his wife pose as the apostles. Nevertheless, Traufler's oeuvre in basswood and pine evokes Leonardo's, with all the disciples placed mysteriously, if photogenically, on one side of the table.

Facing page: When the sun hits the aluminum thirty-three-foot Jesus Christ, blinding rays bounce out in every direction. "Never touch the statues!" a sign warns, encouraging visitors to add their fingerprints to the others already there. Even if Jesus can't be climbed, a visiting kid says, "It would be cool to have our own shrine at home."

Amana Colonies
Collective Farm Tourism

Amid the pristine, rolling fields of Iowa one of the most successful experiments in communal living the world has ever seen took root. The Amana Colonies are seven villages that managed to survive eighty-nine years of shared wealth in a country advocating a very different philosophy.

When Martin Luther's reforms didn't go far enough, the "Community of True Inspiration" was formed in 1714 in the Hessen area of Germany. To put their utopian ideals to the test, many of these pious German immigrants purchased five thousand acres near Buffalo, New York, in 1842. When too many settlers from the "outside world" moved nearby, the group of eight hundred idealists put down roots in the new frontier of central Iowa in 1855.

Named "Amana," meaning "faithful," the communes were completely self-sufficient. The community owned all the property, and living quarters were doled out to families. Chores were delegated to everyone in factories, farms, shops, or kitchens. Groups of up to forty people would gather to eat every meal together in the communal kitchens. While personal possessions may have been verboten, all profits were shared and goods were available to everyone.

The Amana Colonies weren't the only experiment in communal living in the United States, however. The Harmonists also hailed from Germany, near Wurttemberg, and settled in Indiana vowing freedom from owning property and a celibate life, which didn't bode well for the birth rate. The Shakers, so named because they would shake with religious fervor in church, also advocated celibacy and sharing of all material goods, but anyone could opt out of joining their group. Brook Farm, set up in 1841 in Massachusetts, was another famous socialist experiment by transcendentalists who agreed that everyone should receive the same wages and have the same housing and food. The Oneida Community in upstate New York, however, made the general public question these communes when, in 1869, they

With twenty-six thousand acres of farms and forests, the Amana Colonies spread their communal way of living even further when they purchased the neighboring village of Homestead and its railroad terminal.

advocated "complex marriages," in which every man was married to every woman and the community decided which couples would produce the best offspring.

The Amana Colonies outlasted all these other communes but disbanded in 1932 before the term "collective farm" took a turn for the worse through the deeds of Stalin, Mao, and Pol Pot. Known as the "Great Change," the movement to shift the Amana Colonies to a profit-sharing corporation was voted on by all the future stockholders in the seven villages. Although this change was brought about by the

Great Depression, the communities formed the famous Amana appliance company, which employs more people than any other business in the county.

Today, Amana is awash in tourists who soak up the sites of the woolen mills, woodworking shops, wineries, antique stores, artisan shops, art galleries, and butchers selling the famous Amana hams. Most of all, visitors come to feast on the hearty German food—from Kassler Rippchen to Jäger Schnitzel—served family style. While the colonies are bustling like never before, the devout founders surely didn't envision that their communal ideals and mystical Pietism would be ceded to celebrating Oktoberfest.

→ *Amana Colonies: Main, Middle, High, East, West, South, and Homestead.*
On Highway 151 go twenty miles southwest of Cedar Rapids. Or, from I-80, take exit 225 onto Highway 151 north. After five miles, turn right at the "T" to stay on 151. In two miles, Homestead will be on the right, and Main Amana is another three miles farther over the river.

Effigy Mounds

Landmarks of the Ancients

When European pioneers first started settling along the Mississippi River, they found thousands of mysterious burial mounds in prominent spots overlooking the water. Few believed that ancestors of the Indians could have built such intricate monuments, so instead they thought that a long-lost race of "mound builders" lived here in a civilization that then disappeared, much as Atlantis supposedly did. Others theorized that the Vikings ventured inland to teach the Native Americans their burial technique, but this theory fell flat when some of the mounds were dated back six thousand years before the Norsemen even set foot on North America in A.D. 1000. Finally in 1880 the Smithsonian confirmed that these mounds were indeed built by Native Americans after finding Indian-made objects inside. The term "New World" suddenly didn't fit so well when sites such as the three-thousand-year-old octagonal terraces near Epps, Louisiana, were found, measuring four thousand feet across and probably influenced by the Olmec of Mexico.

Besides this unusually shaped fort, the ancient "Monk's Mound" was discovered near the Mississippi River with a base larger than the Great Pyramid of Giza. Set among a hundred other mounds, this monument covered sixteen acres and was one of the main attractions of Cahokia, one of the earliest cities in North America with a population of forty thousand, located in what is now southern Illinois.

While simple conical mounds are the most common and oldest of the mounds, effigy mounds in the shape of animals, usually birds, bears, bison, turtles, and lizards, were discovered mostly from eastern Iowa to the shores of Lake Michigan. Three special effigy mounds include a 600-foot bird-shaped mound found near Madison, Wisconsin; a 210-foot mound in the form of a standing man discovered near Baraboo; and a huge lizard-shaped mound found near Milwaukee. The largest

The Little Bear Effigy is a mini version of the Great Bear Effigy, which measures 137 feet long and 70 feet across from the shoulders to the front legs (but rises up only 3 feet).

effigy, however, is the Great Serpent Mound near Hillsboro, Ohio, measuring a quarter mile long.

Iowa's impressive mounds stand high on bluffs overlooking the Mississippi River just north of Marquette. Of the two hundred mounds, most are conical or linear, but twenty-nine are shaped like bears, which are guardians of the earth, or birds, guardians of the sky. Wingspans of the spirit birds stretch to 212 feet, while the Great Bear Effigy measures 137 feet long.

The earth to build these burial mounds was carried entirely by hand, probably in baskets, and valuable artifacts were placed inside, maybe to help the dead in their journey to the next world. Copper from the Great Lakes, obsidian from the Rocky Mountains, shark teeth from Chesapeake Bay, pearls from the Gulf of Mexico, and mica from the Appalachian Mountains have been found in the mounds, evidence of an extensive trade network.

Little is known about these ancient Native Americans, often called "Woodland Indians" or even "Effigy Mounds People," but evidence shows that humans have been living in this area for about twelve thousand years. The effigy mounds, however, were probably built between seven hundred and fifty and fourteen hundred years ago.

The mystery remains, however, of how these mounds could be built when the animals' shapes can often only be distinguished from the air. And what purpose did these effigies of animal processions serve?

Early surveys of eastern Iowa found more than ten thousand mounds of various kinds, but, after logging and plowing, only about a thousand remain. The National Monument of the Effigy Mounds was founded in 1949 to preserve 191 of these burial mounds so that future generations may ponder the meaning the Woodland Indians instilled in these impressive monuments.

➜ *Effigy Mounds,* 51 Highway 76, (319) 873-3491. From Marquette, drive three miles north on Highway 76 along the Mississippi. Shortly after crossing the Yellow River, the entrance to the visitors center will be on the right (northeast) side of the highway.

While in the Area

A red carpet wasn't the only spectacle rolled out for President Jimmy Carter's visit to the Marquette area in August 1978. In his slick speedboat, Bob Reis zoomed by on the Mississippi River with a special water-skier no one was soon to forget. A huge fiberglass pink elephant named Pinky, sporting a top hat and oversized Buddy Holly glasses, impressed the president and his cavalcade at Prairie du Chien, across the river. Perhaps emboldened by the audacity of the event, Carter valiantly fended off a rabid attacking rabbit eight months later on his trip down the Mississippi with a canoe paddle, making national headlines.

In spite of these bold acts, Carter lost the White House, and Pinky lost his Pink Elephant Supper Club, where he'd been the resident roadside attraction. The

Pinky the Waterskiing Pachyderm entertained Jimmy Carter on the Mississippi River when the president visited the area in 1978.

pachyderm was moved from the closed club and relegated to the task of convincing gamblers to try their odds at the slots or at least load up at the buffets at the Marquette Riverboat Casino and the Isle of Capri Casino riverboat (south side of downtown Marquette on Highway 76).

South of Marquette, a few miles along the beautiful river road of Highway 18, is the quaint town of McGregor. The young sons of native Augustus Ringling used to charge a penny for mini circus shows here in the river city. Later they provided millions of Americans with the world-famous three-ring circus. An old circus wagon still holds the remnants of a calliope under the cliffs off Main Street as a monument to the Ringling Brothers.

Across the street is the second oldest hotel in Iowa, the Alexander (213 Main Street, [563] 873-3454), with excellent Italian pasta *fresca* served up by the Italian American owner, Sal. Otherwise, for the best fried catfish around washed down with the requisite tap beer, stop at the White Springs, a classic roadhouse bar up the road at 30157 Klien Brewery Road (call [563] 873-9642).

Continue up the bank on Highway 18/52 for another seven miles, and billboards with cartoon ghosts will taunt you with Spook Cave (13299 Spook Cave Road, [319] 873-2144). As "America's longest underground boat tour," this watery grotto stays at a constant forty-seven degrees inside the ninety-foot limestone cliffs. To avoid total panic by those easily upset, tours are "fully lit," with only brief intervals of darkness to supplement the eerie sounds that early settlers and explorers supposedly heard coming from this cave along Bloody Run Creek.

Big Treehouse

Swiss Family Robinson Dream Home

In the spring of 1983, Michael "Mick" Jurgensen had six pallets of wood delivered to his property at Shady Oak Campground. He had sketched out a preliminary plan for a little treehouse in the towering old oaks that stood over the green pastures. That first summer he tacked up a modest first floor and a second-story lookout perch, all accessible via ladder.

Since Jurgensen began building, he hasn't stopped. Little by little, new levels have been added for a total of twelve, which rise five and a half stories in the air. Only ladders can reach the twelfth level, while the other eleven have little walkways with a huge wooden spiral staircase winding up close to the top.

Jurgensen took his passion for landscaping, lighting, and gardening to a new level. A fifty-foot-long flower box lines the first elevated walkway; rope lights wind around the wooden banisters; and benches and tables are placed throughout the treehouse for picnicking. Fourteen porch swings sway, providing a relaxing place to pause.

The Swiss Family Robinson could only dream of all the amenities in Jurgensen's never-ending treehouse. Water is piped up into the trees to complement the microwave oven and refrigerator. When the phone rings, rather than climb down from a fifty-five-foot-high branch one can simply grab the recently installed telephone in the trees. To achieve the perfect mood for this summertime dream house, a grill is available for cooking brats while music twinkles through the trees.

Having recently passed the twenty-year mark, the house in the oaks has surpassed five thousand square feet of floor space with no end in sight for Jurgensen's imagination. Someday, maybe the big treehouse will even be zoned as a

Facing page: Visitors from all fifty states and fifty-seven countries have toured the twelve-story treehouse just outside Marshalltown.

bed-and-breakfast, as has been done with hotels in trees in Oregon and Washington state.

→ *Big Treehouse*, Shady Oak Campground, 2370 Shady Oaks Road, (641) 752-2946. From I-35, take exit 111. Take Highway 30 east for thirty-five miles to Marshalltown. Don't turn north into town, but continue on Highway 30 for three more miles east. Turn left (north) on Shady Oaks Road. The treehouse is a quarter mile up on the right (east) side. Summer only, weather permitting.

While in the Area

When the sky grows eerily dark and the low clouds threaten, don't drive thirty miles north of Marshalltown to visit the house that was thoroughly destroyed by a Hollywood tycoon known as *Twister*. For added effect, leaves were stripped from the trees and a barn was collapsed next to the house used in this Tinseltown blockbuster. Sleep at your own peril in the two-story white house turned into a bed-and-breakfast that has kept all the destroyed décor from the film. Next door, an RV and trailer park lie in wait as bait. (C. Welch B & B RV Park, east of Eldora about three miles on Highway 175. Look for signs on the south side of the unmarked road. The house is two miles south of 175 on the dirt road [515] 858-5133.)

Just waiting for its windows to be blown out by an F5 cyclone, the Twister House has been turned into a bed-and-breakfast for those who sleep well in Tornado Alley.

University of Okoboji
A School of the Mind

Garbage cans around Lake Okoboji in northwestern Iowa are plastered with stickers beseeching students to "Help keep your campus clean." This trash is picked up by garbage trucks with "Garbology Dept." painted on the side, and local radio station trucks carry the call letters KUOO, short for K-University Of Okoboji.

Welcome to one of the largest campuses in the world, stretching from the northern point of Big Spirit Lake to south of the town of Milford. The University of Okoboji offers an appealing curricula: degrees in human anatomy require research excursions to the beaches of Big Spirit Lake, and roller coaster engineering students make trips to nearby Arnolds Park wooden roller coaster. Book learning and class attendance are passé. Tuition is free. And everyone graduates at the top of the class.

Photos of a new campus building circulate each year, such as one for the new school of agriculture building that boasts of "seven full-sized tennis courts located over the ultra-modern main level cattle stalls and pig pens." The only class offered, however, is in grain fermentation to quench the students' thirst.

University of Okoboji's sports teams are legendary. The Okoboji Fighting Phantoms are the only undefeated football team in all of college athletics, and the U of O's slogan reflects their fighting spirit: "A Pox on Yale, Poo Poo Purdue and who needs Michigan State for American Truth?" Every year on September 31, the Phantoms play three games in a row against the University of Iowa, Nebraska, and Notre Dame, only these out-of-town teams fail to show out of fear of Okoboji's great record.

If you tour the campus in the winter a local guide might tell you that those shacks on the lake are the dorms, and that they have a terrible problem with water in the basement.

Emil Richter, one of the founders of the University of Okoboji, poses with the ubiquitous sweatshirts and T-shirts of the school that's all in your mind.

The University of Okoboji was started by two brothers, Herman and Emil Richter, and their friend Roger Stolley, with their respective positions being director of student affairs, administrative dean, and director of admissions. Emil explains the origin of the school: "A lot of people wanted to go to college and they knew they'd probably never go. This was the next best thing. When people call in and actually want to register for classes—and there's a lot of them—we turn them over to the community college."

The U of O isn't above bestowing honorary degrees to certain visionaries. "We sent an honorary degree to Ronald McDonald, and he sent us back this eight-by-ten signed photo," Emil explains as he points to a portrait of the hamburger clown/alumnus.

Emil's main occupation, however, is managing the University of Okoboji Student Union, also known as "The Three Brothers" clothing store, in Milford. U of O T-shirts and sweatshirts fill an entire room. "I asked the folks out at Stanford and other universities and they said that they sell about the same number of shirts and stickers that we do," Emil says proudly. This could be in part because a local rumor spread through town that the Okoboji decal in the rear window would get the driver a discount on speeding tickets.

A customer in the Grand Diner in the town of Spencer ten miles to the south isn't sure about all the goings-on around the university. He says, perhaps a little enviously, "Aww, it's just a bunch of guys running around up there. . . . There's really nothing to it, a guy just got a printing screen and printed up stickers. There's no campus, no nothing."

Another man on one of the swivel seats in the diner nods his head in agreement and pipes up indignantly about this alleged university, "It has no logical [*sic*]!"

Emil isn't concerned about this petty small talk from his envious neighbors (without University of Okoboji degrees, obviously). In fact, the school has become more tangible with the establishment of an endowment for community projects around the University of Okoboji worth more than two million dollars set up by ex-Congressman Berkley Bedell in 1988.

As the U of O becomes less ethereal, Emil takes it in stride. "It's almost like a real college," he explains, and then adds cryptically, "It isn't that it isn't."

➜ *University of Okoboji.* From I-90, take exit 73 south into Iowa on Highway 71. Stay on Highway 71 when it merges with Highway 9, going west for seven miles. Continue on 71 south after Spirit Lake another two miles into Okoboji.

16. PELLA

Vermeer Mill
Battling Windmills

No passport is necessary to enter downtown Pella, but buildings around the town square resemble a quaint Dutch burg more than small-town Iowa. Even the chain Casey's General Store has architectural ornamentation reminiscent of Holland, and the Dairy Queen is in a Flemish-style barn.

The capstone of Pella's transformation into a Dutch town was the construction of its own authentic windmill. Shipping a windmill overseas was deemed impractical. The Netherlands followed Denmark's lead in prohibiting export of its windmills after citizens of Elk Horn succeeded in dismantling an old Danish mill and importing it to Iowa.

Nevertheless, the woman at the entrance to Pella's Vermeer Mill discounts the Danish windmill in Elk Horn and rebuts, "Well, well, our windmill has many imported parts from Holland, and they even brought workers over from Holland to build it."

In fact, Dutch builder Lukas Verbij flew in from Hoogmade, Holland, to build this Tallest Working Windmill in the United States using the design of a similar structure in the northern Netherlands province of Groningen. The base of this downtown windmill alone rises four stories so the sails can reach above the other buildings clustered around it. The 124-foot-tall windmill grinds local wheat through the milling stones, and it is then shaped into bread at local Pella restaurants.

The mill's receptionist loads me full of ever-larger brochures of the windmill and other sites in town. When I decline the enormous Tulip Time calendar, she's a little offended. "Haven't you ever been to Tulip Time?" she asks, surprised, and explains that this is Pella's town festival, held in May when eighty thousand tulips bloom. "I've been to Tulip Time every year and I'm from Albia—except for twice when I was sick. I just love Tulip Time."

The Dutch-style windmill rises four stories, and the sails stretch even farther. The Vermeer Mill is the centerpiece of the Historical Village and a model for many mini windmills scattered around town.

In 2002 the Vermeer Mill was finally finished, so Pella has a gathering point for its festival, apart from the mini windmills in parks across town. While the Historical Village next to the windmill adds to the attraction, the finale of this trip to Holland is the Klokkenspel, with eight figures dancing in circles every hour to the music of 147 carillon bells bonging away.

→ *Vermeer Mill and Historical Village,* 714 East First Street, (641) 620-9463. From Des Moines, take Highway 163 east, then southeast, for about thirty-five miles. Take the Washington Street exit into town and follow it for about one mile. At Main Street (Highway T14), turn right (south) and go one block to Franklin Street. Turn left and go one block to East First. The mill is on the southeast corner. Open year-round, but closed Sundays.

Indian Princess Statue
Welcomes the Weary Traveler

Legend states that twelve-year-old Pocahontas saved colonist John Smith when she placed her head on his just before her father, Powhatan, was going to bludgeon him to death. Years later, in 1613, she was lured on board an English ship after fighting raged between the Native Americans and the colonists. It was a trap, and Pocahontas was held captive. Even though she'd already been married at age fourteen to an Indian chief, Pocahontas and settler John Rolfe got married a year later. This union brought peace to Jamestown for the rest of her lifetime. Pocahontas converted to Christianity, traveled to England to lobby on behalf of the colonies, and changed her name to "Rebecca."

Perhaps this little town in northeastern Iowa was trying to evoke these images —especially in the wake of the Dakota and Black Hawk wars—when it assumed the name "Pocahontas." Today, the town has expanded the theme to its Chief Motel with a Native American motif. The Geronimo Restaurant is now for sale; maybe customers were wary of testing their bravery at the dinner table.

The main attraction, however, is the towering Pocahontas statue "posed to welcome the weary traveler into town." It was built as a 1954 project of Albert J. Shaw and Frank W. Shaw, according to a plaque on its base. Fortunately, the statue of Pocahontas steers clear of the Disneyfied version with those oversized eyes.

When I bend down to look at the base of the statue, discovering that she's made of covered chicken wire and two-by-fours, someone hollers over at me, "Don't look up her dress, be respectful! Geez!" I should have guessed that she's carefully guarded, judging by the red and white pansies at her feet.

Not only is the statue of Pocahontas well tended, but the townspeople have made a home for her with a false façade in the shape of a tin teepee on the Quonset hut in front of No Mar Towing Equipment.

Pocahontas/Rebecca was nicknamed an "Indian princess," and the town is even dubbed "The Princess City" after her. The English in the 1600s assumed that Native Americans had royalty and that she was a "noble savage" uncorrupted by luxury and European decadence. Perhaps this image as well was intended in the naming of Pocahontas, Iowa.

→ *Pocahontas Statue.* The town of Pocahontas is located about forty-five miles northeast of Fort Dodge at the intersection of Highways 3 and 4. The "princess statue" is east of town on East Elm Street (Highway 3) at Northeast Sixth Street next to the cemetery.

While in the Area

Just thirteen miles west of Pocahontas on Highway 3 and a couple of miles north on County Road 197 is a contender for the World's Largest Dala Horse. The big orangish-red steed stands high above Albert City but well below their other monument, the World's Largest Concrete Silos. With a motto of "How Swede It Is," Albert City boasts the more tangible lure for passing tourists: Swedish pastries.

Facing page: Pocahontas, later known by her Christian name of Rebecca, stands in front of her tin teepee façade on a little Quonset hut.

Future Birthplace of James T. Kirk

Where the Trek Begins

When mention was made on *Star Trek* that Captain James Tiberius Kirk of the *Starship Enterprise* was born in a small town in Iowa, city council member Steve Miller of Riverside got an idea. In 1985, he wrote to *Star Trek* creator Gene Roddenberry and asked why Riverside, Iowa, shouldn't be the "future birthplace of Captain Kirk." Perhaps seeing a chance to generate a little publicity for their sci-fi series, *Star Trek*'s producers agreed.

When licensing fees to Paramount Pictures became exorbitant, the town nicknamed their spaceship USS *Riverside* instead.

Looking more like a tomb than a birth marker, this holy spot indicates where the captain of the USS *Enterprise* will enter the world. Does this mean a hospital will be built here?

The town festival on the last Saturday in June soon changed its name from the overused "Riverfest" to "Trek Fest" to lure sci-fi fans dressed as Vulcans, Klingons, coneheads, and future cadets of Starfleet. "Where the West Begins" used to be written on the Riverside sign welcoming visitors, but that has since been changed to "Where the Trek Begins." Videos of *Star Trek* are screened after the parade, and collectors trade memorabilia at the swap meet.

Some people in town are a little overwhelmed by all the trekkies converging on Riverside. "I don't watch *Star Trek,* but the festival was pretty fun," says the attendant at the Kwik-n-EZ. "There was a costume contest over there at the park, but I didn't dress up."

A sculptor who is fixing up downtown storefronts has a more optimistic take on the festivities. "It ain't the Green Bay Packers, but it sure is a flying farce that sets us apart from every other Podunk town in Iowa. I think Riverside should take advantage of it and have all sorts of prequels filmed of his life before *Star Trek* and Starfleet."

Any profit from Trek Fest is dedicated to erecting a monument to Captain Kirk's future birth. Unfortunately, Paramount won't let little Riverside erect a *Star Trek* statue without a hefty licensing fee of forty thousand dollars.

"That's extortion!" complains the sculptor. "I'm sure, though, that whatsis-name has some high paid agent that will try to get anything out of it he can."

To skirt these legal obstacles, the town built a twenty-foot-long USS *Enterprise* mounted on a trailer in the town park but named it the "USS *Riverside*." Apart from that, a plaque behind the yellow New Image Salon marks where the future local hero will be born on March 22, 2228. Vials of "Kirk Dirt" from this spot are for sale for three dollars via catalog.

The sculptor says, "The other local legend is that he'll be conceived on the pool table in Murphy's Bar—of course, that probably puts him in the running with everybody else in town! I doubt they'll put up any sort of plaque for that, though."

He also gossips that people in town have been wondering what Kirk's ancestry will be, because his great-great-grandparents probably are alive today.

"There's something strange and special about this town that people just up and do things," the sculptor continues. "I just gotta hand it to the son of a bitch who wrote Gene Roddenberry as soon as that line came out in *Star Trek* that Kirk was born in a small town in Iowa. That's genius. I hope Riverside goes overboard and keeps expanding on this crazy idea."

→ *Future Birthplace of James T. Kirk*, 51 West First Street, (319) 648-KIRK (5475). Riverside is nine miles south of Iowa City on Highway 218. Exit on Highway 22 and go west two miles into town. The USS *Riverside* is along 22 on the right (north), and the marker is downtown behind the yellow salon on the right.

Bily Clock Museum
"Officially Priceless"

"Please go upstairs until the tour has begun," suggests the guide in a way that one dare not disobey. "The clocks can only be visited with a tour guide." This is the museum built around the clock by the Bily brothers, lifetime bachelors who kept busy during the cold Iowa winters by whittling beautiful ticking machines that make grandfather clocks seem simple.

The Bily brothers began working in wood at school with an elaborate Virgin Mary, Joseph, and baby Jesus carved into their school desk during lessons. Luckily, the teacher had a sense of humor and gave the desktop to the boys at the end of the year because no other students would sit there. The Bilys gave their schoolwork to their concerned mother.

With little luck in school, the brothers received only a fifth-grade education. The Bilys had a higher calling, however, to make clocks. For fifty years, Frank and Joseph Bily turned wood into huge ticking statues, such as the Creation Clock from 1913 based on Genesis, and the Capitol Clock, with George Washington appearing under the Capitol dome—in spite of the fact that the cupola was not finished until 1863, long after Washington's death.

Even a peek is prohibited, however, until the tour begins. Instead, visitors are shooed upstairs to admire some of the town's artifacts, including arrowheads, a two-headed pig in a jar, and an 1860s "medical puncture" used to "let blood" to cure all sorts of ailments. Visitors can also ooh and aah over the prowess and diligence required to carve a walnut shell into a minuscule basket and a cherry pit into a tiny pitcher, presumably by the brothers Bily.

"Please don't touch the clocks," warns the docent as she carefully puts on her spotless white gloves to open the clocks, like Vanna White turning letters on the *Wheel of Fortune*. The guide presents marvelous clocks such as the Chimes of

Town curiosities (such as the two-headed pig) are stored upstairs at the Bily Clock Museum, while downstairs the "officially priceless" collection of clocks made by the bachelor brothers can be touched only by a docent wearing white gloves.

Normandy, the American Pioneer Clock, and the Apostles Parade Clock, with the Apostles spinning by once an hour.

Besides a clock version of the World's Smallest Church in Festina, the brothers carved a replica of a church in nearby Nashua: doors open up as a little belt transports two wedding couples inside. I ask if this diorama is supposed to represent the Bily bachelors' dreams of getting married. The guide says this is a possibility and is not amused by my mispronunciation of their name. "It's 'bee-lee' not 'bile-ee,'" she corrects as she wiggles her gloved finger.

Adam and Eve await the serpent and banishment from the Garden of Eden in this Genesis-themed cuckoo clock, called "Creation" by the Bily brothers.

"The Bilys never sold any of their clocks and later donated them all to Spillville as long as the collection wasn't separated," informs the guide. "They are now all officially listed as 'priceless.'" No one dares point out that of course they're priceless if they can't be sold.

"Henry Ford offered one million dollars for this clock and they refused," she continues. Someone whispers that maybe they could have gotten married and moved out of Spillville, and then that doubter acts innocent when the docent looks her way.

An elderly visitor takes out her camera to shoot a photo of this beautiful clock. She asks people to step aside, then carefully aims and focuses her camera. Just when she's finally ready to shoot, the guide interrupts her. "You can't take any pictures in here. Our town council voted that no pictures be allowed in here."

With a warning not to touch anything, the guide leaves us alone after the tour to admire the Paradise Clock carved from 1934 to 1936 from butternut and white oak, and the Violin Clock with a portrait of composer Anton Dvorák, who, the docent was proud to point out, lived in the town one summer.

I later ask a manager if I can shoot some photos for the book, and she says it's fine. When I pull out my camera, the elderly visitor asks me if I'm crazy because the guide might throw me out. Luckily, the protective guide is on break, and some other guests risk taking some photos of the beautiful clocks to show people back home.

→ *Bily Clock Museum,* 323 Main Street, (563) 562-3569. Spillville is in northeastern Iowa. From Decorah, take 52 south for about eight miles. Turn right (west) on Highway 325 for about four miles into town. Cross the Turkey River and drive one block. Turn right on Main Street and go one block to the museum on the left (west) side. Open May through October.

Coffee Pot and Cup Water Towers
A Monument to "Mrs. Olson"

When television ads aired of local girl Virginia Christine pushing Folgers Coffee as "Mrs. Olson," Stanton, Iowa, took notice. When Folgers began printing her Swedish face on their coffee cans, residents of Stanton decided they needed to honor their most famous citizen.

"Mrs. Olson" flew home for Stanton's centennial celebration in 1970 to spearhead her homecoming parade as the Grand Marshal. This momentous occasion led to a beautification project for the town of Stanton. Hundreds of gallons of paint were slapped on the side of the town water tower, as Swedish-style *tole* painting transformed this public works into public art.

A year later, the 126-foot-high Coffee Pot Water Tower was complete, and soon people speculated on how many cups of coffee it could contain. Some figured 125,000 cups could fit in the thirty-six-foot-tall tower, while others calculated that the forty thousand gallons would easily make 640,000 cups of Swedish egg coffee.

Nearly thirty years later, these debates were forgotten as a companion water tower was erected holding 150,000 gallons of water, far more coffee than the town could ever hope to drink. This twin tower took the shape of a Swedish *tole*-painted coffee cup to keep with the theme.

These towers are easily visible from a distance; nevertheless, the nickname of Stanton plugged on signs is the somewhat disconcerting "The Little White City" (because most of the houses are painted white). Why not replace it with "The Coffee Capital" after all their valiant efforts? Perhaps in another thirty years Stanton can hit up Folgers for their next water tower, with the possible motifs of an old-fashioned coffee grinder, a sugar bowl, or a coffee can featuring the motherly Mrs. Olson.

Stanton's coffee pot water tower even has flames painted on the bottom to percolate the 125,000 cups of coffee waiting to be piped into houses all over town.

To accompany the coffee pot, a ninety-six-foot-tall cup was erected in 2000.

➜ *Coffee Pot Water Tower,* southeast corner of Thorn Street and Grand Avenue. From I-29 south of Council Bluffs, take Highway 34 for about forty miles to Stanton. Turn right (south) on the "only paved exit into town." At fork, turn left onto Halland Avenue and go over the bridge. Drive to the top of the hill and go left on Grand Avenue. Look up! To arrive at Coffee Cup, continue south on Halland Avenue (past Grand). Cross the railroad tracks and turn right on Highland Avenue for three blocks.

Cowboy and Steer
Colossi in Fiberglass

An enormous cowboy with a fifty-gallon Stetson and a huge longhorn steer ready to ram passing semis tower in front of the Village Farm and Home store in northeastern Iowa. "All the truckers that come into town list the statues on their invoice because it's easier to remember than our name," says Joe Sweeney, who owns the store along with his brother Jerry.

"Our dad [Ray] probably got them about thirty-eight years ago," remember the brothers. "The bull used to be on a trailer in parades and had a lariat lassoed around his neck."

Now the beast's feet have been cemented in place just south of Waukon, but he undergoes the same torture as many such sculptures when teenagers consider them oversized jungle gyms. "One night some kids were swinging on its horns and we had a heckuva time trying to get a new one. We had a farmer finally fix his horns."

The wrangler nearly bit the dust as well. "When we were putting up the cowboy, a real bad wind came right when we were laying the cement and he fell flat on his face just short of the cement. If he'd have fallen two feet further, he'd be hatless!"

The maintenance of these icons seems to have paid off, because the charging bull and the cowboy with ruby red lips were featured in *Smithsonian Magazine* in October 2000. Perhaps the persistence of these highway icons and recognition by the nation's museum will convince Congress that roadside attractions deserve protection as American landmarks.

One of the Sweeney brothers chuckles and tells me, "This probably isn't appropriate to print in your book, but when the cowboy used to stand behind the steer, some kids hung down two enormous garbage bags with a roll of carpet coming out of the middle of the cowboy right into the back of the cow, if you get what I mean. It was pretty funny, actually, but we had to take it down right away because we can't have that out in front of our business!"

→ *Cowboy and Steer,* Village Farm and Home Store, 1718 Rossville Road, (563) 568-4577. Waukon is in northeastern Iowa. From Decorah, take Highway 9 about fifteen miles east to the intersection with Highway 76. Turn left (north) and follow 76 north, which becomes Rossville Road. The statues are on the right (east) side just south of House of Clocks.

Facing page: Standing outside the Village Farm and Home Store, the wrangler and steer have managed to survive intact (in spite of teenagers swinging on the horns of the angry but helpless beast).

House of Clocks
Where Time Has Stopped

I'm late for my tour of the House of Clocks, but Norris the guide says there's no need for an apology. "My time isn't really worth much anymore," he says as he twists the keys to unlock the enormous warehouse.

The door swings open and out spills the musty smell of an old museum of antiquities. This is the life's work of Ray Tlougan, who began his collection in nearby Spillville. Seeing the curiosity seekers pour into the Bily Clock Museum, Tlougan thought he'd tap into the tourist trade with a clock collection of his own. While the Bily brothers passed the cold winters carving their own clocks, Tlougan salvaged everything from huge store clocks to grandfather clocks and spent hours remodeling them.

Ray Tlougan sold his beloved clocks to Ray Sweeney, who moved the collection to nearby Waukon. Sweeney housed them with his own assortment of antique bric-a-brac and a little pioneer village with a train, old cars, a small church, a cabin, the schoolhouse Sweeney attended as a child, etc. As a farm-store owner, Sweeney had some cash to collect knickknacks, and as a part-time auctioneer, he came across thousands of relics and one-of-a-kind memorabilia to fill out his warehouse.

The moment Sweeney retired he began conducting tours of the clocks—perhaps the largest concentration of old clocks in one area in the world. Since Sweeney died in 1994, advertising for the House of Clocks has diminished along with the hours. Private tours of the obsessive assortment and of the de facto Waukon historical museum can be arranged with a call to Sweeney's sons.

"Here's a gold-plated clock made of cast iron found in a La Crosse, Wisconsin, dump but restored by Ray Tlougan," Norris informs me. He points to the oldest clock in the collection and says, "It's from the 1600s—I didn't think that they had even invented the sundial by then!"

Hundreds of wind-up timepieces line the walls of the House of Clocks. The guide has given up keeping them all on time: "As soon as I'd finish winding all the clocks, I'd have to start all over again!"

Tlougan scrounged for historically important timepieces, such as a clock made for an Egyptian ruler in 1876 and another made entirely from wooden gears. Because no cards describe the clocks and a guidebook is out of the question, visitors must rely on local memory. "Some old German Kaiser owned that one, and no one knows how much it's worth," Norris recalls as he shows a gaudy marble clock with little brass figurines.

The House of Clocks is hardly just clocks, however, and holds such curios as an early terrorist bomb from the Prohibition days of bootlegging moonshine. A description only whets the appetite of the inquisitive for the seedy story behind this old copper kettle still for making whiskey:

> Believed to be in a secret hiding place in Alamakee County. It was told when the federal men came in there was dynamite put in it and left to go off. Evidently, the dynamite didn't go off. The man was supposed to have left the country very wealthy.

Other historical oddities include a surprisingly comfortable chair made of cow horns, a barbed wire collection, and presidential spoons featuring the mugs of every executive from Washington to Kennedy. A disturbing display shows two World War I doughboys keeping two garishly painted Native American mannequins under surveillance. Norris is mostly interested in showing off the ancient jukebox spinning seventy-eights of Strauss's "Beautiful Blue Danube," as a mini mechanical band bops around in unison.

All of these peculiarities pale, however, in comparison to the huge wall of clocks. Norris doesn't understand why anyone would donate their old family clocks. "A lot of folks don't like the ticking of these old clocks. I think it's relaxing and helps me fall asleep. . . . I am hard of hearing, though."

Norris keeps the collection alive, although the clatter of a thousand deafening tick-tocks has fallen silent. "I started winding the clocks one day, and it seemed like quite a chore," Norris says. "As soon as I'd finish winding all the clocks, I'd have to start all over again!"

➜ *House of Clocks.* Thrashing Road, (563) 568-3377. From Decorah, take Highway 9 about fifteen miles east to the intersection with Highway 76. Turn left (north) and follow 76 north, which becomes Rossville Road. Go past the enormous cowboy and steer. Turn right (east) onto the dirt Park Road and drive the half block to Thrashing Road. Park past the enormous building with "House of Clocks" painted on the west side. By appointment only; ask the Sweeney brothers at the store with the big steer. Admission charged.

WEST BEND

Grotto of the Redemption
Immortality in Stone

Seminarian Paul Dobberstein was stricken with a nasty bout of pneumonia in Milwaukee after he joined the priesthood. As he lay dying, he promised the Virgin Mary that he would spend the rest of his days building a shrine to her if she would cure what ailed him.

When he miraculously rose from his illness, Dobberstein hadn't forgotten his vow. While finishing up his priestly duties in Wisconsin, "he began to show signs of the unusual artistic ability that was to characterize all the waking hours of his earthly existence," according to the pamphlet *An Explanation of the Grotto of the Redemption.* This skill was in stones. Perhaps, as this explanation points out with bold capital letters, Dobberstein took the text of Isaiah 54:11–12 (repeated in the booklet) to be his calling:

> Thou, the friendless, the storm-beaten, the inconsolable, shalt have a PAVE-MENT of patterned STONES, and their FOUNDATIONS shall be of SAPPHIRE; thou shalt have turrets of JASPER, and gates of carved GEMS, and all the BOUNDARY STONES, shall be JEWELS.

Having emigrated from Rosenfield, Germany, in 1872, Dobberstein was inspired by Old World grottoes carved into the earth and stacked with stones where devout pilgrims could pray to their maker. When he was stationed in West Bend, Iowa, in 1898, however, there was rich black soil but nary a rock in sight. The priest was undeterred and spent the next decade stockpiling rocks for his dream grotto. He traveled far and wide, hauling back hundreds of pounds of rocks, crystals, and minerals from such places as Hot Springs, Arkansas, and the Black Hills in South Dakota.

Dobberstein's faith only grew with each semiprecious gem he cemented into place for his stone Stations of the Cross, and the grotto grew to fill an entire city

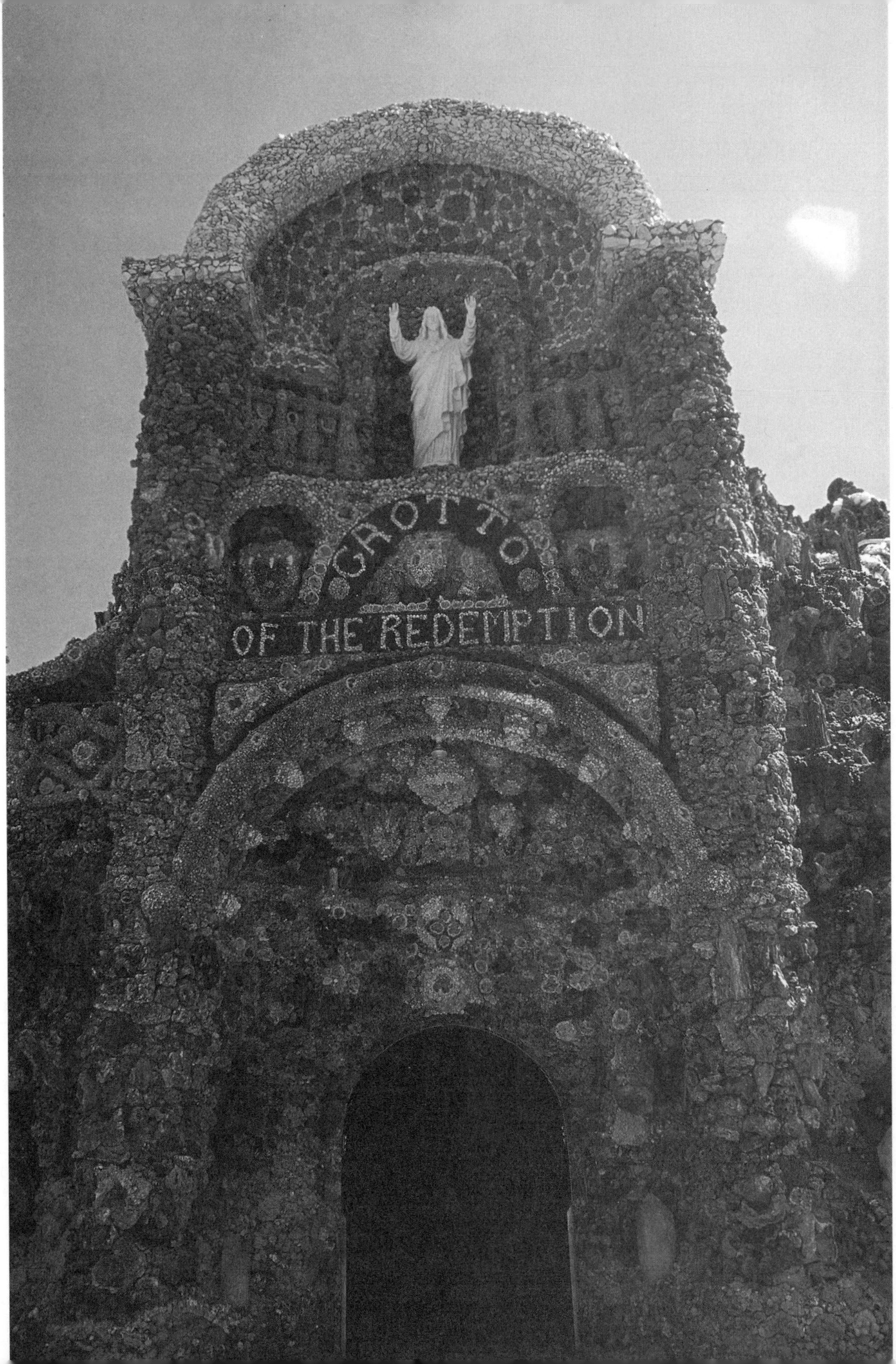
GROTTO
OF THE REDEMPTION

block. He didn't bother with pesky blueprints to complete his vision but instead relied on his geological intuition and divine inspiration to fulfill his promise to the Blessed Virgin Mary. The site became known as "The Grotto of the Redemption," not only for Jesus' deliverance from this earth, but for Dobberstein's revival from pneumonia.

For forty-two years, Dobberstein worked on the Grotto of the Redemption to complete the world's biggest grotto with the largest collection of semiprecious stones known. Pinnacles made of mortar, steeples encrusted with gems, and battlements covered with crystals fill the site. Even the restaurant and the restrooms are plastered with polished stones. Rather than sculpt his own statues, Dobberstein opted for the easy route of plopping relatively bland white figures of angels, Joseph of Arimathea, Nicodemus, and a replica of Michelangelo's *Pietà* as the centerpieces of the nine grottoes.

During his last years, beginning in 1946, Father Dobberstein passed on his vision to Father Louis Greving. They worked together for eight years so Greving could understand the original vision enough to toil for another fifty years on the grotto. A total of ninety-two years of work by these men of the cloth produced the most extraordinary site in Iowa, and a hundred thousand visitors a year would surely agree.

Father Dobberstein "laid down his trowel on July 24, 1954," according to the Grotto's literature. "It was as if God had waited until the last ruddy rays of the setting sun had shed the last warm friendly rays over the twinkling towers of his grottos and then called the tired artist home from his life work."

Dobberstein had accomplished his goal of earthly immortality through rocks, about which he wrote: "Spoken words are ephemeral; written words remain, but their durability depends upon the material upon which they are written; but if carved into bronze or sculptured into stone they are well nigh imperishable."

→ *Grotto of the Redemption,* 300 North Broadway, (515) 887-2371 or (800) 868-3641. West Bend is in north-central Iowa. From I-35, take exit 194 onto Highway 18 going west (toward Clear Lake). After about fifty-eight miles, turn south onto Highway 15. Drive for eight miles, and turn right (west) on Fourth Street North. Go two blocks, then turn left (south) on Broadway Avenue for one block. Open weekdays 9 to 4 P.M., and tours are available June through mid-October.

Facing page: More than four million dollars' worth of crystals and gems make up the Grotto of the Redemption. This holy site was doomed to become just another rock heap when a tornado headed its way in the 1990s. Miraculously, the cyclone jumped into the air and sliced off the tops of trees but spared the grotto.

Covered Bridges
Madison County's Pride

When pioneers started settling in earnest around Winterset, all the little rivers called for bridges for buggies to cross. Rather than replacing the rotting beams every ten years or so, nineteen covered bridges were built in Iowa between 1855 and 1885 to protect the track from any holes that could lead to carriages falling through. The roofs also served to shed any freezing rain destined to make the wood slippery and treacherous.

Only nine of these bridges remain, five of which are in Madison County around the county seat of Winterset. From the picturesque downtown, each of the bridges —from the Holliwell to the Hogback—is within a fifteen-minute drive.

Touring these covered relics smacks of touring a Hollywood set ever since the romance *The Bridges of Madison County* was written, with the subsequent film featuring Clint Eastwood as the roving photographer and Meryl Streep as the misunderstood and lovelorn housewife. Supposedly, many couples now pronounce their love and propose marriage at the Roseman Bridge, where Streep's character left an invitation for dinner for the tough but sensitive man played by Eastwood. The movie location tour continues at the classic Northside Café, established in 1876 off the main square at 61 West Jefferson Street. The final stop is sixteen miles north of town at "Francesca's House," where Streep's persona lived and the guides let truly dedicated fans hop in the bathtub where Eastwood washed.

The upside of all this attention for Winterset is that nearly a hundred thousand people attend the Madison County Covered Bridge Festival on the second weekend in October, and all funds help restore the bridges. The film crew already shelled out the funds to completely restore two of the bridges—the Roseman and the Hogback —so if the movie nostalgia dies down, Madison County will at least have its bridges in pristine shape.

A critic armed with kerosene tried to torch Francesca's House and succeeded in

The Hogback Covered Bridge west of town was renovated in 1992. Ten years later a critic burned the Cedar Covered Bridge and tried but failed to burn the Hogback the following year.

razing Cedar Covered Bridge in the fall of 2002. The book's author, Robert Waller, has offered ten thousand dollars to capture the arsonist, and government offices have chipped in to up the reward to thirty-six thousand dollars. No word yet if a vigilante posse has been set up, but things could change considering the pyromaniac burned another bridge in Delta, Iowa, on the one-year anniversary of the destruction of Cedar Bridge and attempted to set Hogback Covered Bridge ablaze. At this rate, Madison County could be bridgeless within five years unless this rash of negative criticism is halted.

→ *Covered Bridges.* From Des Moines, go west on I-80 for thirteen miles. Turn south at exit 110 onto Highway 169. Drive south for fourteen miles into the town square. Go first to the Madison County Chamber of Commerce off the square at 73 Jefferson Street ([515] 462-1185 or [800] 298-6119) to get a map to all the bridges.

While in the Area

Winterset is home to another local silver screen sensation, whose roles were a far cry from the feel-good romance played by Eastwood and Streep in *Bridges of Madison County*. Marion Morrison was born May 26, 1907, in a little white bungalow at

John Wayne was born not in a frontier town of the Old West, but right here in this quaint bungalow in Winterset.

216 South Second Street but took the more manly sounding stage name of "John Wayne."

His birthplace has been restored to its original condition. The Duke lived in it for his first three years, before his family moved on to Earlham, Iowa. The little four-room house has been converted into a museum ([515] 462-1044) with displays of photos and letters from Gene Autry, Jimmy Stewart, Lucille Ball, and Maureen O'Hara (his fiery costar in *The Quiet One*). While president, Ronald Reagan even stopped by to pay tribute to Wayne and admire one of the fifteen eye patches that the Duke wore in *True Grit*.

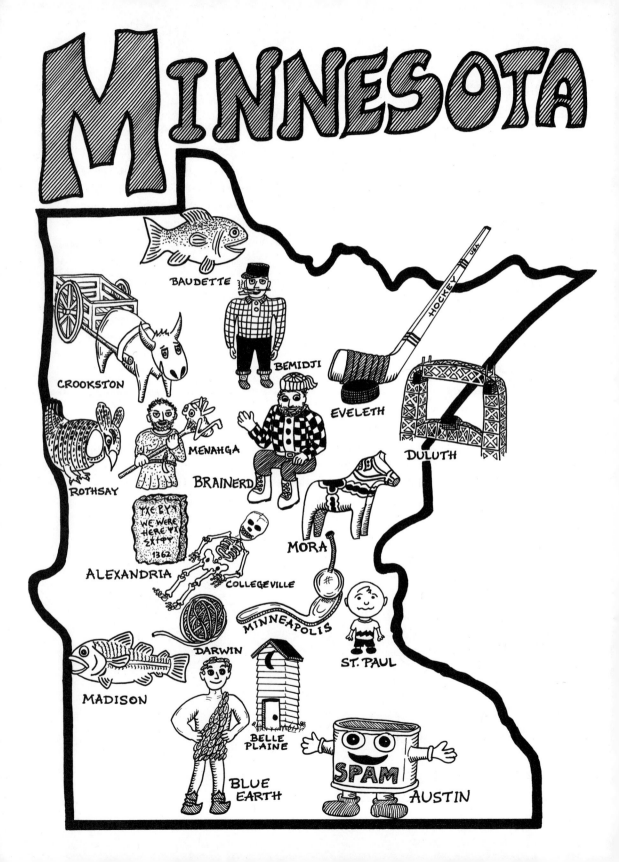

MINNESOTA

BAUDETTE

CROOKSTON

BEMIDJI

EVELETH

DULUTH

ROTHSAY

MENAHGA

BRAINERD

ALEXANDRIA

MORA

COLLEGEVILLE

MINNEAPOLIS

ST. PAUL

DARWIN

MADISON

BELLE PLAINE

BLUE EARTH

SPAM

AUSTIN

HOCKEY

WE BYX
WE WERE
HERE YX
2X1PY
1362

MINNESOTA

Considering the state's name translates as "Land of Sky-Blue Water," one might think that there could be nothing better than relaxing next to one of its more than ten thousand lakes and listening to the loons while the sun sets.

Then, of course, winter strikes. St. Paul holds the record as the coldest state capital; Duluth is the "air-conditioned city"; and International Falls is nicknamed Frostbite Falls. What is there to do from November to April besides wrap baling string to create the World's Largest Twine Ball by One Man? You could build an ice palace like St. Paul does every few years to prove it's not another Siberia. Or you could soak already bland cod in drain cleaner, serve it to your family for Christmas dinner, and then erect an enormous lutefisk statue that can be dressed up for special occasions.

This is not normal behavior. But why raise statues to some self-important governor or statesman when you can create your own idol, like little Menahga did with Saint Urho, who chased the grasshoppers from Finland? Then there's the half-man, half-peapod creature known as the Jolly Green Giant. And don't forget the three huge Paul Bunyan statues. As if that's not enough, towns around these big statues also display relics of the woodsman: his axe, ox, anchor, girlfriend, kid brother, marble, and even his fishing bobber. Perhaps the giant white pines that used to cover the northland inspired tales of this larger-than-life lumberjack.

These monuments reveal what is important to people. Rather than just admiring the otters climbing and sliding on the banks of the river, Fergus Falls built an enormous otter, and now kids climb on it. Rather than just hauling in a lunker of a walleye and feasting on its flesh, towns across Minnesota mounted gigantic statues as evidence of the one that got away. Instead of listening to the loons wail, Vergas and Virginia created huge decoys of the black-and-white bird with red eyes.

These statues may be raised with a knowing smile that they are over the top. Ultimately, though, these attractions represent what is worthy to people—and all the better if they get some grins from visitors.

KENSINGTON RUNESTONE
A.D. 1362

Kensington Runestone
The Mystery Continues

What was dismissed as a hoax during the Depression and sold for a measly ten bucks continues to stump scholars. A huge slab of graywackle stone with ancient writing scrawled onto the surface was suspiciously discovered in 1898 by Swedish immigrant Olof Ohman while clearing stumps from his field near Kensington, Minnesota.

With the Cardiff Giant hoax having duped the public not even thirty years before, the public was wary of another marvel dug up in some field that would rewrite the history books. Ohman's neighbor, minister Sven Fogelblad, confessed he had studied runes, and Ohman was a trained stonemason. Critics were convinced the pair probably forged the writing as an elaborate hoax for a good laugh or perhaps to show that this land belonged to them rather than the Indians after the Dakota Wars in 1862.

If Ohman and Fogelblad indeed carved the stone, they offered no translation of these Nordic runes. Not until nine years after the stone's discovery was the cryptic text finally unraveled, revealing that Norse explorers had supposedly beaten Columbus to the New World:

Eight Goths and 22 Norwegians on an exploration journey from Vinland to the west. We had camp by 2 skerries one day's journey north from this stone. We were to fish one day after we came home found 10 men red of blood and dead AVM [Ave Maria].

Facing page: Go past Scandia Street, Viking Street, and Nissen Street for a close-up view of a replica runestone five times the size of the original at Runestone and Sixth Avenue East. The stone stands on the eastern edge of town along Highway 27, advising people not to question Alexandria's claim of being the "Birthplace of America."

[on the side of the stone] We have 10 men by the sea to look after our ships 14 days' travel from this island Year 1362.

The mysterious stone traveled around the United States and even appeared for a brief stint in the Smithsonian Institution with no specific claim except: "The Smithsonian Institution has appointed no commission, but states, 'Perhaps the most widely known object attributed to the Vikings is the Kensington Runestone.'"

While professors lined up to debunk the stone, Hjalmar Holand, the stone's premier advocate, proposed his theory that this was an expedition sent by King Magnus Erickson of Sweden and Norway in 1355 to find out what happened to earlier explorers in Greenland and Vinland.

Numerous theories have risen and fallen as holes were punched into them by Scandinavian scholars. As recently as 2001, a new book by Thomas Reiersgord speculates that some of the Dakota carried what they thought was "a mysterious stone that had supernatural power . . . [and] . . . identified themselves as the Isanti, meaning the people who possessed 'isan,' the cut stone." The Isanti gave the stone a ceremonial burial with the traditional planting of an aspen tree above it, which Olof Ohman then uprooted during its discovery.

Reiersgord postulates that the "Goths" of the stone were actually Cistercian monks from the Swedish island of Gotland who were often stone carvers and literate. He argues that the "red of blood" doesn't mean the ten men were killed, but that they died of hemorrhaging from the bubonic plague that was ravaging Europe. Therefore, "save us from evil," should actually read "save us from illness."

As further evidence, Reiersgord claims the Dakota worship of the "White Buffalo Woman" stems back to these Nordic monks showing them a portrait of the Virgin Mary. Because these Norsemen probably had bushy white beards, which the Dakota had never seen before, perhaps they called them "White Buffalo Men" and therefore Mary was the "White Buffalo Woman."

New theories about the origin of the stone abound, especially since Ohman stood by his story to the day of his death even after being publicly humiliated. If the runestone indeed was a fantastic fake, why wouldn't Ohman and Fogelblad have taken credit for tricking the world?

Facing page: Even though the Vikings had quit their warring ways by the time the Kensington Runestone was supposedly carved in 1362, the World's Largest Viking was molded to accompany the stone to the 1965 New York World's Fair. The berserker guards the museum at the end of Main Street and is a popular photograph background for proud Scandinavian Americans.

One way to confirm the runestone was valid would be to find another one, and some students did just that a few years ago. With all the intense media pressure, however, they admitted their hoax, casting further doubt on the original stone.

At the end of 2003, the Kensington Runestone traveled to Stockholm for further analysis at the National Historical Museum of Sweden. Specialists in runes ran tests to determine if the stone was indeed more than two hundred years old, as claimed by its advocates. United States ambassador to Sweden Charles Heimbold gave an address in which he asked the question on everyone's mind, "Is it an authentic historical record of an early Scandinavian visit to the New World—over a century before the voyages of Christopher Columbus? Or is it a modern forgery, a strange early Swedish American practical joke?" Once again the stone was debunked, but who wants to believe it's a hoax?

→ *Runestone Museum and Old Fort Alexandria,* 206 Broadway, (320) 763-3160. From I-94, take Highway 29 north into Alexandria. Look for the big Viking statue on the main street (Broadway). Summer only.

Spam Museum

"I think; therefore, I Spam."

E ven the long-awaited inauguration of the new eight-million-dollar Spam Museum suffered from the attacks of the pork-abstaining terrorists. Scheduled for mid-September 2001, the grand opening was delayed a year to properly launch this all-American monument to mass-produced meat.

Hormel has pooled its resources into revisionist history in the state-of-the-art

The Spam Museum fills the old Kmart with cans of deviled Spam swirling overhead on conveyor belts.

During the Spam Jam, the Spam Man dances to the rhythm of the Spamettes singing "S.P.A.M." to the tune of the Village People's "Y.M.C.A."

Spam Museum, which is housed in a building formerly occupied by Kmart. This pork paradise represents Hormel's struggle to keep Spam a relevant American pop cultural icon—like Coca-Cola or Hershey Bars—as opposed to being shelved into the nostalgia of a bygone era as mediocre American cuisine synonymous with unwanted e-mail.

While the museum makes no mention of the pesky labor strikes of the 1980s, much attention is given to comptroller Cy Thomson, who was put through business college by founder George Hormel and then embezzled nearly $1,200,000 by

1916. It is possible to see the checking deposit slips that nearly ruined the world-famous company.

Apart from a miraculous recovery, Spam's biggest feat was, of course, saving the world by winning World War II. After all, Spammy, Hormel's fighting pig, went to war to feed the troops by making the ultimate sacrifice. Sure, doughboys may have turned Spam's company nickname of the "miracle meat" into the "mystery meat that failed the physical," but it was probably a welcome break from K rations. Strangely, *Squeal: the Hormel News-Magazine* claimed, "We have not sold a single can of Spam to the U.S. Army." Was this Hormel's not-so-secret mission to keep the troops fed? Did they just donate all that Spam (unlikely)? Or perhaps they feared becoming a target if stray German bombers ever ventured inland. In any case, Hormel can now boast of their patriotic assignment to rid the world of fascism.

At the time, little was said about Hormel's assistance to the Russkies. Nevertheless, Nikita Khrushchev sang Spam's praises: "There are many jokes going around in the army, some of them off-color, about American Spam; it tasted good nonetheless. Without Spam, we wouldn't have been able to feed our army." If Spam indeed won World War II, did it start the Cold War?

Sadly, the historical photos of the "Hog Kill Gang," the "Meat Cooler Gang," the "Lard Room," and the "Ham Boning Room" were not transferred from the old Spam Museum in a suburban shopping mall to the new cleaned-up, family-friendly digs. Instead, the new state-of-the-art museum encourages interaction. Kids, for example, are able to can their very own Spam. If you do it in fourteen seconds—a very good time indeed—there's little satisfaction. The Austin plant finishes 105 cans in the same amount of time.

While the kids use a little pink rectangular cushion in the shape of the meat inside, "Spam is actually in liquid form when it is pumped into the cans," a guide informs me. "The machine fills six cans at a time, kind of like an old-fashioned six shooter." Behind him, comic drawings of cute pigs show how the happy animals stuff themselves in the pasture on fresh corn. The animals then joyfully enter the factory and magically come out the other side as big cans of Spam ready for your lunch.

The guide explains how 960 hogs are "processed" per hour. While I reel at the thought of all those pigs, an endless conveyor belt overhead is shuttling around a constant line of Spam and I feel like a cartoon character imagining his favorite pork products—Spam and Cheese, Cured Pork Tongue, Smoke-Flavored Spam,

Spam-n-Tongue, Deviled Spam Curds. "My favorite is the red cans of Spam with Tabasco," the guide confides.

"If all the cans ever eaten were placed end-to-end, they would circle the globe at least ten times," he tells us. I picture the earth with a belt of blue-and-yellow cans to rival the rings of Saturn. Hormel claims the dubious honor of being the first company in the world to can a ham. The guide points out a photo of the fifty-millionth pig dressed in ribbons and photographed before being "processed" into Spam.

What put the miracle in this meat is not the sheer quantity but its versatility, according to one display. Multicultural recipes abound, from Spam sushi to Korean kimchi Spam to Spam pizza. The new prize-winning recipe, however, is Spam cupcakes.

A video loop of Monty Python's anti-Spam skit runs continuously, something that was conspicuously absent from the old museum. Apparently, here they subscribe to the theory that any publicity is good publicity, or perhaps Hormel's newfound ironic detachment now lets it poke fun at itself. More perplexing is a life-sized video version of Al Franken hosting a surprisingly normal Spam game show. Sure, Hormel must have paid him a pretty penny to push Spam. But isn't Al Franken Jewish?

The exit for the Spam Museum is skirted by the four-thousand-can Wall of Spam, with a nearly indefinite shelf life and the perfect provisions to save us from the next world war.

Apart from the nation's defense, Hormel's dabbling in the arts has made them the Medici of Austin: the annual Spam Jam is the Uffizi for area artists to express their creativity in pork. One year, Rodin's *The Thinker* was the best of show, a meaty reference followed up years later by an advertisement for then-gubernatorial wannabe Jesse Ventura when the beefy candidate made the mind-body split.

Health nuts may shudder at the site of all this spiced ham at the Spam Jam, but who can resist a free Spamburger amid all the nostalgia for a time when canned food was good food?

The ubiquitous product placement of this four-letter word to promote processed pork at the museum and festival borders on brilliant mental conditioning of all in attendance to ensure sales through the next millennium. At the museum exit, a big-boned gentleman hands out free Spam magnets. He has a strangely vacant smile on his face and wears a T-shirt silk-screened with a witty consumptive twist on Cartesian observed logic, "I think; therefore, I Spam."

→ *Spam Museum*, corner of North Main Street and Spam Boulevard, 1937 Spam Boulevard, (800) LUV-SPAM or (507) 437-5100. Take the Sixth Street exit off I-90. Turn south and go toward the Hormel factory. At the "T" turn right, then stay right at the fork. Just past the bridge is the museum on the right side of the road.

BELLE PLAINE

Two-Story Outhouse
Historic Practical Joke?

Before Thomas Crapper popularized the water closet in England and its use spread to the United States, even wealthy families were constrained to use an outhouse to do their duty. Rather than stoop to using the shiver shack or risk capsizing a jam-packed chamber pot, Sandford Hooper created an architectural marvel that doubles as a running joke.

When the Hooper-Bowler-Hill House was built in 1871, a two-story privy was tacked on a few feet away—just far enough to prevent unwanted fumes from wafting into the bedrooms. The covered "skyway" (the world's first?) on the second story allowed toilet-goers to avoid getting their toes cold by not stepping outside. But what about the poor souls downstairs? The outhouse is ingeniously designed with the top floor set back to conveniently avoid unwelcome surprises from above.

To dispel speculation from neighbors as to the nature of this tall but little wooden building, no crescent moons are carved into the side. Outhouse lore claims that to be discreet and to guide the illiterate, suns were once cut into privy doors to show it was the men's room and moons for the women's. Over time, the gentlemen's outhouse often fell into disrepair from lack of male scrubbing skills, and the moon privy became the go-to spot. In Belle Plaine's two-story outhouse, full-fledged windows were mounted instead of a crescent moon, and to avoid the potential methane blast if a lit lantern was carried inside.

As Samuel Bowler had so many kids, the two-story outhouse boasts five holes. Different-sized seats could be swapped as the children grew, preventing everyone's

Facing page: The two-story outhouse was attached to the 1871 Hooper-Bowler-Hill House to make those late-night runs to the privy a bit more comfortable. From the upstairs bedroom, just walk across the historical skyway to the second story, ingeniously set back to avoid unwanted surprises to those busy on the first floor.

nightmare of slipping through the hole, especially from the second story. To avoid tipping over the tower, the hole was apparently dug deep enough to never require moving this mini skyscraper over new digs.

This redoubtable outhouse has become a de facto symbol of Belle Plaine, and T-shirts proclaim the town "Home of the Two-Story Outhouse." Who wouldn't brag, since this is probably one of the only outhouses in the country to win a spot on the National Register of Historic Places?

→ *Two-Story Outhouse,* Hooper-Bowler-Hill House, 410 North Cedar Street (at East Court Street), (952) 873-6109. From Highway 169, take the Belle Plaine exit north into town and look for the old white house next to the town park. Open Sundays from 1 to 4 P.M. during the summer.

Jolly Green Giant
Who Stole Sprout?

Born in a boardroom as a menacing white giant covered by an enormous bearskin when he first appeared in 1925 on a bag of beans, the Jolly Green Giant soon underwent a face-lift for a more positive corporate image. The original design, lifted from a Grimms' fairy tale, was a Blue Earth Canning Company patented peapod mascot. That was traded for a happier, humanized green colossus to sweep its cans off the supermarket shelves.

This vegetarian giant was content being a two-dimensional drawing relegated to veggie labels until 1978, when Blue Earth showed what it meant by a giant. The year coincided with the culmination of Eisenhower's dream of paving America with a cross-country interstate highway system that connected in Blue Earth. In an attempt to recreate the brouhaha of the golden spike hammering in a cross-country railway in 1869, Blue Earth used "imported gold paint from Germany" to color a strip of golden concrete at the rest stop just west of town.

Local KBEW radio owner Paul Hedberg had an even better idea. From his bully pulpit on the airwaves, he preached of his vision of an enormous green beast towering over Blue Earth. While skeptics scoffed, eleven local businesses stepped forward and pitched in at least five thousand dollars each. Creative Displays (now F.A.S.T.) of Sparta, Wisconsin, finished the thousand-dollar-a-foot Jolly Green Giant in a mere eight weeks and trucked it down I-90 to Blue Earth.

On September 23, 1978, as the crowd looked down on the golden cement patch, a fifty-five-and-a-half-foot giant was erected to look down on them. This historical reference to the golden spike was overshadowed by the corporate reference to the lovable half-vegetable, half-human symbol that put Blue Earth on the map.

As the largest of Minnesota statues, this de facto greenish-golden spike stands as the emblem for the link of the world's longest interstate highway, I-90. Originally, Jolly's personal objects, such as his size seventy-eight shoes, were slated to be

The Jolly Green Giant keeps watch over Blue Earth. This fifty-five-and-a-half-foot colossus is not to be confused with the diminutive two-dimensional version standing over the valley in Le Sueur.

a little amusement park for kids to play in, but corporate mergers have left the giant less of a logo and more of a symbol of fertile farmlands.

The Jolly Green Giant knows it's not easy being green and puts on his four-foot smile, even though his little buddy Sprout was recently abducted, beheaded, and hung from the interstate overpass by ruffians from Fairmount. Jolly's TV sidekick was born in 1973, but little Sprout was always only a three-foot-tall, two-dimensional halfling. Jolly's "Ho, ho, ho" is back, for his dwarfish pal is scheduled to be replaced any day now, but still the giant's eight thousand pounds don't seem to intimidate envious out-of-towners.

The Blue Earth Chamber of Commerce is upbeat about the constant threat of kidnapping by the neighboring malcontents, and they say hopefully that the dull golden cement on the interstate is safe: "I don't think they could steal that one!"

→ *Jolly Green Giant.* Go south of I-90 on Highway 169 a few blocks. Look up for the giant on the right side of the road.

Saint Peregrine

Roman Boy Martyr

The Roman emperor Commodus was the jealous type. Seeing the glory bestowed upon the gladiators as they bludgeoned each other to death and the Roman women swooning over the surviving heroes, Commodus entered the ring himself to show Rome that Caesar was mightier than these mere mortal warriors. Of course Caesar's melee in the Colosseum was probably rigged in his favor, but the bloodshed of his victims was real.

To honor himself on his birthday in A.D. 192, Commodus decreed that all Rome should come to adore him dressed in his new outfit as Hercules, with a revealing scanty lion skin, an oversized club, and his imperial crown. While most Romans had little choice but to hail this narcissistic emperor, Christians were especially appalled by this show of vanity.

Eager to be martyred for Christ, four Christians—Eusebius, Vincent, Pontian, and the boy Peregrinus—ran into the streets and condemned Commodus, beseeching Romans to abandon worshipping the emperor and his gods. The four were summarily scooped up by the Praetorian guard and executed, but not before being thrashed with clubs, burned with torches, stretched on the rack, and flogged with lead whips.

Their preaching was not in vain, however. A rich Roman senator named Julius heard the word and converted to Christianity. His vast wealth was bestowed upon the poor. Commodus thoughtfully gave Julius the chance of worshipping Caesar before executing him, his body flung out on the streets.

Conversions to Christianity continued in the jail cell, as one of the torturers of the four condemned men saw an angel shielding his victims from the flames and dabbing their wounds with a sponge. The torturer quit his thankless job and hurried off to be baptized. Another miracle was performed when Lupulus, a priest for the Roman god Jupiter, visited the convicted and was converted. Once blind, Lupulus miraculously could now see.

The four martyred bodies were gathered by devout Christians and carried to the catacombs under Rome. On a visit to Rome in 1731, Abbot Kilian Kneuer took the bones of Saint Peregrine back to his monastery in Neustadt-am-Main, Germany. The Benedictine monks there were forced to give up their abbey and the holy relics to Prince Löwenstein during the Napoleonic wars, however. Perhaps as divine retribution against the prince, fire ravaged the church in 1854. The bones of Peregrine, again miraculously, remained unscathed.

Then in 1895 a monk from Saint John's Abbey, Father Gerard Spielmann, was on a visit home to southern Germany when he appealed to the new Prince Löwenstein to give the body of Saint Peregrine back to the Benedictines. After a stint in the Bronx, the bones of the boy martyr came to Collegeville to stay in 1927.

Just north of Cold Spring, the home of the bones is the impressive Saint John's Abbey, which has a 112-foot-high modernist bell tower by Marcel Breuer that rings

Saint Peregrine's martyrdom began with his objections to the revealing lion-skin outfit of Roman Emperor Commodus. The remains of the boy saint are lovingly protected at Saint John's Abbey. *Photograph courtesy of Saint John's Abbey.*

out the good word every fifteen minutes. Abbott Jerome Theisen even "baptized" the now-sacred white tower and its biggest bell, weighing in at a hefty four tons.

Founded in 1856, the church has the largest stained-glass window in the world, depicting religious holidays and a kaleidoscope of ever-expanding circles meant to be none other than God. One of the designs for the church was submitted by Frank Lloyd Wright, but the monks opted for a simpler design of poured concrete.

After lounging on Lake Sagatagan at the "monastic beach" (the public is steered to the "students' beach"), the monks can browse through one of the largest collections of medieval manuscripts in the world, containing documents from such places as Malta, Italy, Ethiopia, France, Austria, and Germany. The story goes that a monk received a vision that he needed to put as many manuscripts and incunabula on microfiche as possible.

The abbey's pride, however, are the bones of Saint Peregrine in the reliquary chapel. The abbey's saint is not to be confused with Saint Peregrine of Forlì from 1265, who inflicted self-mortification, such as refusing to sit, out of penance for his sins. The resulting varicose veins in his legs turned cancerous, but Christ descended from a crucifix to heal him the day before the impending amputation. The phenomenal cure of his "odiferously cancerous foot" earned him the title of "Patron Saint of Cancer Victims."

However, Saint John's Peregrine is not one of the "incorruptibles," as he is sometimes called. "Our Peregrine is quite corrupt," according to Saint John's Brother Richard, who then clarifies, "Incorruptibility is not a required condition for canonization."

While Saint Peregrine may not have performed any recent miracles or have as many pilgrims as more well-known martyrs, the boy saint can rest in peace knowing that his assassin, Emperor Commodus, died the same year he did. Without a strong, arrogant leader, Rome sank into chaos, with numerous generals declaring themselves the new divine Caesar. It was more than a hundred years before Constantine would declare Rome to be Christian.

→ *Saint Peregrine,* reliquary of Assumption Chapel, Saint John's Abbey, 38120 County Road 159, (320) 363-3514. Take the St. John's University exit off I-94, then follow the signs.

CROOKSTON

Red River Ox Carts
Fifteen Miles per Day

Early European settlers along the Red River Valley of the North often resorted to trapping to augment their income from farming. Selling the valuable furs, however, required transporting them long distances. To the north, Hudson's Bay Company practically owned Manitoba and monopolized all fur trade. Exporting of Canadian furs was illegal, and the Hudson's Bay Company paid a pittance.

Only Babe the Blue Ox could pull the World's Largest Ox Cart, outside the Polk County Historical Society in Crookston.

Joe Rolette was the "Father of the Pembina Trail, Savior of St. Paul, a Giant among Pioneer Giants, and a Real Life Paul Bunyan," according to brochures about the fifteen-foot statue of this French Canadian who served on the Minnesota Territorial Legislature. The fifty-foot-long ox and cart were saved in 2002 when the boys at Delta Theta Sigma fraternity rebuilt and painted the statues after they were damaged by a windstorm.

Trappers were left with little choice but to carry their catch all the way to St. Paul to connect with the American Fur Company, where John Jacob Astor's empire usually paid more than double what the Canadians paid.

Carrying the pelts to this future capital of Minnesota posed a problem. Steamboats reached only as far as St. Paul in the 1840s, and James J. Hill hadn't laid tracks up north yet. Because there's not a hill in sight around the ancient lake bottom of Lake Agassiz, the Red River Valley was perfect for simple carts pulled by oxen.

Initially, round sections of large trunks made up the wheels, but the trees rarely measured over three feet in diameter. Soon, spokes were added to a rim for five- to six-foot-wheels to prevent the wagon from flipping over if a tree stump or stone blocked the path. When the wheels spun around the ungreased axle, the screeching could be heard for miles and the din was said to drive passengers nearly mad.

In a pinch, these clumsy-looking carts could be turned into a raft for river crossing, and sometimes the wheels were simply slipped off the axle and used for flotation. Most important, these versatile carts with oversized wheels could trek over the thick prairie grass and marshy thickets without getting bogged down, and at night they doubled as tents when canvas was flung over the top for shelter.

Soon hundreds of ox carts made the summer trip from Pembina in Dakota Territory along the border with Canada down to St. Paul. Caravans of dozens of carts transported everything from pelts to produce to market. The squeaking carts trudged along at a painfully slow pace, however, averaging fifteen miles on a good day with no problems. The voyage from Pembina to St. Paul easily lasted a month or more, so a trip to the town was not to be taken lightly.

Ox carts helped bring new settlers into the fertile Red River Valley, and the deep tracks of the carts are still visible along some stretches of the trails they followed. Two deep grooves remain where the wheels made their mark, and a wider track between the two shows where beefy oxen lugged the load. Many of these trails have since been covered by concrete to become major roads and highways.

To honor these early pioneers, Crookston celebrates Ox Cart Days every year in August. A giant replica of oxen driver Joe Rolette and a Red River Ox Cart, created by E. A. Konickon, is complete with an ox clad with horseshoes and an electrical outlet attached to one of the wheels. Outside the county historical museum stands an even bigger replica, dubbed the World's Largest Ox Cart, which some say was used by none other than Paul Bunyan and Babe the Blue Ox.

→ *World's Largest Ox Cart,* Polk County Historical Society, 719 Robert Street East, (218) 281-1038. Crookston is in northwestern Minnesota. From downtown, take Highway 2 a half mile southeast. The museum and ox cart are on the left (northeast) side of the highway.

→ *Pembina Trail Memorial,* Highway 2 North. From downtown, take Highway 2 one mile north. The Joe Rolette statue and ox cart are on the left (west) side of the highway in front of the Red River Valley Shows building.

Twine Ball
Largest Made by One Man

Between the man with the beard of bees and the guy from India with the longest fingernails, *Guinness* wrote up the world's largest ball of twine, crafted by Francis Johnson. These visionaries were the ones that made the *Guinness Book of World Records* famous and encouraged others to set another weird world record for something that no one had ever even imagined before.

Folks in Darwin, however, weren't so sure about being thrown in the limelight for this stringed oddity. As an obsessed collector of anything he could get his hands on (five thousand pencils, two hundred feed caps, buckets, padlocks, pliers, etc.), Johnson began the secret twine ball project in his house. Four hours a day were dedicated to his string to keep him busy during the cold Minnesota winters. After the unusual project outgrew his house, the ball was relegated to the barn, where he hoisted it with a railroad winch to achieve a more perfectly even wrapping technique.

For the world to get a look at his masterpiece and see what he'd been doing all these months, Johnson's ball was rolled into his yard next to his cupola, painted bright yellow and blue due to his overflowing Swedish pride. A photo was snapped of this new world record, and suddenly tourists started stopping at tiny Darwin for a peek.

Fame can be difficult, however. Once the photo of Francis Johnson standing next to his twelve-foot twine ball ran in *Guinness*, Frank Stoeber of Cawker, Kansas, knew he could collect more string. Stoeber wound and wound 1.6 million feet of baler twine night and day. Victory was in sight as his ball reached eleven feet in diameter. With just one foot diameter more spun around, he could ring up *Guinness* to take his place in the annals of history. Tragically, on the eve of his glory, Stoeber had a heart attack and died in 1974.

Rather than letting this tragedy end in defeat, Cawker, Kansas, rallied for an an-

The twelve-foot-diameter, eleven-ton masterpiece of eccentric Swede Francis Johnson put little Darwin on the map. The famous ball even has its own mailbox for fan letters.

nual Twine-a-thon Festival to add more string to the ball in tribute to Frank Stoeber. The twine ball was placed on Cawker's Main Street under a little shelter for all to admire.

Perhaps competition for the dubious title inspired residents of Darwin to build a Plexiglas silo in the main square and raise banners along the light poles for "Twine Ball Days." Only with special permission can the twine ball reliquary be breached to lay hands on the famous ball and inhale the hallowed air of the musty twine.

In 1989, Francis Johnson passed on to greener pastures after spinning twine for thirty-nine years. A few years later, Ripley's Believe It or Not had a ploy to exploit the famous ball in one of its galleries of the grotesque and fascinating. The town of Darwin united around the eleven-ton twine ball and refused Ripley's. The freak show chain was undaunted and turned to a Texan to make one even bigger. J. P. Payne from Mountain Springs, Texas, hired a crew to surpass Darwin's record with a twine ball measuring thirteen feet and two and a half inches. "It's probably bigger but doesn't weigh as much; it's not of twine and not done by one person," rebuts the woman at the Twine Ball Souvenir Shack in Darwin. She laments these other copycat balls, saying, "They took us out of *Guinness.*"

What originally raised eyebrows toward this bizarre collection of string by an eccentric Swede has become the symbol of tiny Darwin, Minnesota. The local café has adopted the name the Ball of Twine Inn and showcases Johnson's collection of pliers. The ball of twine even has its own little mailbox.

→ *Twine Ball.* From Highway 12, turn south into Darwin. The twine ball is on the left in a little park.

DULUTH

World's Largest Aerial Lift Bridge

Elevator to the Heavens

Follow the sounds of the squawking seagulls to the world's largest aerial lift bridge, visible from nearly any high point in town. The traffic halts as a new barge rolls into Duluth Harbor and the middle section of this iron bridge rises into the sky. After a few minutes, cars sputter across the metal grates of the bridge out

Stories abound about horrible tragedies of people getting stuck on or jumping from the world's largest and fastest lift bridge in Duluth. These urban legends probably were invented by bored motorists with vivid imaginations waiting for the bridge to come back down.

to Park Point and its beautiful sand beach along the south shore of Lake Superior. No wonder the lift bridge has become the symbol of Duluth.

While the middle span ascends and descends, motorists waiting in their cars inevitably ponder how dangerous this bridge could be if someone were caught in the wrong spot. Rumors spread about unfortunate fatalities caused by this enormous moving guillotine. Duluthian Scott Lunt swears it's not just hearsay. "Oh it happened, and I have seen the pictures. In fact, my old partner Fuzzy at Gold Cross was on call. . . ." Lunt recalls the legendary day when the bridge accidentally turned guillotine. "When the bridge started going up she became confused and tried to run off the bridge."

Even so, Canal Park at the foot of the bridge is ground zero for Duluth's tourist destination. Cappuccino cafés, trendy shops, and Grandma's ever-expanding restaurant are favorite hot spots on the small peninsula overlooking Lake Superior, the world's largest freshwater lake. Duluth's freshwater Great Lakes Aquarium has struggled to survive—some critics have suggested it should have an enormous fish fry to recoup losses. The building has stayed in business and basked in the limelight by hosting such offbeat events as the local Geek Prom.

Displays at the Lake Superior Maritime Visitors Center next to the bridge in Canal Park explain that this enormous lake contains 20 percent of the world's fresh water. A lesser-known fact is that Russia's Lake Baikal holds double the amount of water. The usual retort is that Lake Baikal covers only 12,500 square miles, whereas Superior is nearly triple that area at 31,700 square miles. The Maritime Center is operated by the U.S. Army Corps of Engineers and features reconstructed ship cabins and tours of a huge steam engine.

→ *World's Largest Aerial Lift Bridge,* Canal Park, and Lake Superior Maritime Visitors Center, (218) 727-2497. From I-35, turn on Canal Park Drive. The road dead-ends at the visitors center, which is open summer only.

→ *Great Lakes Aquarium,* 353 Harbor Drive, (218) 740-3474. From I-35, take exit 256B and go southeast on Lake Avenue for one block. Turn right (west) on Railroad Street and drive for three blocks. Turn left on Fifth Avenue West, and the aquarium is on the right along the shore.

Built in 1939, at its peak Enger Tower stands five hundred feet above the lake.

While in the Area

Another site fraught with rumor in the air-conditioned city is the mysterious hexagonal bluestone tower on the top of the bluff. One theory claims it's a lighthouse designed to prevent the wreck of a second *Edmund Fitzgerald*. Another hypothesis says it's a huge tombstone in memory of a man overcome with grief for his dearly departed. A third guess argues that the six-story stone building was an early prison—like the Tower of London—to house Chicago bootleggers nabbed by Duluth's untouchables.

In reality, Enger Tower was constructed to honor a Norwegian immigrant who came to the New World penniless and struggled to become a successful businessman in this northern port. Prince Olav flew in from Oslo to dedicate the sixty-foot tower, which sees both sunrise and sunset, a rarity in this hilly burg.

The park also boasts an enormous Peace Bell from Japan. Scrounging for any metal for the war effort, the Japanese army had fated the bell to be melted for matériel to help the land of the rising sun. When the bell escaped the furnaces, American seamen aboard the USS *Duluth* nabbed the big bell from Ohara, Japan, as a spoil of war. The booty was sent to the ship's namesake for display. In the interest of peace in the 1950s, the bell was returned to Ohara, which made a replica to display in Duluth. In 1994, the new bell was dedicated as the Peace Bell and rings out over Duluth from near the base of Enger Tower.

EVELETH

World's Largest Hockey Stick
Notwithstanding the Weather

On September 7, 1995, Eveleth was all abuzz. A 107-foot hockey stick was on its way from Christian Brothers in Warroad to be erected in this Hockey Capital of the United States. Sirens wailed and police lights swirled as the Minnesota Highway Patrol escorted this huge piece of wood on its four-hour voyage.

A week later, the stick was mounted and ready for face-off with a seven-hundred-pound hockey puck above Hockey Plaza. Across the street on the side wall of the hardware store, a thirty-foot-tall goalie mural awaited audience tauntings of "Sieve!" once the might of this world's largest hockey stick was let loose.

Once erected, however, Eveleth's new symbol proved not to be big enough; the Canadians had a stick double the size. Luckily in November 1995 the *Guinness Book of World Records* wisely disallowed the Canucks' claim because their stick wasn't regulation. Eveleth's stick withstood the challenge and was deemed the biggest on earth.

Six years later, the stick showed signs of sagging. Some worried that the seven-thousand-pound stick could come down with a crash and crush some poor hockey fan snapping a photo—definitely not good for the tourist trade. The original thirty laminations of the "Pro 1000" stick weren't enough to fend off the elements and the woodpeckers. The day before the Fourth of July 2001, Eveleth's place in the *Guinness Book of World Records* was erased.

The city rallied for a comeback, however, and sold off slices of the old stick for five dollars a pop to fund a new one. In June 2002, Sentinel Structures of Peshtigo, Wisconsin, finished the new stick and shipped it to Eveleth with a police escort. The 110-foot stick stands once again over the face-off circle, with a surrounding fence to look like hockey dasher boards. While some hockey buffs don't brave venturing beneath the ten-thousand-pound stick, the City of Eveleth assures visitors that the stick is absolutely safe and purely regulation.

Little did tourists to the hockey capital know that the World's Largest Hockey Stick was an accident ready to happen. Luckily, hockey fans in Eveleth replaced the 110-foot-long monument with a safe (but authentic) stick.

→ *World's Largest Hockey Stick Constructed Like a Real Hockey Stick,* Hockey Plaza, 122 Grant Avenue. Eveleth is fifty miles north of Duluth on Highway 53. Turn off into town and the stick is down Main Street at Grant Avenue.

While in the Area

More famous than the huge stick, however, is the U.S. Hockey Hall of Fame perched on the hill above town. While northern Minnesota may seem like an odd spot to put such an important national monument, "no other town of Eveleth's size in the country has contributed so much to the sport of ice hockey," boast the brochures.

The town's first hockey team was formed in 1902, and, in 1956 alone, four of the members of the U.S. Olympic hockey team hailed from Eveleth. Inside, you can hum along to the Gear Daddies' song "I Wanna Drive a Zamboni" while admiring the fourth ice machine ever built. In the museum's Great Hall, view a hockey game from the terrifying perspective of the goalie's mask and hope that your teeth are still intact. The highlight, however, is the ice rink, where you can show off your slapshot and dream of being the next Gretzky inducted into these hallowed halls.

→ *U.S. Hockey Hall of Fame,* 801 Hat Trick Avenue, (218) 744-5167 or (800) 443-7825. Follow the signs off Highway 53 just north of town.

World's Largest Otter
Another "Monstrosity"?

"How I got interested was that I traveled all over the country and took pictures of big statues," teacher and sculptor Bob Bruns recalls. "You know that every town has something big, usually a big statue, they can be proud of." From his collection of little statuettes, Bob picked out a little mallard that he used as a model for a colossus for Wheaton, Minnesota.

Bob convinced the Wheaton Lions Club to bankroll a big bird. "Two brothers started it in 1959 and finished it in 1961. A couple of other guys did the wire mesh, then someone stuccoed it, and then a group of people painted it three times over the years," Bob says. Around the base of the duck, a mantra for life was painted: "Fishing," "Farming," "Hunting," and "Living."

Following the erection of the twenty-six-foot-tall bird based on a five-inch figurine, Bob moved on to Fergus Falls to build an even bigger otter from an even smaller statuette. Bob says, "The otter was a little ceramic figure about two inches tall—about the size of one of your fingers. We built it from January to June in 1962. I moved over there as a teacher, and they all knew that I had done the otter. We had two classes of fifteen kids from the vocational school who did the frame and all the welding. Both Steve Jaenisch and a teacher named Tom Willitt did a lot of the work. In the end, the otter sits thirty feet long and twelve feet tall."

The otter instantly became a jungle gym for anyone visiting its lair in Adams Park. "We built it so the otter looked like it was ready to leap into the lake," Bob says, and then laughs. "Every time I drive by it in the summer, there's always kids climbing on it. I don't think kids could get up on the duck in Wheaton, though. The mallard's wings weren't originally so vertical, but we made it that way so kids wouldn't climb up on it and hurt themselves."

Inspired by this new symbol of Fergus Falls's status as the county seat of Otter Tail county, miniature replicas of the sculpture popped up along Main Street.

"Do not climb on the otter," warn signs next to Fergus Falls's mammalian monument, but visitors can't resist leaning a picnic table against the animal to get on its head.

"When they renovated the downtown, they put in some small otters near the planters under the old-fashioned street lamps. They were upright otters that came out ten or twelve years ago. If a car happened to jump the sidewalk, though, it would run one of the little otters right over. Kids liked to tip over the otters, and they became the object of vandalism."

Local teenagers viewed this lineup of otters as their canvas, spray painting them all the colors of the rainbow. Some even brought their heads home on a platter, perhaps in reference to John the Baptist's noggin offered to Salomé. "Everyone was

doing it that summer," said a local teen who asked to go unnamed. "I think Fergus tried to put out new otters the next year, but then gave up."

Bob's wife laments, "There's no more little otters unless they have one in the town museum." She then pointed out how St. Paul now has the little Peanuts statues and Washington, D.C., has the donkeys and elephants. "It's true, towns all over the country are now doing the same thing as Fergus Falls."

"For us, these big statues are normal. Outside of Paul Bunyan, we have a lot of big things around here, like the Pelican in Pelican Rapids and the loon in Vergas." Then she adds with a laugh once her husband is out of earshot, "We call them all 'monstrosities!'"

→ *World's Largest Otter.* Take the Highway 210 exit north off I-94. Turn left on Pebble Lake Road, and the otter will appear soon after in Adams Park.

→ *World's Largest Mallard.* Wheaton is in west-central Minnesota. The duck is at the intersection of Highways 75 and 27 next to Traverse County Fairgrounds.

Facing page: The twenty-six-foot-tall mallard of Wheaton was erected for just $1,200 in 1959 and stands as a lit beacon to truckers tooling down Highway 75.

Cordwood Pete and Tamarack
Paul Bunyan's Kid Brother

Although the local opera house was razed, a legendary local fellow who was once lost has been raised from the dead. Under the foundation of the old opera house theater, which was later Hartz Store, a time capsule was discovered dating back to the late 1800s. Inside, the tale was told of a squat French Canadian lumberjack named Peder Le Dang, weighing in at a puny hundred pounds and standing barely four feet, nine inches. Taller lumberjacks nicknamed Le Dang "Cordwood Pete" because the little lumberjack would rather split cordwood than saw big logs.

When Pete would hit the hooch, however, he'd brag that he was the mightiest man in Minnesota for his size, which was probably true considering his height. No other lumberjack would fight the feisty French Canadian, but they all admired his spunk.

The local lawman kept the peace, but Pete kept raising a ruckus. With a little sleuthing, Sheriff Holt discovered that Pete had grown up in Bangor, Maine—the same town as Paul Bunyan—and fit the description of this gentle giant's little brother Peder. When confronted with the evidence, Pete admitted the relation but never wanted to live in the shadow of his big brother. Perhaps he was embarrassed that his sibling nabbed all the flapjacks at the breakfast table, leaving little Pete practically a midget.

The woodcutters in Maine mocked him for his size, and they didn't let poor Peder join in any lumberjack games at the annual rendezvous. When Pete heard that Paul was making a name for himself in Minnesota, he took the next train west to the end of the line, which was Fosston in 1883.

Cordwood Pete snuck into his brother's camp one night and pinched Paul's double-bladed axe. During the getaway, Pete swung the axe and couldn't stop it. Before he could gain control of it, he'd felled one hundred acres of forest in a single day. The railroad took notice and hired this diminutive lumberjack with the

Part man, part myth, Cordwood Pete was forgotten for decades until a time capsule from the 1800s was uncovered to help complete Paul Bunyan's family tree.

mighty blade. Rather than a big blue ox to haul the wood, Pete relied on his trusty little donkey, Tamarack. Soon fifty miles of trees were toppled as the clear-cut continued, until Pete had to give Paul back his axe.

Peder "Cordwood Pete" Le Dang lived to be eighty-four years old and is buried just east of Fosston in the Rose Hill Cemetery. An appropriately small chainsaw statue of Pete and Tamarack has been erected in downtown Fosston.

→ *Cordwood Pete and Tamarack.* Fosston is forty miles west of Bemidji on Highway 2, which becomes First Street once in town. Turn north at Johnson Avenue North (Highway 6), and the statue is immediately on the right (east) side of the road.

World's Largest Turkey

It Only Takes a Spark . . .

Big Tom the Turkey was being spruced up by park staff for the annual Frazee Turkey Festival in July 1998. The colossal poultry stood as the town symbol on top of a hill overlooking a bend on Highway 10 and was the showpiece for the town get-together. When workers secured the base of the fiberglass fowl with an

Roast turkey may be the town specialty in the Main Street cafés, but workers hadn't planned on turning the town symbol into the "World's Largest Turkey Roast."
Photograph courtesy the Frazee Chamber of Commerce.

acetylene torch, a stray spark caught the flammable material. In seconds, the whole bird was in flames.

Passing motorists pulled over and snapped photos of this impromptu bonfire, while the men with the torch stood by helpless as dinner was overcooked. Although turkeys often die by drowning when they look up during a rainstorm, the big birds usually have the good sense to flee fire, unless they're firmly secured to the ground.

"Those guys sure got teased after they did that!" says the guide at the tourist bureau. All that remained for the celebration were the charred remains of the gobbler and a new papier-mâché egg, meaning a new beginning. The culprits made the best of their blunder by printing T-shirts with the snapshot of the burning bird and the caption, "World's Largest Turkey (Roast)."

"Good thing we already had another one on order!" adds the tour guide. The new turkey was installed a few months later, to accompany the smaller turkey downtown next to a large map of the region.

Now visitors can stop and snap a photo with the new Big Tom and pretend they're the president pardoning this year's gobbler. Afterward, any of the cafés downtown will serve up the perennial special: roast turkey.

→ *World's Largest Turkey.* From Highway 10, turn north onto Route 29 and look up the hill to Lions Park.

Facing page: Big Tom the Turkey was already ordered when his predecessor went up in flames.

MADISON

Lou T. Fisk
World's Largest Cod

Madison boasts that its residents eat more lutefisk than anybody, anywhere, including Norway. Even though the town is as landlocked as possible from the cold North Atlantic breeding grounds of cod, Madison is home to a national champion lutefisk eater. Standing nearly seven feet tall, Jerry Osteraas triumphed at the National Lutefisk Eating Contest in Poulsboro, Washington, in 1989, surpassing his personal record of six pounds at one sitting.

If you're not Norwegian and aren't sure exactly what "lutefisk" is, just ask anyone in town. At first, they'll perhaps utter their disbelief at your ignorance, then they'll likely grab your hand and bring you to any supermarket in town to show you the fridges full of the lye-soaked codfish. With fresh cod a rarity, residents of Madison can enjoy their favorite white fish anytime they want thanks to toxic sodium hydroxide.

Any fish stored in "lut," which doubles as drain cleaner and paint remover, must have a funky flavor, but this preserved cod actually has only a light fishy flavor that is covered up by side dishes of extra fatty bacon or mashed green peas. The favorite recipe in Madison, however, is simply lutefisk smothered in butter.

In honor of this strange passion, a twenty-five-foot fish was erected in 1983 and aptly named "Lou T. Fisk." As a goodwill gesture to other U.S. cities named Madison, Lou toured the country in 1987 and even paid a visit to nearby Glenwood—perhaps to challenge that town's claim as the Lutefisk Capital of the World. Madison had to settle for mere national prominence with the title "Lutefisk Capital, U.S.A."

Madison's Lou T. Fisk statue is no longer mobile. Nevertheless, locals still "praise cod" by dressing him up in lederhosen during Oktoberfest, in army fatigues for military parades, and as a (cannibalistic?) fisher-fish for the fishing opener.

This belief in cod extends to the town festivals. Rather than Crazy Days for the town sidewalk sales, Madison has "Lutefisk Madness" to eat up its lye-soaked manna. Stinker Days are held at the end of July with a one-mile Uff-Da Walk and a Lou T. Fisk three-mile run. Participants are either rewarded or punished with this Nordic delicacy after they cross the finish line.

Finding the fish icon is no problem. Look for the huge torsk adorning the town water tower, and the chainsaw sculpture of a lutefisk pointing the way to downtown from the World's Largest Cod.

→ *Lou T. Fisk, the World's Largest Cod,* (320) 598-7373. Exit Highway 75, and the fish statue is next to the road at Fair Street in J. F. Jacobson Park, across from the After Five Supper Club.

Greeting guests along Highway 75, Madison's Lou T. Fisk statue was a wise investment of eight thousand dollars in 1983. F.A.S.T. Corporation of Sparta, Wisconsin, formed the fish in fiberglass and sent the cod to landlocked Madison.

Saint Urho
Patron Saint of Finland

Teased once too often by his Irish coworker about how Finns lacked worthy holy men like Saint Patrick, Richard Mattson concocted fabulous tales of how Saint Urho chased out the poisonous frogs from Finland to save the grape crop. As the story goes, the young priest Urho in medieval Suomi carefully calculated the height of frog jumps. From the swamp where these venomous critters hopped, Urho constructed a sluiceway right into ships' holds waiting to take them to sea. As the ship hailed from Finland, ice was shoveled into the hold to freeze the frogs to keep them from escaping. The boats set sail and ended up docked in France, where the people sautéed the amphibians in some *herbs de Provence*, and they soon became a French delicacy.

While this was the version of events that Mattson invented while manager of Ketola's Department Store in Virginia, Minnesota, Bemidji State University Professor Sulo Havumaki had his own take on this mythical messiah. Perhaps seeing that frogs had little to do with a grape harvest (never mind that grapes hadn't taken root in Finland), Havumaki insisted that Urho rid Finland of a grasshopper plague with the legendary chant: "Heinasirkka, heinasirkka, menetaalta hiiteen!" ("Grasshopper, grasshopper, go away!"). Urho's words frightened the hoppers, who flung themselves into the sea like a pack of lemmings.

In 1975, a contest was announced to develop the "true likeness" of the mysterious Saint Urho. Chainsaw artist Jerry Ward plied his craft on an enormous chunk of wood and sculpted Havumaki's version of the Finnish Pied Piper with an enormous pitchfork impaling a giant grasshopper. The monument was unveiled on March 19, 1982, and the publication *A History of St. Urho* pictures the historic event with the headline "The Erection of St. Urho."

The twelve-foot-tall oak icon could handle the grasshoppers but fell victim to the elements. F.A.S.T. of Sparta, Wisconsin, came to the rescue to replicate Urho in

Once a chainsaw sculpture but now made of fiberglass, Saint Urho of Finland keeps the grasshoppers at bay and saves the grape crop.

long-lasting fiberglass; the original wooden Urho has been banished to the Menahga cemetery mausoleum.

Ever since the discovery of this ancient holy man in the 1950s, Finns don royal purple and Nile green clothes on March 16, conveniently upstaging Saint Patrick's Day. Some sing the "Ode to Saint Urho," penned by Mattson and his Irish buddy Gene McCavic in "Finglish":

> Ooksie kooksie coolama vee,
> Santia Urho is ta poy for me!
> He sase out ta hoppers as pig as birds;
> Neffer peefor haff I hurd dose words!
> He reely told dose pugs of kreen.
> Braaffest finn I effer seen!

The North Shore Neighbors, a band from Finland, Minnesota, were inspired to record the song and released a forty-five rpm single in 1978 entitled "St. Urho's Polka and Finland, U.S.A." To prove their pride, Finland, Minnesota, erected its own twenty-two-foot-high Saint Urho totem pole looking out for grasshoppers to scare into Lake Superior.

All this Finnish patriotism caused Minnesota to be the first state in the Union to officially recognize Saint Urho's Day in 1975. By the 1980s, all fifty states marched in Minnesota's footsteps, and a nationwide Saint Urho's Day was declared. More recently, as the tale of Urho's feat of freezing frogs has spread, a movement has gotten underway to declare Urho "the patron saint of refrigeration."

→ *St. Urho statue.* Take Highway 71 just south of town, and the pitchfork-wielding colossus and the Menahga Museum are on the east side of the road.

Cherry Spoon

Nation's Largest Outdoor Sculpture Park

A huge spoon with a cherry squirting water has inexplicably become a symbol of Minneapolis. Any tour of the town must pass Claes Oldenburg and Coosje van Bruggen's *Spoonbridge and Cherry* for a photo op with the skyline jutting up in the background. Huge hedges separate courtyards to create a labyrinth, leading

Claes Oldenburg and Coosje van Bruggen's *Spoonbridge and Cherry* has become the de facto symbol of Minneapolis—and even has inspired artist-designed mini-putt golf in the garden.

visitors to each new courtyard holding abstract sculptures that kids can't resist climbing all over. The graceful Irene Hixon Whitney Bridge extends over busy Hennepin Avenue to connect the garden with Loring Park and its dandelion fountain and statue of the flamboyant Norwegian land speculator and violinist Ole Bull.

The Minneapolis Sculpture Garden is the largest urban sculpture park in the world and has been a boon to attendance at the Walker Art Center, even if the garden's lack of Minnesota sculptures is always a sore spot to local artists. Could the world-famous modern art museum be worried that a five-story Jolly Green Giant peering into downtown would dwarf their statues and become the highlight of their collection? Or would a talking Paul Bunyan clumsily lifting his limbs through a system of pulleys scare away art aficionados or attract even more folks to this high-class art park?

The perfect cure for cabin fever in subzero temps is a walk in the greenhouse to sniff blooming flowers and admire the glass fish above the fountain constructed by Frank Gehry, the designer of the stainless steel Weisman Art Museum on the campus of the University of Minnesota. After strolling through the garden (open year-round), venture into the actual Walker Art Center. With a little luck, maybe the notorious ghost that haunts the old Guthrie Theater next door will rattle its chains for you.

The walking tour continues over the blue-and-yellow bridge into Loring Park. In winter, skaters risk the thin ice on the pond, and in summer the Walker stages bands and films in the park on Monday evenings as spectators swat mosquitoes.

→ *Spoon Bridge and Cherry*, Walker Art Center and Minneapolis Sculpture Garden, 725 Vineland Place, (612) 375-7600. Coming east on I-94, take the Hennepin exit and follow it south. The Walker Art Center is at the junction of Hennepin and Vineland on the west (left) side of the road.

Facing page: With razor-sharp glass scales, Frank Gehry's fish jumps from the fountain in the conservatory of the Minneapolis Sculpture Garden.

Weisman Art Museum
"The Tin Can"

When the Guggenheim Museum opened its doors in 1997 and revitalized the industrial port of Bilbao, Spain, international art critics applauded architect Frank Gehry's masterpiece. Meanwhile, Minneapolis tried to show the world that Gehry had already built a similar museum on the University of Minnesota campus.

The Weisman Art Museum met mixed reviews upon completion in 1993, and even today university students give it the unflattering moniker "the tin can" because of the stainless steel walls jutting out in every direction.

Frank Gehry seems to thrive on the criticism, however. His original sketch for the Weisman is projected on one of the interior walls of the museum and looks just like a three-year-old's scribble. "It's at this point that the client gets nervous," he pointed out in a speech in Modena, Italy. In hopes of building his first project in Italy, Gehry presented a design to the people of this northern Italian city of a similarly outrageous gate of the city and was promptly rejected.

During the gentrification of Times Square, Gehry proposed revamping one of the old triangular buildings into an enormous clock for Warner Brothers with all the Looney Tunes characters popping out the windows on the hour every hour like an enormous cuckoo clock. "I thought it would have been a fantastic idea, but it wasn't what New York had in mind for Times Square," Gehry recalled. Once again, the project never saw the light.

Respecting Gehry's vow "not to build another brick lump," Minneapolis has helped Gehry establish himself as one of the premier architects in the world. Gehry's *Standing Glass Fish Sculpture* towers twenty feet over an indoor pool at the Walker Art Center's sculpture garden, the largest urban sculpture park of its kind in the world. According to the *New York Times,* the Walker's 1986 exhibit with the

Architect Frank Gehry vowed not to make another brick lump, and the Weisman Art Museum at the University of Minnesota lives up to his promise.

fish brought Gehry "a national audience." Some critics even claim that the design for the Weisman was inspired by Gehry's fascination with fish.

When Gehry's star rose after Bilbao and the American Center in Paris, the University of Minnesota added matching stainless steel bridges across Washington Avenue to fit in with the Weisman. Now, new galleries with an artsy café are slated to be tacked on when the funds present themselves.

In keeping with the architectural risk of Gehry and the diversity of buildings on campus, the university commissioned Antoine Predock to build the bizarre trapezoidal McNamara Alumni Center, with five hundred beams, lots of copper, almost no right angles, and forty thousand feet of rose-colored granite. Still, the students aren't impressed. Rather than accepting the university's hopeful nickname for the building, "the geode," irreverent pupils refer to it as the "Death Star" from *Star Wars*. Only time will tell if the geode will be a gem or Darth Vader's debacle.

The East Bank of the University of Minnesota is full of these architectural oddities and beauties, from the refurbished Coffman Union and Walter Library to the copper-covered Rapson Hall and ultramodern Weisman.

→ *Weisman Art Museum,* 333 East River Road, (612) 625-9494. From I-35, take the Washington Avenue exit going east. As you cross the Mississippi River look on the right for the shiny museum.

While in the Area

After touring the striking, if sometimes austere, architecture of the university, a stop at the opulent Loring Pasta Bar (327 Fourteenth Avenue Southeast, [612] 378-4849) in Dinkytown is the icing on the cake. Owner Jason McLean worked on theater set designs and gutted the landmark Grey's Drug Store at the corner of Fourteenth Avenue Southeast and Fourth Street all the way through the second story to the roof. Wrought-iron railings, swirling sculptural trees dotted with little lights, and thousands of bricks cemented in Dr. Seussian patterns make this surreal atmosphere a throwback to decadence only imagined by Hollywood directors.

Another must-see café inspired by McLean's vision is the Kitty Cat Klub (313 Fourteenth Avenue Southeast, [612] 331-9800), down the block below Annie's Parlour. Push aside the love beads, enter the "blue room," and sink into the cushions on the floor to imagine being in the fog of a turn-of-the-century Parisian absinthe den.

The basement of the Kitty Cat Klub has been transformed into the new digs for the El Dorado Conquistador Collection, the largest collection of foam bas-relief conquistador artwork in the land. This anti–art exhibit was spurred by the Broadway smash *Man of La Mancha,* when industrious entrepreneurs cashed in on the craze by mass-producing foam conquistador and matador bas reliefs to the delight of not-so-refined consumers across America. Cervantes had hit prime time, and all things Spanish were the rage. Black velvet matadors, brass plates imprinted with galleons, and foam conquistadors were swept off store shelves by greedy connoisseurs and eventually donated to the Salvation Army. The quixotic curators have saved these masterpieces—made of everything from pressed plastic to black velvet to hardened foam—from certain obscurity. The mythical city of gold and bad art has been found, at last, in a Dinkytown basement.

MORA

Dala Horse
Big Money in Horse Trading

In search of a symbol, Mora looked back to its namesake in Sweden. Little Lindstrom just to the east shaped its water tower into a Swedish coffee pot with "Vilkommen till Lindström" surrounded by colorful swirls of Scandinavian *tole*-painting. Mora opted instead for a more classic icon of Sweden: the bright orange Dala Horse.

These wooden horses were created in the Dalarna province of Sweden, probably by lumberjacks who whittled away the long, dark evenings by the home fire after a long day of knocking down trees. These statuettes likely date back to the 1500s, but the first written record of them is from 1624.

During the winter of 1716 when King Charles XII of Sweden was marauding across Europe, the remaining starving troops at home were forced to seek shelter among civilians. One of the soldiers carved a little horse and painted it an orange-red—a common color in the area because of the copper mine at Falun. He gave the statuette to the little boy of his host family in appreciation for their hospitality.

Other soldiers saw how a gift horse got them a bowl of soup. The carvings spread across the country, becoming almost a de facto currency. The Swedish army survived the brutal winter, and some soldiers even whittled and painted rooster and pig figurines. The Dala (Dalecarlian) horse, however, won the race.

While many life-sized versions of the horse were built around Sweden as a sort of equestrian jungle gym for kids, the Jaycees in Mora, Minnesota, wanted a giant version of the statue. The plaque at the base of the twenty-two-foot-high orange horse hails it as "a reminder of their cultural heritage" and perhaps more importantly as "a tourist attraction." The other traditional color of blue for these Swedish horses was nixed, because no passerby could miss the brilliant orange beast blazing next to the baby blue sky.

Minot, North Dakota, recently followed Mora's lead and erected a Dala horse of

This three-thousand-pound steed towers more than twenty-two feet tall, making it the World's Largest Dala Horse—in spite of rumors that Sweden and Minot, North Dakota, have bigger ones.

its own for its Scandinavian Heritage Center. By adding an extra five feet to its steed, Minot toppled Mora's claim to the World's Largest Dala Horse. Nevertheless, the Swedish immigrants who struggled to settle on this harsh prairie are honored by these gargantuan versions of their little wood carvings.

→ *Dalecarlian (Dala) Horse.* The huge orange horse is just south of downtown Mora on Highway 65 next to the town swimming pool.

Booming Prairie Chicken
Photo Op Extraordinaire

With bicentennial fervor sweeping the country, the Booming Prairie Chicken was unveiled along Interstate 94 on June 15, 1976, just outside downtown Rothsay. Much as the pioneers came to this land after the colonies declared themselves independent, the "prairie chickens moved ahead of the settlers to inhabit the

The mating ritual of the booming prairie chicken begins with rustling in the underbrush. Bizarre noises emerge from the fields as the male puffs up the curious orange sac in his neck and struts around to impress the females.

Inspired by a stuffed pelican, two metalworkers welded together the bones of this oversized bird in 1957. A thick layer of cement covered the skeleton, and the pelican was ready to watch the fish jumping at the little waterfall on Mill Pond.

prairies of Minnesota," according to brochures for Rothsay. The birds may not have done their part to cut the thick sod of the virgin prairie, but they surely gave the homesteaders a good supper.

Just a year before the pecking poultry statue was inaugurated, the town of Rothsay broke new ground by officially declaring itself the Prairie Chicken Capital of Minnesota on June 10, 1975. While choosing a chicken as the town symbol may seem like a move for only the most self-confident of towns, the prairie chickens' mating ritual, with the booming sound of the male strutting to impress the female, is one of those rarely seen spectacles of the plains. Some may say, then, that the nine-thousand-pound statue stands as an enormous fertility symbol both for the blooming fields and the teenagers necking in its shadow.

Sculptor Art Fosse's hard work of bending steel pipes for the ribs and slapping on thousands of pounds of cement has paid off. The World's Largest Prairie Chicken is now the subject of the town postcard and a popular pull-off along the interstate. Who can resist getting their photo taken with a gigantic bird pecking your noggin?

→ *Booming Prairie Chicken.* Rothsay is about twenty-five miles north of Fergus Falls on I-94. The chicken is visible from the interstate on the south side.

While in the Area

Just five miles north on I-94 and twelve miles east on Highway 108 is another town that's crazy for birds: Pelican Rapids. Not only is there an annual turkey roast in mid-July with special roasting pits to hold the spits filled with plucked birds, but the remaining turkeys are raced in heats. The biggest bird in town, however, is the white pelican overlooking the waterfall at Pelican River. Built in 1957 out of metal and coated with thick cement, the town symbol stands over the park at Mill Pond, where contenders for the bizarre Ugly Truck Contest show off the most ramshackle pickups in the county.

ST. PAUL

Peanuts Park
You're a Statue, Charlie Brown

When Charles Schulz, the creator of *Peanuts*, talked about his life, you'd think he had been a failure, or a "goat" as Charlie Brown would say. Charles Monroe Schulz was born on Chicago Avenue in Minneapolis to Dena and Carl Schulz, a barber who nearly lost his St. Paul shop at Selby and Snelling during the Depression.

Schulz was a below-average student at St. Paul Central High on Lexington Avenue. "I don't know which was worse—the Army or Central High School," he told Curt Brown of the *Star Tribune* in 1997. "I was a bland, stupid-looking kid who started off bad and failed everything and hated the whole time."

He contributed cartoons for the high school yearbook, but they were rejected. "At our twenty-fifth reunion, I was on the list of people nobody knew what happened to." As the story goes, the greeter at his Central High School reunion didn't believe he was the creator of *Peanuts* until he doodled a little Charlie Brown on a sheet of paper.

Schulz was drafted into the Army infantry division in 1943, and his mother died while he was in basic training. When he returned from the war, he earned just eighty-five dollars a week teaching drawing at the Federal Schools, which became the Art Instruction Schools, in Minneapolis.

The Little Red-Haired Girl with whom Charlie Brown was infatuated was in reality Donna Johnson Wold, one of Schulz's coworkers at the school. She spurned his marriage proposal and chose a fireman instead because her mother insisted Schulz would never amount to much.

Although the St. Paul *Pioneer Press* did publish his cartoon *Li'l Folks* for a couple of years, in 1950 it deemed his weekly fee of ten dollars too much for the simple drawings. Schulz packed his grip with a pile of his drawings and took the train to New York in search of greener pastures. United Feature Syndicate signed Schulz up

149

for five years, and the morning paper *The Minneapolis Tribune* (later the daily *Star Tribune*) quickly snatched up the rights to run *Peanuts* in the Twin Cities. Schulz had his comeuppance, as the *Pioneer Press* hasn't been able to run his work ever since that fateful day in 1950.

While Schulz's youth may have been bumpy, he became the most successful cartoonist ever—with the possible exception of Walt Disney. He was the highest paid cartoonist in history, eventually grossing twenty million dollars a year. The state of California has declared two Charles Schulz Days and immortalized him with his own star on the Hollywood Walk of Fame. The Italian Minister of Culture bestowed Schulz with the Order of Merit, and France proclaimed him a Commander of Arts and Letters during his retrospective at the Louvre. *Peanuts* is now published in twenty-six hundred newspapers worldwide and read by two hundred million readers in seventy-five countries. Although Schulz may have been humble with his fair share of tribulations, ultimately the goat became a hero.

Finally, the city of St. Paul recognized its most famous native son in 2000, the year that he died, with a series of five-foot polyurethane statues scattered around town. For four years, local artists painted more than one hundred of each of the molded figures of Snoopy, Charlie Brown, and Lucy and Linus Van Pelt. Some of these colorful little statues have remained on display around town, such as in front of O'Gara's bar, where Schulz's father's barber shop once stood. While some locals griped about St. Paul turning into "Snoopyville" or the "Peanuts Gallery," two million tourists have scoured the city over the years to snap photos in front of each character.

Speculating that polyurethane isn't forever, St. Paul has erected a permanent memorial to Schulz next to Landmark Center. Charlie Brown leans against a kite-eating tree with Snoopy on his lap; Linus tries to convince Sally that he is not her sweet baboo; Peppermint Patty chats with Marcie, who has her nose in a book; and Lucy the fussbudget plans her marriage to Schroeder, who blissfully ignores her and plunks out Beethoven on his toy piano.

When Schulz died on February 12, 2000, he never knew about the memorial. He never quite realized his fame and the ways he managed to touch so many lives around the world through comics. As he told the *Star Tribune*:

> I'll never be an Andrew Wyeth, and that's kind of sad. I wish what I did was fine art, but I doubt it is. It's well researched and authentically drawn, but I

Facing page: Of all of Snoopy's personas, a mustached mafioso never came forth from the pen of Charles Schulz. This amorous pup promotes pizza on West Seventh Street.

do not regard what I am doing as great art. Comic strips are too transient. Art is something so good it speaks to succeeding generations. . . . I doubt my strip will hold up for several generations to come.

How wrong he was.

→ *Peanuts Park. Landmark Plaza,* on the east side of Landmark Center (75 Fifth Street West) next to Lawson Commons, (651) 265-4923 or (800) 627-6101. Coming from Minneapolis, take I-94 and take the 10th Street/5th Street exit. Follow 5th Street West almost one mile to Landmark Center. The triangular park is wedged between Fifth Street West, Market Street, and St. Peter Street.

VINING

Swollen Toe Sculpture
Gas Station Art Park

"I think there's already enough Paul Bunyans around," says sculptor Ken Nyberg of tiny Vining. "I want to do something else." And indeed he has. Scattered around town are Ken's giant creations of everything from a metal square knot to a spilling cup of coffee held up by the thickest java juice around.

Nearby crawls a giant insect tempting fate in the jaws of an even larger pair of pliers. "Some people think it's a beetle, a cricket, or even a woodtick," Ken says, preferring to let people interpret his work in their own way.

While well-known artists such Claes Oldenburg make a mint enlarging everyday objects to mammoth proportions, Ken's similar creations coming from his Quonset hut are for fun, he says. Oldenburg and Coosje van Bruggen's *Spoonbridge and Cherry* may be the toast of Minneapolis, just as Ken's portable *Lion* is the pride of the local Lion's Club. Another city symbol, Philadelphia's clothespin by Oldenburg, could easily parallel Vining's clothespin, wedged between a couple of buildings on Main Street.

Ken spent ten years as a construction worker before he found his part-time passion of creating colossal sculptures on the weekends and in the winter. Collecting steel scraps from his job, he welds them together in unusual patchwork patterns. A door handle to nowhere towers more than twenty feet outside his workshop. What's it called? "Oh, you can call it whatever you want," Ken responds, amused by all the different theories and titles that are bestowed upon his handiwork.

Ken's magnum opus is an enormous foot with a swollen toe greeting visitors to Vining along Highway 210. When he's asked to shed some light on this unusual sculpture, Ken is typically cryptic: "Can't really go wrong with a foot since there's billions of them, and they're all different." This may be difficult logic to contest, but it's not much of an explanation.

The doorway to nowhere stands outside Ken Nyberg's atelier just north of Vining.

Perhaps as a reference to Philadelphia's huge clothespin sculpture, Vining's version in yellow is wedged between two buildings on the main drag.

When pressed, Ken admits, "I didn't want to do anything with a person in it." Rather than make a foot, he even thought of doing a statue of a big middle finger once, "but I don't think many people would like that."

Instead the disembodied limb in ten-gauge steel has drawn speculation from around the country. "A doctor wrote me a letter calling it a 'Hawaiian hitchhiker's toe.'" Ken laughs at the bizarre prognosis.

The owner of the Citgo station at the edge of town was so inspired by the sculpture that he renamed his store The Big Foot Gas Station and has allowed Ken to display his other sculptures near the pumps.

While admiring his Big Foot statue with the painfully distended toe, Ken simply remarks, "Different, isn't it?"

→ *Swollen Toe Sculpture and Ken Nyberg's other sculptures.* Vining is about twenty-five miles east of I-94 and Fergus Falls on Highway 210.

Big Fish Tour
Perfect for Postcards

"The one that got away." "The lunker to end all lunkers." Fishing and the accompanying exaggeration are part of the Minnesota way of life. Where else but in Minnesota is there a Fish House Parade (in Aitkin), an Eelpout Festival for the ugliest fish imaginable (in Leech Lake), or Bullhead Days (in Waterville)? Residents of Waterville couldn't figure out how to get rid of their town's reputation for these whiskered fish, so they decided to celebrate them instead with a big fish fry.

Early tourism ads for Minnesota boasted happy hunting and fishing grounds, and even now the state is first in the country for per capita sales of fishing licenses. There's a boat for one of every six residents and more than fourteen thousand lakes from which to reel in the big one.

Because of this obsession with fishing, towns around the state have boldly claimed all kinds of superlatives. To name a few of them: Walker is Muskie Capital of the World, Alexandria is Bass Capital of the World, and Mille Lacs is Walleye Capital of the World (although that title is contested by Fairmount). Hand-colored postcards dating back to the 1920s feature fishermen riding enormous rainbow trout and other creatures of the deep. This tradition was revived in the 1960s with photo montage postcards. Many feature the caption, "The Fish Are Hungry Here!" and depict enormous fish gobbling up unsuspecting boaters.

Were these cards sent as a warning to gullible city slickers to keep them from venturing north to eat all the fish? Or to lure them with lollapalooza lunkers? Perhaps these goofy postcards were the muse that inspired industrious towns to erect enormous fiberglass fish along Main Street. These piscatorial icons spread the good word to passing tourists and let them dream of landing the leviathan of a lifetime.

Baudette, Bemidji, Bena, Cambridge, Clarks Grove, Deer River, Erskine, Finland, Garrison, Isle, Madison, Medina, Minneiska, Nevis, Orr, Park Rapids, Pres-

Special outriders supplied here for safety of Canoeists.-1

An early postcard boasts about the lunkers in the lakes.

ton, Rockville, and Rush City all have huge fish statues. These huge fish sculptures make for the perfect photo opportunities to show modern versions of *The Old Man and the Sea*—although this time visitors come home with a photo rather than just bones and exaggeration.

The following is a gill line loaded with some of Minnesota's outstanding giant fish.

Willie the Walleye

Since Lake of the Woods is a haven for fishing pilgrims, nearby Baudette paid tribute with its 9,500-pound fish statue, built in 1959. Every year at the beginning of June, the town hits the streets for Willie the Walleye Day, to taste this year's catch and to pay homage to its forty-foot-long fish.

→ *Willie the Walleye.* Right next to the SuperValu at the intersection of Highways 11 and 172 in Baudette on the Canadian border.

This decal for Baudette proudly proclaims the town's mascot to be Willie the Walleye (not to be confused with Wally Walleye in Garrison, North Dakota).

The Original Big Fish of Bena

"Please Don't Steal the Teeth!" reads the sign on the door to the Big Fish in Bena. Owner Rita Wichmann complains, "All these people stop by to take their picture with the fish and want to take something home with them, so they take the teeth as souvenirs. I suppose we really should sell T-shirts."

Originally built as the Big Fish Drive Inn in 1958, the fish's fame soon extended beyond Minnesota, having appeared at the beginning of one of the *National Lampoon's Vacation* movies with Chevy Chase and in a Charles Kuralt "On the Road" CBS television news segment.

In spite of this fame, the owner is fed up with the fish. After more than thirty years of annual upkeep, she wants to sell it and retire.

Pull up to the side of the muskie, and a person appears from inside the fish to take your order for fishburgers. Alas, the drive-in fish has now been relegated to be a mere storage closet, but the owners still lovingly slap a fresh coat of paint over the tar paper every couple of years.

"What can I say good about it?" she says. "It's a pain, not a moneymaker."
Even so, her attached Big Fish Supper Club lures in hundreds of summer anglers.

→ *The Big Fish Supper Club,* 456 Highway 2 northeast, (218) 665-2333. The fish is just east of Bena on Highway 2, which is halfway between Bemidji and Grand Rapids.

The Mystery Pike of Deer River

The older woman behind the information desk in the little tourist cabin next to the temporary tepee had all the details of the annual powwow, but when asked about the Northern Pike statue, she turned down the volume on her TV and said, "Oh, I don't know. It's been around here as long as I can remember. Every town needs something, I guess." At least pesky park rangers won't scold you for climbing all over this cement creature to snap a Polaroid.

➜ *Mystery Pike.* Deer River is thirteen miles northwest of Grand Rapids in northern Minnesota, and the pike is just north of downtown on Highway 2 on the east (right) side of the road.

Deer River's pike, the centerpiece of Wild Rice Days, is for kids to climb on and marvel at how big the fish are up north.

Picnic Pike

The huge jaws on this northern pike overlooking a sandy beach on Cameron Lake ominously warn swimmers of the dangers that lie beneath the waves. Mostly, though, the big striped northern pike offers something for the youngsters to climb on while their parents barbecue on the picnic grounds.

→ *Picnic Pike.* Erskine is thirty miles east of Crookston. The fish is just east of town off Highway 2 on the south (right) side of the road at the lakefront park.

Although the spotted pike of Erskine tries to make swimmers scared of these creatures from the deep, no one seems to pay it any mind as divers plunge into shallow Cameron Lake.

As big as a car, Garrison's walleye makes any other fish story pale by comparison. The fiberglass creature stands as a beacon to lost anglers on Minnesota's most famous fishing lake, Mille Lacs.

Walleye Capital of the World

For one rare moment in 1965, Minnesota legislators were nearly unanimous on something. They declared that the walleye was the official state fish, but some spoilsport—who was probably stumping for the bullhead—voted nay in the 128 to 1 tally.

The town of Garrison didn't wait around for this political wrangling, and instead declared itself the Walleye Capital of the World. After all, this little fishing village is wrapped around the most popular walleye lake in the state, Mille Lacs.

Soon Garrison saved its pennies to construct a beautiful, portable fiberglass fish (only slightly bigger than those avowed caught by anglers in the lake) to accompany Miss Garrison in the annual town parade. This whale of a walleye has since been affixed to a cement base and serves as a beacon for boaters and ice fishermen lost on the lake.

➜ *The walleye* is just south of the intersections of Highways 169 and 18 on the shore of Mille Lacs.

Saddle up on Kabetogama's Bucking Walleye

On Lake Kabetogama along the Canadian border, a sixteen-foot concrete walleye was erected in 1949 as part of an advertising sign. Sculptor Duane Beyers hailed this bucking beast as the "World's Largest Walleye," a claim now easily surpassed, but most likely it's still the World's Largest *Saddled* Walleye. The outstanding feature of this fish is the little ladder behind it that allows tourists to hop on top to pose for a snapshot.

➜ *Bucking Walleye.* Located twenty-five miles southeast of International Falls at the intersection of Highways 53 and 122, near one of the entrances to Voyageurs National Park.

Anglers can climb the secret staircase in back to pose on their dream walleye, just like in old postcards.

A sign in the mouth of Nevis's tiger muskie under the town picnic pavilion warns "KEEP OUT."

World's Largest Tiger Muskie

Governor Luther Youngdahl's official duties called him to Nevis in September 1950 to inaugurate the World's Largest Tiger Muskie with jokes about fishing and Swedes.

Ribs of wood and scales of concrete make up this thirty-and-a-half-foot-long fish. In 1990, a real fifty-four-pound muskie was hauled in on a Minnesota lake, breaking all previous state records. Partially in honor of this feat, the next year the Nevis fish was repainted and a new roof was put over its head. This way, everyone coming to Muskie Days in July could marvel at the fish (and, of course, pose in its mouth).

→ *World's Largest Tiger Muskie,* downtown Nevis. Take Highway 34 from Walker fifteen miles west along Highway 34. Nevis is on the north (right) side of the road, and the muskie statue is in the town park on the left upon entering town.

Preston's Parade Trout

In honor of the fish-filled streams in southeastern Minnesota, Preston chainsawed a huge wooden trout, but Mother Nature's harsh weather soon took its toll. Preston has magically transformed its trout into timeless fiberglass and bolted it to a trailer for better mobility. The trailer trout is lugged to local festivals so Preston can show off its pride to its neighbors, and hopefully lure some tourists to its rivers.

→ *Preston's Trout.* Usually parked near downtown Preston at Highways 16 and 52, except when Trout Day rolls around on the third Saturday in May and it's paraded through town.

Preston's trout is mounted on a trailer and can be conveniently stored during the winter to preserve its fiberglass sheen.

Paul Bunyan Tour
Relics of the Giant

Forget fish stories; the real test of exaggeration lies with the tall tales of Paul Bunyan. First put to paper in a promotional brochure for the Red River Lumber Company in 1914, the legend of Paul Bunyan has been embellished around campfires ever since. Towns across Minnesota pay tribute to this tree-cutting giant with unbelievable tales and enormous artifacts to prove their stories. Here is a compendium of all things Paul.

Bemidji's Paul and Babe

Minnesota's largest and most famous citizen was born on the shores of beautiful Lake Bemidji. Five storks huffed and puffed to deliver the baby giant, and a herd of cows worked around the clock to feed him.

The year was 1937. Bangor, Maine, claimed to have Paul Bunyan's official birth certificate, so Bemidji mayor Earl Bucklen decided to cement his town's title by posing for a stocky statue of the lumberjack. The statue towers three times Bucklen's height and weighs in at a whopping two and a half tons.

To keep poor Paul company, his trusty ox, Babe, was built to stand beside him. The ox was made from wood and wire topped with canvas and mounted on a Model T Ford. The eyes were bright-beam headlights, and the exhaust pipe curved around to the beast's snout, where huge clouds of smoke billowed out. The portable Babe was the highlight of holiday parades—at least until strands of Christmas lights were snagged by his enormous horns during one exhibition.

After touring the country, Babe came home to his master's side on Lake Bemidji. Inside the nearby little tourist office, Paul Bunyan paraphernalia—his moccasins, back scratcher, dice, toothpick, toothbrush, yo-yo, axe, and even his phone —is littered everywhere, proving that Paul wasn't much of a housekeeper.

According to the tourist office, hundreds of people stop each day to visit the wood-cutting duo, making these giants the most photographed statues in the state.

→ *Paul Bunyan and Babe the Blue Ox,* Bemidji Avenue and Third Street, Bemidji. (800) 292-2223. From Highway 2, take Highway 197 (Paul Bunyan Drive) right into the center of town. Statues are on the east (right) side of the road next to Lake Bemidji.

World's Only Talking Paul Bunyan

With strip malls and big-box shopping centers rising around the giant talking lumberjack, property taxes soared through the roof for Paul Bunyan Land in Baxter on the edge of Brainerd. Rather than fight with the sprawling suburban stores that were leveling forests faster than the famous lumberjack could, the aging amusement park decided to sell off its most valuable asset: Paul Bunyan.

Above: A close-up of this mechanical marvel from 1949 shows his eyelids blinking and his slack jaw ready to greet the kids. *Facing page:* Bemidji claims its *Paul Bunyan* and *Babe the Blue Ox* are the most photographed statues in the state. In front of the tourist office, which features the Fireplace of States, the rigid eighteen-foot-tall giant stands in an eternal staredown with a fiberglass statue of Shaynowishkung, a.k.a. Chief Bemidji, across the street.

This early postcard of Brainerd's talking Paul Bunyan shows the mighty man pre-facelift. His double-blade axe was soon replaced with a more modern red telephone.

Even South Dakota expressed an interest in the talking monument, but Minnesotans were outraged that this symbol of the state would flee over the border. Governor Pawlenty jetted to Brainerd in a last-ditch effort to save the giant. Paul referred to Pawlenty, the relatively small man, as "Little Timmy."

Even though Paul Bunyan Land was doomed to close, the owner, Don McFarland, generously agreed to give the twenty-six-foot-tall Paul to a historical farm east of Brainerd, so visitors can still hear their name called by the five-thousand-pound man with the size eighty footprint. Babe has been left behind in Baxter as the mascot for the Blue Ox Bowl.

→ *World's Only Talking Paul Bunyan*, This Old Farm, 17469 State Highway 18, Brainerd, (218) 764-2915. From Brainerd, go east on Highway 18 for about fifteen miles.

World's Largest Lumberjack

In the little town of Akeley, a colossal cradle that once barely held the massive child still rocks. One week after Paul Bunyan came into this world, he outgrew his diapers and ended up wearing his dad's pants. Paul's britches were bursting at the seams, and wagon wheels had to be used to button up his enormous new duds.

All this and more can be learned from a quick tour through the Complete History of Paul Bunyan, on display behind the lumberjack's crib at the Red River Museum in Akeley. Outside the building, sculptor Dean Krotzer moved mountains of fiberglass in 1984 to construct the largest Paul of them all, reaching forty-two feet into the air—and that's crouching down. As though begging for alms, the kneeling giant stretches out his gloved hand and tourists hop in it for a photo opportunity.

→ *World's Largest Paul Bunyan*. In front of the Red River Museum in Akeley, at the crossing of Highways 34 and 64 in north-central Minnesota.

Hackensack's Lucette

Halfway up the Paul Bunyan Trail from Brainerd to Bemidji stands the lumberjack's well-endowed spouse, Lucette Diana Kensack, erected in 1952. Paul Bunyan married? Well, she's got a gold ring on her fiberglass finger, and the Hackensack Chamber of Commerce has the "official" marriage license under glass to prove it.

Perhaps Paul wanted to make an honest woman of his sweetheart after his puny progeny, Paul Jr., was born. Brainerd had already named Paul's belle the more obvious Pauline, and even has Pauline's Restaurant near where Paul Bunyan Land stood.

Poet Robert Frost warned in his poem "Paul's Wife" that "She wasn't anybody else's business, / Either to praise her, or so much as name her," but Frost also claimed she was sawed from a white pine log.

Hackensack wasn't afraid to name Paul's buxom bride and erect a statue in her

The story of Paul Bunyan's birth has yet to be written—perhaps the childbearing of a giant doesn't make for a good yarn. Suffice it to say that Paul Bunyan's enormous umbilical cord was cut in the northern town of Akeley. Paul's colossal cradle in a small manger lies next to this statue of the lumberjack.

honor. Mother Nature took its toll, however, and a swift wind zipped across Birch Lake and took poor Lucette's head off in the winter of 1991. Luckily a new head was mounted just in time for Hackensack's annual summer Sweetheart Days.

→ *Lucette Diana Kensack and Paul Jr.* Drive past the Up North Café and the Yellow Brick Road store, and the statues are two blocks from the highway overlooking Birch Lake.

Paul Bunyan's bride (she's got the ring to prove it) and his relatively runty progeny. Poet Robert Frost speculated on the origin of Paul's sweetheart with an Arthurian Lady-of-the-Lake bent.

Blackduck's original black duck rode in Bemidji's parade in 1938 near Paul Bunyan's triple-barreled rifle, which shot fireworks. The old coot was moved downtown, while this sporty new duck landed at the entrance to town along Highway 71.

Blackduck's Black Duck

As an odd addition to the Paul Bunyan myth, little Blackduck created a fiberglass version of its name in 1937 as a hunting trophy of the lumberjack. The duck ran on wheels during the summer, and in the winter runners were mounted on the duck as the newly crowned queen of Blackduck rode through town on its back. Paul Bunyan's enormous three-barreled shotgun followed the float and fired sparks into the air.

Taxidermists have since mounted Paul Bunyan's prize black duck in the center of town, while a new decoy tricks tourists along Highway 71 into stopping by for a visit. Paul Bunyan's three-barreled rifle has been moved from the roadside to safe storage in a gun locker.

➜ *Blackduck's Black Duck.* Take Highway 71 for twenty-five miles northeast from Bemidji. The new duck is at the wayside rest area off the highway; the old is next to the Do Duck Inn and the fire station on Main Street.

Paul Bunyan's Bobber, Anchor, Fish, and Wheelbarrow

While fishing for Notorious Nate the Northern with a sixty-foot bobber made by a Swedish blacksmith, Paul snagged the pike in Lake Whitefish and heaved it seven miles away to downtown Pequot Lakes. The crater Nate made when he dropped from the sky is used to this day to boil pots of beans for the annual Beanhole Days, and the bobber just happened to land in braces and now doubles as a water tower.

Recently, sportsmen have wanted to paint the bobber to look like a golf ball in honor of the area's golf craze, but critics have wondered who would make Paul Bunyan's golf club.

Slightly more plausible is Paul Bunyan's 225,000-pound anchor next to Big Stone Lake outside of Ortonville in western Minnesota. "I remember when they

Paul Bunyan's walleye was hauled out of Rush Lake with these stats: "Weight: 1999 lbs. 15 1/2 oz. Bait: 35 lb. tiger muskie. Line: 1 inch manila rope. Rod: 62 ft. white pine. Reel: 3 ton logger's winch."

Paul Bunyan's bobber happened to fall into metal braces in Pequot Lakes and now doubles as a water tower. The red-and-white bobber provides the backdrop for Beanhole Days, which have a smell that can be sniffed for miles.

brought that stone up here," the guide at the Big Stone County Museum recalls. "They needed two trucks to haul it up here." With an anchor like that, no lake besides Superior could hold Paul's boat.

One of the walleyes Paul nabbed with the famous bobber stands guard at a Conoco station just off Interstate Highway 35 at Rush City. While not the largest in the land, this 1,999-pound lunker is nothing to scoff at. Notorious Nate the Northern and Paul Bunyan's walleye grew fur to survive in the cold Minnesota winters under ice.

Another one of Paul's minor feats was accidental, when Babe the Blue Ox accidentally tipped over his wheelbarrow, which stands outside the Itasca Trading Post, and started a river we now call the Mississippi.

→ *Paul Bunyan's Bobber,* at the stoplight on Highway 371, downtown Pequot Lakes. Paul Bunyan's Walleye, outside the Conoco station off I-35 at Rush City. Paul Bunyan's Anchor, next to Big Stone Lake outside Ortonville.

The guide at Big Stone County Museum talks up Paul Bunyan's anchor with appropriate embellishment by telling visitors, "You should see the boat!" Paul Bunyan's boat? Where is it? "They're still looking for it," he teases.

Baby Paul Bunyan wouldn't pick up his toys, so his marble was lost until miners found it near Chisholm and put it in front of the castle-like mining museum.

Paul Bunyan's Marble

Amid a yard filled with enormous old machinery and railcars from the mines and in front of the castle-like entrance to the mining museum lies an enormous ball of granite misplaced during one of Paul's childhood games. Probably dug up at the Glen Open Pit Mine next to Iron World, the marble rivals the size of Pellet Pete, the chunk of taconite anthropomorphized into the mascot of the mining-themed putt-putt course.

→ *Paul Bunyan's Marble,* Minnesota Museum of Mining, 900 West Lake Street, Chisholm, (218) 254-5543.

Paul Bunyan, R.I.P.

While Paul's personal belongings are scattered across the state, the most creative artifact lies in little Kelliher. A forty-foot-long rise in the earth became the burial site of the giant lumberjack in 1899 in Paul Bunyan Memorial Park just south of town.

"What do you mean, 'Paul Bunyan's grave'?" a group of guys in Kelliher respond when asked where the famous lumberjack's tomb is. As they head into Thor's Sports Bar, they laugh, "You mean the poor guy's dead? Maybe you should come into Thor's and see a live band!"

Paul's launching pad into lumberjack heaven is marked by a simple tombstone with the inscription, "Here Lies Paul, And That's All." Babe the Blue Ox, on the other hand, was buried in South Dakota, forming what is now called the Black Hills.

→ *Paul Bunyan Memorial Park,* one block south of downtown Kelliher on Highway 72.

CLOQUET
VOYAGEUR

Voyageur Tour
From Perseverance to Pierre

Jessica Lange may hail from Cloquet, but rather than raising a huge statue of King Kong in honor of her role as the damsel in distress, the town decided to delve further into its past and pay tribute to the French Canadian traders. As a bicentennial project, the World's Largest Voyageur was erected on an island in the St. Louis River with a little wooden fort next to it that doubles as an amphitheater during the summer months. Logging chic runs rampant at Lumberjack Days in the beginning of July, as voyageur acts are performed to charm the tots in the shadow of this fiberglass woodman.

➡ *World's Largest Voyageur,* Dunlap Island Park. From I-35, take the Cloquet exit onto Highway 33, which turns into Sunnyside Drive. At the intersection of Cloquet Avenue (Highway 45) look for the Frank Lloyd Wright gas station on the southeast corner. Turn left and follow the road out to the island in the St. Louis River.

Perseverance the Voyageur

According to interpretive displays in Pine City, people have been living along the banks of the Snake River since 6000 B.C. The Ojibwe named the area "Chengwatana," meaning "steep end of a spur of hills"; settlers later simplified it to "Pine City."

A huge thirty-five-foot redwood log was transported into town in the 1970s, but no one had the heart to chop up the beautiful lumber, which came from an

Facing page: Cloquet's most famous monument may be the Frank Lloyd Wright gas station, but the town was founded by voyageurs immortalized in fiberglass by this World's Largest Voyageur.

Carved from California redwood, Perseverance the Voyageur in Pine City stands as possibly the world's largest chainsaw sculpture.

old-growth California forest. The wood changed hands a few times and was finally carved into what is perhaps the world's largest chainsaw sculpture, an enormous voyageur placed in Riverside Park to commemorate the first European explorers in the area.

→ *Perseverance the Voyageur,* Riverside Park. From I-35, take the Pine City exit going east. Drive through town, cross the Snake River, and look for the voyageur statue on your left just across the bridge.

Pierre the Voyageur

Two telephone poles were leaned against each other and then a ton of stucco was slapped on to create the twenty-foot-tall Pierre, the French Canadian Voyageur. As the good-luck mascot for the Voyageur Motel, this statue of classic Americana guards the fishing store, which has a genuine jackalope mounted for the gullible city slickers. Once upon a time, lucky Pierre's eyes gyrated back and forth as cars whizzed past on Highway 61, wishing happy trails to all who came his way.

→ *Pierre the Voyageur,* Voyageur Hotel. From Duluth, take Highway 61 along the North Shore, toward Two Harbors. When approaching town, look for the twelve-foot rooster on your left, and the Voyageur is another quarter mile past it on the left before downtown.

Crane Lake Voyageur

A roadside attraction as far off the road as possible could be a claim to fame for the giant voyageur on what was once the highway through the lakes of the French Canadian trappers and traders. Pass the tiny town of Buyck (pronounced "bike") with its log cabin post office and enjoy the scenery on this dead-end road with a U.S. port of entry that is accessible only by water. To mark this bucolic surrounding, a paddle-wielding voyageur greets visitors with a plaque proclaiming, "The gay garb of these couragous [sic] happy men is typified by our memorial as he stands here proudly surveying the lands and waterways he once roamed."

→ *Crane Lake Voyageur.* From Orr on Highway 53, turn onto State Route 23 and drive for about twenty-five miles into the wild toward Canada on State Route 24.

Made from telephone poles and cement, Pierre the Voyageur used to have bobbing eyes that would jiggle to and fro to watch cars whiz by on Highway 61 into Two Harbors.

Crane Lake's dandy voyageur stands over one of the few U.S. ports of entry accessible from Canada only by lake.

Big Vic and Big Louie

Two protest statues of voyageurs symbolize the fight to wrestle the plotted land along the Canadian border east of International Falls to create Voyageurs National Park.

Vic Davis had no intention of giving up his beautiful Cranberry Island on frigid Rainy Lake, so he sold off square-foot sections of the island for $19.95 in hopes the Feds would be bogged down by the bureaucracy of recouping each bit.

To call attention to his battle with Washington, Vic commissioned F.A.S.T. (Fiberglass Animals Shapes & Trademarks) in Sparta, Wisconsin, to make an enormous fiberglass voyageur statue in 1980 to helicopter to his island. The government struck back with bureaucracy of its own and slapped a probably trumped-up fine on the pilot for unintentionally wandering into Canadian airspace while searching for the border island.

The twenty-five-foot-tall Big Vic statue was confiscated by the Feds, and Davis got on the line to the good folks at F.A.S.T. for a replica he dubbed "Big Louie," after Louie Reel, "a voyageur rebel in the 1800s," according to Davis. Louie the 3,100-pound fiberglass giant went into hiding when Vic got wind the government was itching to get their hands on it.

Big Louie resurfaced years later when the threat of government confiscation subsided and Davis advertised it for sale as "suitable as tourist attraction, lawn ornament, or government protest." The government eventually donated Big Vic to the nearby town of Ranier. Local revisionist historians claim its name is not Big Vic but that it is instead named after the founder of the first voyageur outpost in Ranier in 1788. Vic Davis's mother thinks differently: "You can tell them they're full of hot air! The statue is named 'Big Vic' and don't let them tell you otherwise!"

→ *Big Vic the Voyageur,* Ranier. From International Falls, go east on State Highway 11 about three miles until the intersection with Highway 332. The statue is at the entrance to the town of Ranier on the left (north) side of the road.

→ *Big Louie the Voyageur,* Barnum. From Duluth, go south on I-35 for about thirty miles, and the statue is on the west side of the interstate at exit 220.

Facing page: Big Vic the protest statue has found his home at the entrance to Ranier near Voyageurs National Park.

Big Louie, the twin of Big Vic, now stands over I-35 just south of Duluth in Barnum.

NORTH DAKOTA

With only 650,000 inhabitants, North Dakota sometimes seems empty. Abandoned farmhouses dot the edges of the fields as testament to early immigrants, and now their untold stories are left up to the imagination of the visitors. One rise in the land leads to another endless vista of hypnotic green-and-gold fields, like sheets of silk waving in the wind.

When farmers at the White Maid Ice Cream Stand in Napoleon can't understand what on earth we're doing in North Dakota, we joke that we won a contest: "First prize is a week in North Dakota; second prize is two weeks." Once the ice is broken, they heartily advocate for their state. "Have you seen the turtle in Dunseith?" "You can't miss the cow in New Salem." "Have you heard about what that guy's building on the Enchanted Highway?" The list of favorite attractions is long. Following a discussion about our long journey criss-crossing the state, a teenager says, "I'd love to take a big trip across North Dakota—there's so much to see." At first I think he's joking, but his face shows he's not.

After traveling a week in the Peace Garden State, I understand him. North Dakota is dazzling in the exact opposite way from New York City. The horizon forms a perfect circle and is broken only by an occasional grain elevator, the true colossi of the plains. No wonder that when North Dakotans build something, they want to make it big, really big. What other explanation can there be for the forty-five-foot can pile in Casselton, the giant decaying gorilla in Harvey, or the World's Tallest Structure in Blanchard? The population of North Dakota may be small, but the ratio of big roadside attractions to people is extraordinary.

These giants standing above the fields may seem like a mirage on a scorching hot day. After shooting photos to prove they exist, I drive into a small town on the prairie, an oasis in the desert. Stopping at the Main Street café for a cup of coffee and fresh rhubarb pie is like receiving manna from heaven. The people are friendly and the pace refreshingly slow. This is North Dakota, pure and simple.

The tallest structure in the world is in one of the flattest places, the Red River Valley. Just outside Blanchard, this TV tower rises 2,063 feet to transmit Tinseltown's sitcoms to televisions across the state.

BLANCHARD

KTHI-TV Tower
World's Tallest Structure

No, it isn't the Sears Tower, the Space Needle, or those buildings in Kuala Lumpur. The tallest structure in the world doesn't rise above a new burgeoning city but is outside of the small town of Blanchard in rural northeast North Dakota. KTHI-TV and KVLY 11 raised this 2,063-foot tower in 1963 to send their signal to boob tubes across "an area larger than the District of Columbia, Hawaii, Massachusetts, New Jersey, and Connecticut with 1000 square miles to spare," as they say in literature promoting the colossus.

Two million feet of steel guy wire bow up toward three sets of stanchions to support the tower, which stretches more than a third of a mile into the air. To a person standing at the foot of this huge antenna, the top is nearly lost in space and the shadow extends out of sight across the field.

While this amazing architectural feat may seem unique, another such tower stands just to the southwest, its lights blinking as well to avoid taking down any passing B-52s from the nearby Grand Forks airbase. These two towers are easily visible from twenty miles away and would be seen from a hundred if these "guyed masts" weren't so thin.

Although the World's Tallest Structure screams to be a tourist trap, "No Trespassing" signs shoo away the curious. Visitors can't help but want a thrill ride up the mini elevator within the pylon that can shoot workers part way up the tower. KTHI warns, however, that the top will sway ten feet on a windy day and "the signals atop the tower are so strong they can hurt the fillings in a person's teeth."

Even so, the television stations tout their tower as "taller than the combined height of the Great Pyramid Khufu at Giza, the Eiffel Tower in Paris, and the Washington Monument. If a twenty-second commercial started at the same moment a baseball was dropped from the top of the KVLY tower, it would end nearly four

seconds before the ball hit the ground and [the ball] would be traveling 250 mph."
How can any tourist in the area resist a peek?

→ *KTHI-TV Tower.* From I-29, take exit 100 east onto County Road 200A, which
   merges into County Road 18 in Blanchard. Go west past Blanchard a half mile,
   and the tower is to the left (south) about three and a half miles on a dirt road
   into the middle of a field.

Tommy Turtle
Monument to Snowmobiling

In the depths of the frigid northern North Dakota winter, snowmobiles often outnumber the cars in Bottineau. With three hundred miles of trails connecting to Canada—with no customs or port of entry hassles—this is the preferred pastime. Why not raise a monument to snowmobiling?

Bottineau's Tommy Turtle is careful to be a good role model for future snowmobilers by always wearing a helmet and eye protection. The floorboards of the reptilian mobile are easily accessible, and the dashboard doubles as a graffiti palette for teens eager to proclaim their love.

In honor of the Turtle Mountains north of town, a thirty-two-foot-tall grinning turtle was erected at the controls of a thirty-two-foot-long snowmobile. Tommy Turtle puts safety first by wearing a helmet propped on his protruding head, even though he could just retract it into his shell in a pinch.

Two hotels in town, the Norway House and the Super 8, offer picture-perfect views of the snowmobiling tortoise as the centerpiece of the town. The receptionist doesn't even blink when I ask, "Could we have a room with a view of the turtle?" Apparently, this is a common request.

Tommy Turtle guards the Bottineau baseball field, but today the wind is whipping across the plains at a wicked clip. "Oh, it's always windy here," laments the tired-looking waitress in the Norway House. I don't dare ask how anyone could play wiffleball, let alone baseball, with twenty-five-mile-per-hour gusts.

Kids don't mind the cold as they climb all over Tommy and teenagers express their nocturnal creativity by using him as a canvas to graffiti their names. In fact, the town seems smitten with their impressive statue, and even the bowling alley has named itself "Tommy Turtle Lanes" in homage to the happy terrapin.

→ *Tommy Turtle,* 103 South Eleventh Street East. From Minot, take Highway 83 north for thirty-seven miles when it merges with Highway 5. Drive for forty-three miles on Highway 5 into Dunseith. Tommy is on the far side of downtown on the left (north) side of the road behind the Norway House and next to the Bottineau Visitors Center.

CASSELTON

Can Pile
Biggest Birdhouse in the State

During the Depression, Highway 10 was one of the major routes across the North Dakota prairie. At the eastern edge of this long stretch, the Sinclair Brick Station kept its lights on 24-7 to pump gas and change oil to keep Tin Lizzies chugging away.

The service men in matching green uniforms would chuck the empty oil cans into a little chicken wire enclosure around an old windmill. As the stack of cans swelled, more chicken wire was raised to hold even more cans. Gradually, the pile rose forty-five feet on a skinny eighteen-foot base.

The former owner "started that in about 1938. First he made three of them, then he got it in his head to build a big one. I don't know how he got up there to make it so tall," recalls George Loegering, the current owner and caretaker of this leaning tower of tin.

"He raised chickens in there for a while, then he raised homing pigeons," George points out as he shows me a little hut inside the pile with a ventilating duct. Now hundreds of sparrows make the cans their home. "It's now the biggest birdhouse in North Dakota," laughs George.

Once the original gas station was razed, George had to shift the can pile to make room for his manufacturing business. "To move it, I first lowered the soil one foot all around it. Then we jammed railroad ties under it in a sort of guillotine move. We had three tractors—well over 100,000 pounds of machinery—and we couldn't budge it, so we hooked up a bulldozer as well to push it from behind.

"Right after I moved it, a tornado came through and—see that house across the street? It blew the roof clean off of it and scattered it all down the road and blew part of our building off, but the can pile just got a little tilt to it."

George looks up fondly at the can pile. "I painted it a couple of years ago." He

197

then turns to me and notes, "It's a landmark of a bygone era. No one will get rid of it at this point."

→ *Can Pile.* 15514 Thirty-seventh Street Southeast. Take exit 331 off I-94 at Casselton and go north on Langer Avenue. Turn left (west) immediately along the frontage road, which is Thirty-seventh Street Southeast (Highway 10), and the pile is about a block up on the south side.

Facing page: The World's Largest Stack of Empty Oil Cans is an attractive solution to a landfill. Not even a tornado could topple the tower in 1979. The can pile now has a distinctive tilt, but the sparrows and swallows that have built hundreds of nests in the cans don't mind.

Dakota Dinosaur Museum
Yesterday's Giants

Dense forests used to cover the land that is now North Dakota, and herds of scaly triceratops grazed peacefully on the lush flora. To interrupt the peace, perhaps a hungry Tyrannosaurus rex tromped into the scene in search of a soft spot to chomp on a triceratop's heavily armored body.

While the dinosaurs brutally fought for survival, an even deadlier foe was hurtling through the atmosphere. Approximately sixty-five million years ago an asteroid smashed into the earth and won the battle. The global climate changed dramatically due to thick clouds of dust; the continental plates shifted over the earth's crust; and the only remnants of dinosaurs today—apart from birds and lizards—are bones uncovered in arid areas like western North Dakota.

Before the 1800s, the existence of these gigantic reptiles roaming the earth was unknown to humans, which seems impossible when examining the ten full-scale dinosaurs at the Dakota Dinosaur Museum in Dickinson. A pink, red, and gray triceratops model marks the entrance—no one knows if the dinosaurs were colorful, however. Inside, behind glass, stands the high point of the collection: a fifteen-hundred-pound triceratops skull found in Baker, Montana, in 1992.

Another featured herbivore, found nearby in Hell Creek, South Dakota, is the pachycephalosaurus, nicknamed "bone-head" because the thick bone in its skull kept T. rex at bay. A complete skeleton of Albertosaurus, named for Alberta, Canada, tries to make a lunch out of a velociraptor, even though these smart little carnivores, made famous in *Jurassic Park,* were found in a different continent.

Apart from dinosaurs, the museum features saber-toothed cat skulls found in South Dakota and rabbit skeletons dating back thirty-two million years. Compared to these ancient mammals, humans seem like the new kids on the block. Nevertheless, a fascinating display of hominoid skull replicas shows our possible

After uncovering a fifteen-hundred-pound triceratops skull, the museum sculpted this rideable dinosaur with colorful reptilian scales to guard the entrance.

great-great-etc.-grandparents, including Neanderthal man, Homo erectus, Homo habilis, and Australopithecus africanus, all looking out of the glass from millennia of evolution.

While traveling across the green plains of North Dakota may seem uninspiring to some, thinking about the monstrous creatures now underfoot that used to dominate the area makes me thankful for that huge asteroid.

→ *Dakota Dinosaur Museum,* 200 Museum Drive, (701) 255-DINO. From I-94, take exit 61 south onto Highway 22. Turn left (east) right away on Museum Drive. The museum is about a half block away on the left (north) side. It's open Memorial Day through Labor Day, with reduced hours in the spring and fall.

While in the Area

For the perfectly kitsch Western-themed feed hall, exit the interstate nineteen miles west of Dickinson toward Belfield. The Trapper's Kettle restaurant (803 Highway 85 North, Belfield, [701] 575-8585) crosses an old pioneer village with a country kitchen, complete with cast-iron skillets hanging over the stoves; even the soup of the day is served in mini iron kettles. Just opening the door is disconcerting, as the handles are rusty old bear traps, which are supposedly disarmed. Miners' lanterns dangle from huge pieces of driftwood hanging from the ceiling, and wooden snowshoes and paddles divide the luxurious booths. The overflowing salad bar in a wooden boat doesn't satisfy one unappreciative customer, who complains, "Seems like a waste of a perfectly good canoe, if you ask me."

Even relaxing at the table is challenging for greenhorns, though, since animal traps are inlaid into the wood and covered with a quarter inch of shellac. Thanks to these dangerously effective metallic snares, disembodied heads of unlucky animals stare down at your supper. Antelope, beaver, cranes, deer, elk, fox, mountain goats, hares, jackalope, moose, mink, and so on generously make up the décor for hungry diners. To top off the hunting trip, the menus explain "how to talk trapper," so you can sound like a true frontiersman while munching on that patty melt.

The connected hotel next door continues the frontier feel with a wooden fort surrounding the pool and new horse stalls to board your horse for the night.

W'eel Turtle

Rims as Art

George Gottbreht saved stacks of wheel rims from junked vehicles at the local truck stop. Over sixteen years, he hoarded more than two thousand of these metal rims from truck stops, convinced that someday he'd find a worthy cause. Then, in 1982, Gottbreht had a vision to turn his unusual collection into art that the whole town could appreciate. He plotted a plan to stack his rims into the shape of the reptile with the same moniker as the local state park: The Turtle Mountains.

The receptionist at the gift shop next door to the mountain of rims in the shape of a turtle compared the two competing tortoises standing in nearby towns. "Bottineau's turtle looks like a grasshopper riding a snowmobile! George built Dunseith's turtle for just $5,000 . . . and got master welder Curt Halvorsen to do the work. Bottineau's cost $32,000, and the turtle in Boissevain, Canada, cost $9,000. It's OK, I guess. But we really have the best turtle of them all."

The W'eel Turtle stands eighteen feet high but stretches forty feet long, making it arguably the World's Largest Turtle. Even so, visitors sometimes don't recognize what this strange stack of black rims represents. "People thought it was a cricket at first," the receptionist admits, perplexed.

To clear up any confusion, "They installed a motor so its head would bob up and down. Kids climbed up on the turtle all the time, and with that neck nodding up and down, they didn't want any of them to get stuck in the motor and . . . well . . . you know . . ."

A gruesome beheading was averted, but the W'eel Turtle is still an irresistible jungle gym for tots, especially when dolled up with a red-and-white Santa cap for Christmas.

→ *W'eel Turtle,* junction of Highways 3 and 5. From Highway 2, turn north at Rugby onto Highway 3. Drive thirty-two miles north to the intersection of

At first glance, Dunseith's turtle looks like an orderly stack of blackened wheel rims, but the two thousand metal rims form what must be the World's Largest Turtle. The reptile's head used to bob in rhythm thanks to a motor, but the contraption was soon deemed unsafe to the toddlers who couldn't resist climbing on the turtle's noggin.

Highway 5 and Highway 281. The turtle is on the northwest corner next to Dale's Truck Stop.

While in the Area

As part of the largest undefended border in the world, 150,000 flowers are planted every year twelve miles north of Dunseith off Highway 281 in the International

Peace Garden (call [701] 263-4390 or [204] 534-2510). Founded in 1932, these twenty-three hundred acres of forest and garden are a "testimony to flowering peace between the U.S. and Canada."

Highlights include the eighteen-foot floral clock and the fourteen chimes of the Carillon Bell Tower gonging every fifteen minutes. Debris salvaged from the collapse of the World Trade Center is stacked up along the edge of the main walkway, awaiting a design from students in North Dakota and Manitoba. From this vantage point, only two of the white pillars of the 120-foot-high Peace Tower are visible, and they look eerily like the fallen Twin Towers.

While the Peace Garden may be a symbol of openness between two nations, don't plan on smuggling moonshine after sniffing the roses. Bossy border patrols bring flowerchildren back down to earth with a thorough search of their cars after the brief stay in this bucolic paradise.

Stretching into two countries, the International Peace Garden is at its best when flowers are in summertime full bloom. During other seasons, visitors can tour exhibits like this work-in-progress memorial to the victims of September 11, made of scarred beams salvaged from the Twin Towers.

Thor the Viking
God of the Ski Resort

High on a hill overlooking a ski area and the little Scandinavian town of Fort Ransom stands a twenty-one-foot-tall statue of a Viking perusing his conquest. Down in the valley, the Viking View Resort and the Viking View Ranch make clear the ethnic roots of this little village.

The jolly Viking sports a greenish beard and a helmet more like a court jester's cap than that of a fearsome berserker. The hammerless "Thor" wields instead an axe and a large spear/flag pole with an American flag, in case anyone would question his loyalties.

In search of the history behind this symbol, I'm met only with shrugs in the quaint town of Fort Ransom. "He's there to represent our Norwegian ancestry," the waitress at Oley's Cupcakes tells me uninterestedly as she dishes up rhubarb meringue pie to hungry customers. "I guess the town decided it needed a symbol."

No one seems to buy the claim from the travel book *Dakota Day Trips*: "Legend has it that Vikings visited the Fort Ransom area after they landed in North America." Even if southeastern North Dakota wasn't exactly what Leif Erickson had in mind when the sagas were written about Vinland, his Nordic descendents have definitely staked their claim now, nine centuries later.

Thor's battle to conquer this Midwestern Valhalla has not left him without scars, however. His hand has been nearly severed; fiberglass bandages wrap much of his body; and metal cables brace him in place after his losing battle with the gusts sweeping across the crest of this windswept hill. From the bottom of the valley, however, the marauder seems unscathed as he stands proudly in the light powered by a Trojan Deep Cycle car battery and solar panel recharger.

→ *Thor the Viking,* northeast of town in Viking Park. From I-94, take exit 73 south onto Highway 32. Drive for twenty miles until the road comes to a "T." Go right

Fort Ransom's Thor has been stripped of his thunderous hammer and given an axe and an American flag instead. The town mascot stands twenty-one feet tall above the crest of the hill overlooking the little Norwegian American town and ski resort.

(west) on Highway 46 for about five miles. Before the river, turn left (south) onto the gravel "Scenic Backway" for about ten miles; the Viking is on the left on top of the hill.

GARRISON

Wally the Walleye
No Small Fry

Some visitors may wonder why a walleye is perched on a stand on the plains of North Dakota. Residents of Garrison, however, see no mystery in the matter. The nearby reservoir, Lake Sakakawea, is loaded with lunkers, and people come from across the state to haul in the big ones. So many big fish thrive in this body of water that Garrison boasts—with Dakotan bravado—that it's the Walleye Capital of the World.

To back up this bold claim, ten thousand dollars was raised to erect a suitable monument, a twenty-eight-foot walleye leaping upward in the town park. Strangely, the fish bears a striking similarity to the fish statue in Garrison, Minnesota, which also lays claim to the title of Walleye Capital of the World.

The residents of Garrison, North Dakota, named their 820-pound keeper "Willy the Walleye," but they soon had to backtrack when they learned that Baudette, Minnesota, had already named its pride "Willie the Walleye." With a simple vowel movement, the walleye was named the more apt "Wally."

While Wally has withstood being toppled by thunderstorms, the poor fish has been humiliated by insistent birds building their nests and raising their babies in the mouth of the beast. Tourists stop to snap a photo after a visit to the North Dakota Fishing Hall of Fame, a longhouse museum packed with pictures of fish from the lake—small fry next to the whale of a walleye outside.

→ *Wally the Walleye and North Dakota Fishing Hall of Fame,* North Main Street City Park, (701) 463-2600 or (701) 463-2843 . From Highway 83, take Highway 37 west six miles to Garrison. Turn right (north) off 37 onto Trooper Avenue. Follow signs to the business district and turn right on Main Street. The fish is at the end of Main where it comes to a "T" in Garrison City Park.

What better place to build a nest than in the comfort of a fiberglass fish's mouth? Wally the Walleye hails from Garrison, North Dakota, and is not to be confused with Willie the Walleye in Baudette, Minnesota—or the walleye from the same mold in Garrison, Minnesota.

While in the Area

Just to the northeast of Wally the Walleye, Garrison has another curiosity looming above the town: hot and cold water towers. When the town needed more storage space for water, the local waterworks decided that rather than replacing the existing tower with a bigger one, it would build a second identical one. The two twin towers stand side by side, one hot, one cold, but both supplying the same fresh water to taps across town.

Half a mile east from downtown on the south side of Highway 37 stands a scary-looking Golf Giant named "Big Gene," perhaps because of mutant genetics gone horribly awry. This demonic golfer dwarfs the trees and has the handle of his mashie lodged firmly in his tin tummy. As the wind blows, this homemade golfer swings his enormous club menacingly at the birds that have made nests in his hands. If only he had an oil can, he could improve his slice, or perhaps he needs a wire cutter to break the cables that bind him. Looming fifteen feet high with a look of anger (or is it fear?) on his face, if this metal behemoth is set free he will certainly give golfers rushing for tee time pause to ponder before shooting a round at the Garrison City golf course.

Rather than tearing down the existing water tower and putting up a larger one, Garrison built a twin tower with the running joke that they were piping both hot and cold water to taps across town.

Big Gene the Golfer is chained in place like a giant Gulliver for fear that his frightening expression could translate into action against the Lilliputian human golfers.

GRAND FORKS

B-52 Bomber
Third Largest Nuclear Power

During the Cold War, a Soviet attack seemed imminent. The Air Force assumed the reds would attack via the quickest route possible, over the North Pole and through our undefended northern border with Canada. Suddenly, quiet North Dakota was flung onto the front lines of this nuclear standoff.

To defend ourselves from communists taking this transpolar attack route to conquer North Dakota, construction on the five-thousand-acre base in Minot began in 1956, with an SAC (Strategic Air Command) set up there two years later. In addition to protecting the United States, an added perk was that these bases in Minot and Grand Forks offered an opportunity for us to attack the Soviets if they misbehaved. When B-52 bombers landed in 1961 to make this their home base, North Dakota became a nuclear power to be reckoned with.

A squadron of bombers armed with the most powerful weapons ever known was deemed an insufficient deterrent from the Russkies. In 1962, intercontinental ballistic missiles (ICBMs) were scattered across eight thousand square miles of the state. Protecting the bounty of North Dakota's bonanza wheat fields required a new kind of silo, an underground one able to withstand a nuclear blast and armed with a missile able to level Moscow. "Peace through superior firepower" was the credo.

Soon, one hundred and fifty such silos were sunk next to grazing cattle and housed 450 W78 warheads on the missiles. The missiles fulfilled a third of the "nuclear triad," composed of atomic submarines, long-range bombers, and North Dakota's ICBMs. With the 1,140 nuclear warheads at Grand Forks and Minot aimed at the Bolsheviks in Russia and China, North Dakota had the heaviest concentration of nuclear weapons on earth. People joked that "if North Dakota seceded from the Union, it would be the third largest nuclear power in the world."

Today, North Dakota has lost that status due to wimpy concessions in the

The B-52 G Stratofortress bomber has been decommissioned outside the Grand Forks Air Force Base. Although tourists frequently snap photographs of the gray giant that could carry sixty-six thousand pounds of bombs a third of the way around the globe and back, the military ironically prohibits any photographs being taken toward the base.

START I and II treaties and the transferal of many missiles to submarines. Silos were salvaged and imploded, and the holes had to remain exposed for ninety days so Russian satellites could verify the destruction. By the end of 2001, all silos had to be destroyed. Farmers who lost their land in the 1960s to help defend their country now had a chance to reclaim it.

Today, the remnants of the red scare are a tourist site. At Grand Forks Air Force

Base, a decommissioned Minuteman III ICBM LGM-3OG marks the entrance, along with a B-52 G Stratofortress bomber with all its stats:

Mission: Long Range Heavy Bombing.
Range: 8,800 miles.
Max. Weight: 488,000 lbs.
Max. Speed/Altitude: 660 mph/50,000 ft. (almost 10 miles).
Armament: H2.50 Guns/66,000 lbs. of bombs.

Visitors can snap photos of this gigantic plane, but I called ahead to make sure I could get a good shot of the B-52 Stratofortress. "Um, sure, I guess so," the military operator told me. "Someone at the gate might come up to you and ask what you're doing, but just tell them you want some pictures to show your family. You can't take any pictures of the base, though." It's nearly impossible not to take pictures of the base, considering the plane is in front of the base. Perhaps they're a little jumpy about the next communist threat from North Korea, China, or Cuba.

➜ *B-52 Bomber,* Grand Forks Air Force Base, (701) 747-3000. From Grand Forks, take Highway 2 west for fourteen miles. Turn right (north) at the signs for the base and drive about half a mile. The B-52 and ICBM will be on the left (west) side.

While in the Area

Just over the border into Minnesota stands a classic art deco landmark named Whitey's Café and Lounge (two blocks east of the Highway 2 bridge over the river on Highway 2, 121 DeMers Avenue, East Grand Forks, [218] 773-1831). The old saloon's pride is the "wonderbar," a horse-shaped, stainless steel bar boomeranging through the room and surrounded by plush booths with an old-fashioned jukebox supplying the soundtrack. While waiting for your fresh walleye, peruse the framed photos of a time when the whole town—including Whitey's—was submerged in the mucky water of the Red River of the North.

GRASSY BUTTE

Old Sod Post Office
Streets Paved with Glass

Out on the prairie, building materials were scarce. In the town of Hay Stack Butte, which later became Grassy Butte, thick sod was cut and stacked for walls to provide insulation from the devastating cold of the winter and the scorching heat of the summer. In 1912, a large soddy with cedar beams holding up the ceiling was built by Donald McKenzie and his wife to serve as a store.

The Old Sod Post Office serviced this frontier town known for lots of liquor during Prohibition, when cowboys would smuggle moonshine from the north into Grassy Butte. The bottles broken on the dirt streets were not easily swept up and earned Grassy Butte the nickname of the "town with streets paved with glass."

A couple of years later, the Quinion family moved out from New York and ran the sodhouse as the local post office. Ranchers would brand their postal sacks just like their cattle to avoid confusion about whose mail belonged to whom.

Postmen risked their lives getting letters to Grassy Butte when blizzards whipped across the plains. "My brother-in-law used to ride a wagon here whether it was zero degrees, twenty below, or forty below," remembers Jane Heiser, who manages the building now and makes sure there are plenty of freshly baked cookies for visitors.

"I think they were just a little more dedicated back then," Jane laments, and then questions modern mailmen's toughness, noting, "Now they can just drive in their nice warm trucks."

Apart from the danger of yesteryear's weather, Grassy Butte was known as a rowdy drinking town and earned the dubious reputation of "the town with streets paved with glass" because of all the smashed whiskey and beer bottles. During Prohibition, liquor was smuggled across the Canadian border into North Dakota and often ended up fueling a drunken rendezvous in Grassy Butte. "This was a pretty rough town back then, even into the fifties and sixties. People used to get boozed up and break bottles in the streets," Jane recalls.

The Old Sod Post Office in Grassy Butte (population sixteen) ceased its postal duties in 1964 and has won a spot on the National Register of Historic Places. Some of the old postboxes have been converted to birdhouses, and the soddy has been preserved as the town museum.

→ *Old Sod Post Office,* (701) 863-6769. From I-94, take exit 42 north. Drive for about thirty-five miles on Highway 85, and Grassy Butte is on the left (west) side of the highway. The sod post office is the first building on the right. Open daily in the summer.

HARVEY

Og the Gorilla
King Kong of the Prairie

In the middle of a cornfield just south of Harvey a gigantic statue of an ape shakes his fist at a two-dimensional bee buzzing around his head. "You know, at first it was 'come to Harvey and monkey around,' but the school board didn't like that much," according to the waitress in Hornbachers Café. "Then they put a big bee on his head, so the motto goes that even a gorilla can't beat the Hornets."

How this oversized primate ended up in the middle of North Dakota and why only his top half survived is a bit mysterious. Built in Dickinson out of chicken wire and metal frame, the gorilla's body took shape when it was covered with foam insulation that peels now more like papier-mâché. Og the Gorilla traveled across the state with a stint at Rawhide City in Mandan, scaring tots at the frontier village King Kong–style. Once the pioneer village shut its doors, Og was out on the street looking for a new home.

Enter Bert Miller. His Lelm Implement Dealership in the small town of Harvey could always use the help of an oversized ape, and Og's owner was happy to get him off his hands.

Og was halved at the belly button, and Bert wanted to mount the upper section of this monster at his farm implement dealership. His insurance company nixed the idea when worry arose that an arm of the two-and-a-half ton hominoid could crumble and crush a kid.

Bert didn't give up on his homeless ape, and instead the beast was placed on a platform in a field to stand thirty-six feet tall from navel to the top of his angry fist. With one fell swoop, Harvey's "Home of the Hornets" nickname was replaced by "The Gorilla City." Bert gave the ape an annual sixteen-gallon coat of paint—usually pink. "I guess he just likes colors," says the Hornbachers waitress. "He's got a real colorful windmill, and he painted his house blue and pink. Maybe he's color-blind or something."

The wrath of the big white ape of Harvey may be short lived, as his arms are held up by old refrigerators and his bold façade is slowly crumbling.

The paint has since faded from Og, making him an unusual albino ape sans pink eyes. His mechanical arms that once made menacing waves have since been halted and are now held up with old refrigerators (the doors have been removed to prevent kids getting caught inside).

"Aw, he's got a lot of money, but I guess [Bert] just doesn't want to sink any more into Og," the waitress laments. "A couple of years ago, there was this big campaign in town to clean up Harvey. You know, get all the old cars out of your yard so when people pass through they'll see it as a nice place. Well, what about old Og out there in the field? Someone has to fix him up!"

➜ *Og the Gorilla.* Go one mile south of Harvey to the intersection of Highways 52 and 3. Og is in a field on the southeast corner.

World's Largest Buffalo

Sixty Tons of Concrete

When a white buffalo was born in the town of Michigan, North Dakota, in 1996, excitement erupted around this sacred symbol of the Lakota people. According to local Native American legend, the White Buffalo Calf Woman presented the Lakota with their most sacred pipe and spent four days teaching them how to smoke it. As she left toward the west, the Lakota watched her change her buffalo form from being black to brown to red and finally back to the sacred white buffalo.

Now this holy animal is back and has found its way to the shadow of Jamestown's iconic World's Largest Buffalo, another symbol that was met with consternation when it first appeared. When construction began on this statue, people in town wondered what on earth was happening on this hill overlooking the highway. Once they realized it was a giant buffalo, the question changed to a simple "Why?" Never mind the bullheaded skeptics, though, because this three-story cement brown statue allegedly lures in more than one hundred and fifty thousand travelers every year. Soon Jamestown assumed the nickname of its biggest citizen: "The Buffalo City."

On the little road to the statue stands the National Buffalo Museum with a ten-thousand-year-old bison skull as its centerpiece. Next stop is a tour through the frontier village, complete with Louis L'Amour's writing shack, which was moved to the site. Imagine this cowboy author—who doubled as an elephant handler, seaman, and boxer—in this little hut penning his 117 Westerns that earned him the Presidential Medal of Freedom and Congressional Gold Medal, the only writer to earn such an award.

Behind the shack, the albino buffalo "Mahpiya Ska" (White Cloud) and other buffalo are "allowed to roam freely in the pasture as their heritage would dictate," except for those fences, of course. The main attraction is the roadside behemoth standing forty-six feet long and twenty-six feet tall and extending its long dark shadow over the quietly grazing White Cloud.

→ *World's Largest Buffalo,* at the end of Seventeenth Street Southwest, (800) 22 BISON. From I-94, take exit 258 north onto Highway 281. Turn right toward the Frontier Village at the intersection with Seventeenth Street Southwest and go to the end. Or take the scenic drive to the buffalo by turning off I-94 at exit 260 and going north. After a few blocks, when you see the Stop-n-Go, turn left. Go over the bridge and turn onto Buffalo Scenic Drive, a dirt road that winds up to the statue.

While in the Area

To understand the amazing feat of connecting the coasts by railway, stop for a peek at the Hi-Line Bridge on the north side of Valley City, thirty-five miles east of Jamestown. This single-track bridge stretches 3,838 feet across the Sheyenne River in three spans, making it one of the longest and highest railroad bridges still in use in the country.

Facing page: People in Jamestown were skeptical when the forty-six-foot-long and twenty-six-foot-tall statue was erected next to the interstate, but the sixty-ton beast was soon embraced as the symbol of the "Buffalo City."

MANDAN

On-A-Slant Indian Village
Mystery of the Mandan

Welsh legend tells of the son of King Owain of Gwynedd, Madoc, who sailed west from Wales in 1170 in a round Celtic boat called a coracle. His entourage of ten boats stopped briefly in Ireland before venturing across the Atlantic in their little boats to, of all places, Alabama. One boat was sent back to Britain to tell the others, while the other nine paddled upstream into this new world. After skirmishes with the Cheyenne and an ambush at the falls of the Ohio River, the group of Welshmen wandered up a great river to settle, or at least that's how the story goes.

When early settlers told of "white Indians" living along the Missouri River, revisionist historians invented all kinds of theories about the Mandan. Scandinavian scholars suggested that these were surely the descendents of the remaining Norsemen who had carved the Kensington Runestone. Irish historians postulated that it confirmed Saint Brendan the Bold's story of his sixth-century voyage to the "Fortunate Isle," where he found some of his brethren who were related to another monk from Ireland, Saint Finnbar.

The Welsh, however, won the war of words with the least unlikely story after the discovery of the Mandan with coracle boats covered with hides, round Welsh-like homes, and a language with a few words vaguely similar to the Celtic language of twelfth-century Wales. Suddenly, Madoc became the Welsh Christopher Columbus—beating the Genovese sailor by more than three hundred years—and the existence of the "Welsh" Mandan proved that Wales had a legitimate claim on the New World.

"Not true!" rebuts Rheanna, the guide at On-A-Slant Indian Village. "People say they were related to the Welsh because they lived in earth lodges and they fished. Research has revealed that the fairer skin of the Mandan was a form of albinism." The explanation that the Mandan were albinos, as improbable as it sounds, has stemmed the tide of new theories.

The fascinating lifestyle of these Native Americans and the fact that most of them were killed by smallpox brought by Europeans only perpetuates the mystery of the Mandan. When Lewis and Clark arrived in 1805, On-A-Slant had been recently abandoned. Even so, legend states that On-A-Slant was the birthplace of Chief Sheheke, who was called "Big White" by Lewis and Clark, and who traveled back to Washington, D.C., with the explorers.

On-A-Slant was built into a hill along the Missouri River across from present-day Bismarck and once housed about one thousand Mandan in seventy-five lodges. "Mandan villages were a central marketplace in the Northern Plains visited by many nomadic tribes," according to Rheanna. "Many Mandan were multilingual and spoke one of the world's most complex sign languages."

The earth lodge entrances at the On-A-Slant Indian Village lead to a surprisingly cozy interior, with a skylight in the roof that could be covered with a canoe in stormy weather.

Four of the earth lodges were rebuilt by the Civilian Conservation Corps from 1933 to 1934, with the largest lodge stretching eighty-four feet in diameter. "Earth lodges were seasonal homes and occupied in warm summer months," Rheanna explains. "Each house had a large drying scaffold in front for meat and hides. They'd put a canoe over the smoke hole when it rained."

Extended families of between twenty and forty people lived in the same area. "Newly married couples went to live with the bride's mother and her relatives. Even though it was a woman-based culture, men would only converse with men. Women were about sixteen and men about thirty when they married. Then men would often automatically be married to the woman's younger sisters as well, so there was about one man to three women."

In the middle of the village stands what was thought to be a jail but is now assumed to be a ceremonial stockade. Like the story of Noah, Mandan legends told of a flood covering the world, and these small walls stood as a symbol against the rising water. It's yet another similarity to Old World stories and more fodder for further stories about the origin of the Mandan.

→ *On-A-Slant Indian Village,* (701) 663-4758. Go south on Highway 1806 from Mandan for seven miles. The earth lodges are inside the park. Take exit 155 (left lane), which turns into Main Street. Turn left (south) onto Sixth Avenue East. Go past the twenty-five-foot-tall Indian head chainsaw sculpture on Fifth Street Southeast. Drive for seven miles total. Open summer only.

While in the Area

Across the Missouri from Mandan is the big city of Bismarck, or, as John Steinbeck wrote in *Travels with Charley*:

Here is where the map should fold. Here is the boundary between east and west. On the Bismarck side it is eastern landscape, eastern grass, with the look and smell of eastern America. Across the Missouri on the Mandan side it is pure west, with brown grass and water scorings and small outcrops. The two sides of the river might well be a thousand miles apart.

Facing page: Bennett Brien's bison guards the lawn of the Skyscraper of the Prairie, the North Dakota capitol.

Nothing shows this more than a peek at the lush grass lawns and the art deco capitol building nicknamed the "Skyscraper of the Prairie." (From I-94, go south at the State Street exit for one mile, 612 East Boulevard Avenue, [701] 328-2480.) Rising nineteen stories into the air, the unusually stark capitol boasts the North Dakota Rough Rider Hall of Fame, an homage to those people who have received the state's highest honor. On the main floor hang oil paintings of Lawrence Welk, Angie Dickinson, basketball coach Phil Jackson, journalist Eric Sevareid, authors Larry Woiwode and Era Bell Thompson, and actress Dorothy Stickney. Don't miss the observation deck on the top floor or the rusty metal bison statue next to the Sakakawea monument on the grounds in front of the skyscraper.

Scandinavian Heritage Center
"Why Not Minot?"

As host of Høstfest, "North America's Largest Scandinavian Festival," Minot was in dire need of a worthy Scandinavian site to gather around. On May 19, 1997, all that changed with the construction of a huge heritage center with a monument to each of the five Scandinavian countries.

Located south of downtown on Broadway, past shopping centers and strip malls, the Scandinavian Heritage Center stands as an immigrant oasis harkening back to a simpler era amid all the trimmings of modern consumer culture. A skeptic at the gas station isn't quite so sure, shaking her head and looking a little embarrassed when asked about the Heritage Center. "You can't miss it—unfortunately—because there's that big orange Dala horse standing out there."

Naysayers notwithstanding, the center has huge support, evidenced by the fact that nearly every column and bench is adorned with a plaque from a different donor. Undoubtedly, drawing on five nationalities in this ethnic enclave has helped get this gathering place on its feet. Giving equal time to each group has perhaps been more tricky.

The Swedes have the reddish-orange Dalecarlian Horse; the Danes have a small windmill from 1928; the Icelanders have a statue of explorer Leif Erickson; and the Finns have a sauna built in Phelps, Wisconsin, for Finnfest '97 USA. Norway gets the limelight, however, with a stunning reproduction of a wooden *stavkirke,* a type of church supposedly constructed by Viking shipbuilders after they were cured of their nasty habit of pillaging and converted to Christianity.

For the feel of the Old Country, authentic Norwegian houses were also shipped over to this outdoor museum. A beautiful *stabbur* storage hut from Telemark stands next to the Sigdal House, built in Norway in 1770.

The Sons of Norway organization funded the giant modern Thor Lodge as a visitors' Valhalla. Once past the display of the red, white, and blue "Tim Allen Sig-

227

nature series" groundbreaking shovel, stop for a photo op at the knotty Norwegian trolls carved with Husqvarna chainsaws.

The very attentive greeter insists on making sure everyone has everything they need and more. One man doesn't take any brochures and explains to her, "I don't want to have anything else to carry; I try not to collect anything." She doesn't miss a beat but quickly responds, "Oh, that's okay. Here's a bag for you." He hurriedly puts back the "Why Not Minot?" pamphlets when she isn't looking and tries to sneak out the door. Not fast enough! She catches him and warns, "Don't think you can get out without signing the guest book!" He grudgingly returns but skips writing down his address.

After he's convinced to put down his address to receive more brochures in the mail, she's satisfied. As he ventures outside to shoot some photos of the Dala horse, she tells him cheerily, "Please come back for Høstfest!"

→ *Scandinavian Heritage Center,* 1020 South Broadway at Eleventh Avenue, (701) 852-9161. From downtown, go south on Broadway (Highway 83) about one mile. The center is on a hill on the right (west) side. Open weekdays.

While the location of the Scandinavian Heritage Center along the busy strip of South Broadway may seem odd, the Norwegian-style stave church is breathtaking, especially when visitors consider that only wooden pegs hold the beams together.

The jury is still out on which Swedish Dala horse is the largest: the orange steed of Minot, pictured here; the horse guarding the swimming pool in Mora, Minnesota; or the one fed on Swedish pastries in Albert City, Iowa.

Thresher's Row
Dinosaurs of the Prairie

On the knoll of a field in the middle of North Dakota, thirty-four old threshing machines in a row rise above the prairie to be silhouetted on the stark skyline. John Grenz collected these antiquated farm machines once used to separate the wheat from the chaff and placed them in a procession on his farm. The silhouettes evoke images of elephants on parade or the famous closing scene of Ingmar Bergman's dark film *The Seventh Seal*.

The wind whistles through the threshers, which have names like "Belle City Built" and "Hart" from Peoria. Loose parts clang against the Mobil Oil signs used to repair the rusted-out metal, as though the machines are trying to squeak back to life.

At the White Maid Ice Cream Stand, farmers correct my pronunciation. "They're called 'thrashers,' not 'threshers.'" A woman is astonished I've come all the way to Napoleon to see the threshers. "Those old rusty things on the hill?" she exclaims. "They keep falling down, and remember when we had to go and set them back up?" she asks her husband. Then she whispers, "I suspect they got a little help falling down from someone."

Her husband nods with a smile. "I knew how to work those thrashers until 1962." His wife rolls her eyes as he reminisces. "We'd go around to different farms and thrash for them. It was hard work, but those were good times."

In spite of her skepticism, she's quick to point out that *National Geographic* ran a story on Thresher's Row a few years ago. Can they be visited now? "Sure, you can walk right up to 'em. No one will bother you out here."

→ *Thresher's Row,* (701) 754-2891. Take exit 45 off I-94. Go twenty-five miles south on Highway 3 into Napoleon. Go east two and a half to three miles on Highway 34, and the threshers are on the north side of the road. The most dramatic view, however, is looking at them from the east side, so drive past them a bit.

Like elephants on parade, old threshing machines stand on the crest of a hill and make prehistoric-sounding groans as the wind whistles through the cracks and metal siding clangs erratically.

While in the Area
Just past the outfield of the baseball diamond in Nord Park (Fifth Street and Avenue E) is a giant statue of a baseball. A closer look at the oblong ball, however, reveals that it used to be a big bomb from the military. To watch the ball games, kids sit on the shell, confident it has been disarmed.

Nord Park was named for Napoleon's "most famous baseball player," Pete Nord, and his son erected this unusual memorial. The Navy was selling off dud shells sans

TNT. In a sort of swords-to-plowshares gesture, the younger Nord bought the bomb to turn it into a gas tank. Instead, he donated it to the park after painting it to look like a baseball.

Apart from the baseball bomb, Nord Park was lucky enough to have Satchel Paige barnstorm into town before blacks were allowed in the big leagues. He and three fellow players—a catcher, a first baseman, and an outfielder—would take on any nine guys and almost always win due to Paige's pitching.

Another roadside landmark was raised along I-94 thirty miles north of Napoleon. The World's Largest Crane peeks its beak at the traffic along I-94 in the town of Steele to try to lure weary customers into the Lone Steer Motel and Steakhouse (615 Mitchell Avenue North, Steele, [701] 475-2221). Owner Susie White told the Associated Press in 1999, "I look out the window sometimes and see people drive up and they laugh and laugh at the bird. But they're stopping, and that's what's important." If Susie can attract just a fraction of the five thousand cars that zoom by on the interstate each day, the crane will keep the Lone Steer smiling.

An old military bomb becomes a baseball in this swords-to-plowshares monument next to Nord Park's diamond in Napoleon.

Salem Sue, a monument to milk, peers from her perch along the interstate just north of New Salem.

Salem Sue

World's Largest Holstein

Tired of the poor quality of cows in North Dakota, dairy farmers shipped some Holsteins into New Salem to show how it's done. Soon the booming milk production broke all records, and the town has never forgotten.

To give thanks, New Salem raised forty thousand dollars to hire a company in LaCrosse, Wisconsin, to build the largest bovine the world had ever seen. Salem Sue was still not whole in 1974, but after a five-hundred-mile journey, her three pieces were united at her new home atop a hill looking north from New Salem.

Standing thirty-eight feet tall and fifty feet long, Salem Sue is visible for more than five miles along Interstate 94. No wonder more than seven thousand visitors stop every year to pay homage to the cow and plop a buck in a bucket to help pay for the cow's grooming. To keep Sue looking fine, the Lions Club hosts a pancake feed under the udders each year to finance a new paint job every eight years.

The town's bovine pride overflows as shown by *The New Salem Journal*'s subhead, "Home of the World's Largest Holstein Cow," running below the masthead. To honor their statue and its diminutive kine, local athletics and the high school football team assumed the name of "Holsteins." Struck by the statue, a native New Salemite was moved to pen "The Ballad of the Salem Sue" to the biggest muse in the land:

> Her presence shows that New Salem grows
> With milk-producers' yields;
> We've got the cow, world's largest cow
> That looks across our fields.

→ *Salem Sue.* From I-94, take exit 127 south toward town. Turn right (west) at the signs for the World's Largest Holstein and drive up the winding dirt road to her base.

Earl Bunyan

Brother of the Lumberjack

As Paul Bunyan was busy just knocking down a few trees in northern Minnesota, his brother Earl wrangled more than two million cattle out west. Earl's exploits were deemed mere cowboy exaggeration by envious lumberjacks. This little-known younger Bunyan, however, headed up more than twelve thousand cowboys on his ranch, which extended across much of what is now North Dakota. At the time, this was about a tenth of NoDak's population.

Fred and Berd LaRocque dreamed up tall tales of this colossal cowboy while running the S & L Bar in Sanish, North Dakota. Born into the world in Devil's Lake, Dakota Territory, Fred lassooed as a young cowhand on Matador Ranch in Saskatchewan and across Montana and the Dakotas. In 1916, Fred married his betrothed, Bertha "Berd" Northam, a city gal from Chicago who agreed to move to the country.

After ranching for years, Fred convened the first meeting of the "50 Years in the Saddle" group on May 26, 1957, which surely furthered the hyperbole surrounding the now legendary Earl Bunyan.

The next year, Fred and his cronies raised a statue in homage to the "Cowboy of the Plains," as the simulated wood plaque attached to the base calls him. With the black gold discovered underground, the oil business boomed. Fred convinced some oil men—probably regulars in his S & L Bar—to weld Earl together out of old drill stems for his legs and wagon wheels for his hips and chest. Chicken wire

Facing page: Paul Bunyan's brother Earl headed west to the ranches of North Dakota—where of course Earl's ranches were the biggest. His statue rises three times the size of a normal man, one of whom is buried beneath the monument. Fred LaRocque wrangled cows in the early days of the Dakotas, exaggerated the tales of Earl, and created this cowboy tombstone for himself and his wife.

was wrapped around the rest of his body, and then the whole shebang was covered with a hefty coat of cement.

Earl wields a huge "EB" branding iron, ready to sear his mark into his legions of cattle. The twenty-one-foot wrangler walks with a cane, or perhaps it's another cow prod to keep the dogies moving along. While his brother Paul is a brawny lumberman, Earl watches his figure and wears skin-tight blue jeans with an over-sized, ten-gallon Stetson.

Although homesteaders took over Earl Bunyan's big ranch, this Cowboy of the Plains still stands proud in New Town and doubles as a tombstone. A plaque at his feet commemorates his creators: "Fred and Berd LaRocque were cremated and their ashes are under this memorial."

→ *Earl Bunyan.* At Highway 23 and College Road. From I-94 in Dickinson, take exit 13 north on Highway 22 for sixty miles. Turn right at Highway 23 and go eleven miles. Earl is just east of New Town on the south side of Highway 23 outside the old S & L Bar.

Paul Broste Rock Museum
"An Astronomical Cavalcade"

"I will make an infinite room!" declared Paul Broste. Motivated by "psychic inspiration," as he wrote in now-faded ink, he set to work to build his monument to perpetuity out of the oldest objects on the planet: rocks.

Broste was born in a one-room log cabin with a sod roof in 1887 in the middle of North Dakota. With the stark plains surrounding him, he began a collection of one of the only things around, the fieldstones that kept popping up to the surface year after year. While annoyed farmers threw these pesky rocks into a ditch, Broste saved these nuisances, recognizing the splendor under their rough exterior.

"Paul Broste said, 'I'm going to cut my rocks round like earth so they have no beginning and end and they're infinite,'" says Jake, the museum guide. Broste wanted to make spheres, so "he would cut them square and then keep cutting the corners off until he could grind them. No! He did not use a tumbler," exclaims Jake in anticipation of a question from a visiting Texan.

Broste then went out to his junked truck and cut the old axle tube crosswise. He set the cut rock on it and started spinning with another section held on top, eventually making a bowling ball–like stone after many hours of grinding. "He had something to do on the long, cold winter nights," Jake points out.

Now that Broste had made the perfect stone sphere, he still wasn't satisfied. He took another trip out to the trash heap and "tore the wagon wheels and springs off of a truck so he could display them." He bent and twisted the metal to make bizarre stands for his rocks that he dubbed "sphere trees."

Together with the town of Parshall, Broste built a museum to display his 280 rock spheres as well as the granite, gneiss, limestone, lapis lazuli, franklinite, and rhodonite that he'd collected from eighteen different countries. The fortress-like museum, made of Broste's collection of fieldstone with Mexican onyx floors, stands as a completely unique architectural style reminiscent of the Alamo.

The Paul Broste Rock Museum is made entirely of North Dakota fieldstone and serves as a fortress to protect the five thousand rocks inside.

Inside his new digs, Broste could finally realize his dream of infinity. His "Astronomical Cavalcade," a.k.a. the Infinity Room, is lined with mirrors, giving the impression of multiple universes stretching as far as the eye can see. Metal spirals clutching rock spheres—some as big as basketballs—spin upward in the center of the room in a perfectly balanced structure. "We had to hang wires from the ceiling to hold it up," explains Jake. "We realized that when we cleaned it, the whole thing would fall over!"

His rock mobile of perpetuity swirls up and down in the shape of a huge

The Astronomical Cavalcade in the Infinity Room is perfectly balanced, unless you remove one stone and then they will all come down with a crash. The double- or triple-helix here preceded Linus Pauling's discovery of DNA's design, raising speculation that perhaps Broste wasn't quite so far-out when he wrote, "An astronomical cavalcade in cosmic space is indeed infinity—no end of space, no end of time."

double-helix, and perhaps his "psychic inspiration" could have won him a Nobel if he had applied it to DNA rather than rocks. Broste wanted to make the universe with different rocks representing different planets. According to Jake, "He got a little carried away and I think he made the whole Milky Way!"

Broste tried to shed light on his celestial vision with a typewritten paper posted at the entrance to the "Infinity Or Atronomical [*sic*] Cavalcade: Commonly referred to as 'Mirror Room' ":

> The stand or structure that holds the sphere is an abstract conception of space. It is made of solid iron bending and turning in such a way that it flows and twists wandering aimlessly suggesting the vastness of space. . . . If you look in the mirror your eyes would not find a wall nor end. The mirrors reflect back and forth into infinity . . . the spheres on these flowing rods represent plants. Consequently an astronomical cavalcade. An astronomical cavalcade in cosmic space is indeed infinity—no end of space, no end of time.

After Broste had achieved his eternity, he lived out his days in the rock museum, painting disturbing portraits of famous people. Abe Lincoln, FDR, Henrik Ibsen, and Shirley Temple adorn the walls next to black-and-white drawings of skeletons, cars with bull horns, and sea monsters. Jake points to a picture of the Stygian Shore with the damned crossing the river Styx. "These are illustrations he drew from some books. Can you imagine what the neighbors said about him? 'Keep away from him!' "

Paul Broste, farmer, philosopher, and rock collector, died in 1975 at eighty-seven years old. "Paul has achieved immortality," Jake says as he holds up a magazine. "It took decades, but *Rock and Gem* magazine finally gave him credit for making the rock sphere."

➜ *Paul Broste Rock Museum*, North Main Street (but signs mistakenly say "S. Main"), (701) 862-3264. From Minot, take Highway 83 south for seventeen miles to Highway 23. Go right (west) for forty-two miles to Highway 37. Turn left (south) and go two miles into Parshall. Turn right (west) on Central Avenue. Go about five blocks—just past the Juicie Burger—then turn right (north) on Main. The museum is just past Parshall High School on the right (east) side. Open mid-April to mid-October.

Enchanted Highway
Big Is Beautiful

"**P**eople are not going to come off the road for normal-sized sculpture, but they will come for the world's largest," states sculptor Gary Greff when describing his artistic vision. Eleven enormous metal statues are slated—six of which have been completed—leading off the interstate and, ultimately, thirty-two miles south to his hometown of Regent.

"I started with the idea of how to keep this small town alive. At one time, maybe in the 1940s, close to six hundred people lived in Regent. Now it's down to two hundred. Farming has dwindled down to less people with bigger farms. We had to figure out a way to bring people from the interstate," Gary says. Big sculptures were the answer. "It's our only chance of survival. Tourism is what will save the town."

As far-fetched as this may seem, Gary claims, "Twenty thousand to thirty thousand visitors come down the road each year. A bed and breakfast started because of it. There are plans for a motel and theater production."

Traveling along the "Enchanted Highway," these huge sculptures pop up one after another in the distance. Teddy Roosevelt tames a bucking bronco; a covey of pheasants with a sixty-foot-long rooster peer out nervously; a giant deer darts into the air; and the World's Largest Grasshopper harks back to the insect plagues of the 1870s, only with guidance from *Godzilla*.

Easily the most original of Gary's sculptures is the seventy-five-foot-tall Tin Family with Tin Ma, Pa, and Junior sporting ten-foot grins. Drill bits hang down as icicle earrings off the metal mother, the corn-fed teenager licks a lollipop as a propeller spins atop his hat, and father farmer clutches a giant pitchfork as a possible spoof on Grant Wood's *American Gothic*. The medium is the machinery left behind to rust or be recycled. Abandoned oil drums are welded together for arms; feeding troughs jut out for feet; and huge hubcaps give a deer-in-the-headlights

Tin Ma makes up a third of the happy trio of the Tin Family. This was Gary Greff's first colossus, but he still has big plans. "There are six up now, but it will take at least another fifteen years. If I could just hire a good welder! For the first few sculptures, we had a lot of farmers come to weld, but that's sort of dwindled out."

Visible for ten miles, *Geese in Flight* lures tourists off I-94 down the Enchanted Highway to Regent. Each goose in the gaggle takes forty feet of sheet metal with a backdrop of a ninety-foot-tall sunburst (some say it's a dreamcatcher or the eye of Big Brother). Gary completed the geese in only four years, but he laments, "It takes me at least three years to finish one sculpture, and the NEA wants one every year!"

gaze to the eyes. "Mostly, I go to old junkyards and find a bunch of old oil well tanks," reveals Gary, just as Michelangelo went to the quarries of Carrara to choose his marble. Gary goes a step further, however: "I drive over them with a tractor to flatten them out."

Gary is modest about his craft. "I didn't have no art classes. I just had a dream and a vision and said, 'Well, the only way you'll learn is by doing it.' Some people call it 'pop art,' but I prefer 'folk art' because I'm just taking a picture of something or a model and there's no way I can do anything different. I just make it bigger."

While it's doubtful Gary found a model of the happy Tin Family before building it, he doesn't want to be pigeonholed in one particular genre. "I try to do a different design for each one," he says.

Perhaps the most impressive of Gary's sculptures is *Geese in Flight*, along I-94 at the entrance to the Enchanted Highway. With the backdrop of a setting sun, the geese fly south—a subliminal suggestion to travelers to turn toward the town of Regent. Towering one hundred and ten feet tall and weighing in at 78.8 tons, the gaggle of geese made it into the *Guinness Book of World Records* as The World's Largest Scrap Metal Sculpture. "We used over twelve oil well tankers and five miles of weld. The National Guard was even called out for two weeks to help out!" laughs Gary.

While *Geese in Flight* will probably be the biggest along the Enchanted Highway—unless it's toppled from its place in *Guinness* and Gary makes an even bigger scrap metal sculpture. In any case, he plans to weld a giant fish leaping from a scrap metal pond and a seventy-foot-tall buffalo to dwarf Jamestown's. Gary sums up his sculptures, "A photo doesn't show how big these sculptures are. You don't understand until you stand right underneath and look up and say, 'That's one big piece of metal up there!' "

➜ *Enchanted Highway.* From Dickinson, take I-94 east for nine miles. At Gladstone, take exit 72 south. Sculptures are staggered along the highway all the way to Regent.

Geographical Center of North America

"In the Heart of It All"

When the U.S. Geological Survey was issued in 1931, the town of Rugby appeared smack dab in the middle of the entire continent. Actually, the exact center was in the middle of a pond eighteen miles south of town on Highway 3 to Balta, then six miles west. No one cared to go stand in some marsh just to get to the heart of North America. After all, the geographic center of the United States is thirty miles north of Belle Fourche near Castle Rock, South Dakota, and hardly anyone bothers to go there.

Rugby remedied the situation by fudging the figures a bit and raised a cairn of stones the next year along the highway to mark the middle of it all. This two-story obelisk of rocks contains fieldstones, granite, and other special rocks found in the area.

From the center of the continent, a sign plots the distance to faraway places from this important spot: "Acapulco, MX 2090 mi.," "Arctic Circle 1450 mi.," "Lubec, ME 1500 mi.," and "Neah Bay, WA 1100 mi." Who would want to go to all these exotic places when you're "in the heart of it all"?

→ *Geographical Center of North America,* Intersection of Highways 2 and 3. Rugby is in north-central North Dakota, halfway between Minot and Devil's Lake on Highway 2. The rock cairn is at the southeast corner of the intersection with Highway 3, which leads north into town.

While in the Area

About a half block to the east of the rock cairn stands the Northern Lights Tower, erected for the natural wonder that occurs sixty to six hundred miles up in the night sky. Colored metal pillars rise eighty-eight feet into the air to give the

The real center of North America is in a bog a few miles south of Rugby, but who wants to get their feet wet just for bragging rights? Besides, can it really be "the center of it all" if it's just some mucky old swamp? Instead, the residents of Rugby raised this rock cairn along the highway for a quick-stop photo shot.

Rising eighty-eight feet, the colorful beams of the Northern Lights Tower simulate the charged particles from the sun that give us the curtainlike aurora borealis.

impression of these curtainlike lights given off by electrically charged particles from the sun that travel toward the Earth's magnetic poles.

When the real aurora borealis doesn't cooperate, evening ceremonies are occasionally held in Rugby, with simulated northern lights beaming up to the sky to show the four stages of this natural phenomenon.

Behind these multicolored beams, the Geographical Center Prairie Village and Museum (104 Highway 2 East, [701] 776-6414) boasts some oddities of its own. Most notably is an unnerving "replica" of Clifford Thompson, formerly the World's Tallest Man, who was born in nearby Silva, North Dakota, to Norwegian parents. The victim of an overactive pituitary gland, twelve-year-old Thompson shot up to eight feet seven inches and soon had to have all his clothes—except his neckties—tailored to his massive size. Luckily, he found employment—where else but in the circus?

STRASBURG

Lawrence Welk's Birthplace

"Wunnerful, Wunnerful!"

"Lawrence's brothers and sisters could not stand him playing his accordion, so he had to practice in the barn. The animals were his audience," says our guide, Eileen, with a chuckle as she points up to an accordion-playing mannequin in the window of the hayloft. Polkas and schottisches stream out of speakers hoisted to the eaves to fill the farmstead with the jovial music just like Welk did in his day, or at least once he learned his licks.

Welk was the sixth of nine kids, born on March 11, 1903, in the farm's sodhouse with its three-foot-thick walls. "The Welk boys would trap in the winter and skin those little animals for some extra money," Eileen informs us. "They slept in the loft and had to climb upstairs from the outside. That brass bed was actually used by his parents."

Attention is paid to the most minute details. The original Lawrence Welk outhouse is in its original condition, and the one-seater comes complete with a vintage catalog for reading material.

In the family kitchen, Eileen is especially careful to point out what is original and what is just from that era: "This cabinet is not an original Welk but is nearly identical to one that the Welks had with the popular spoon design. And these were donated plates; we have the Welk plates inside." She then shows how the family burned buffalo chips and horse manure blocks for cooking supper, and, to make the point, a model of a blueberry pie with a dusty latticework top is laid out to cool.

The dining room is the centerpiece, with silk flowers and an elegant tea set ready for guests while a cardboard cutout of Lawrence Welk wielding a baton and wearing a white tux stands ready to conduct his "champagne music." As snapshots are taken, Eileen views this as a chance to impart some important history. "Lawrence had appendicitis at eleven years old. He told his parents that it was embar-

A cardboard cutout of the maestro of champagne music stands in the corner of the Welks' dining room. The table is set for tea, and Lawrence's accordion is ready to squeeze out a waltz.

rassing to have fallen so far behind the other kids in school, so he convinced them to let him stay home. He also convinced his parents to buy him an accordion out of a Sears catalog and he'd give them all the money from any wedding or show until his twenty-first birthday. He stayed true to his word, but left home on his twenty-first birthday."

Welk left for the big city of Bismarck having spoken only German his whole life. "He couldn't even talk that much English, that's how determined he was!"

Eileen continues running down Welk's whole history, which she knows by heart. "Lawrence couldn't read sheet music at first and had to be let go from his

Banished to the barn, little Lawrence Welk played for the animals because his early music was not appreciated by his family. Piped-in champagne music wafts from the hayloft to fulfill the fantasy of the boy mannequin with an accordion strung around his neck.

first band, but he did later learn to read music. They said that he could play every instrument in the orchestra in case there would be someone sick in the band."

In the next building, Eileen shows some of Welk's records, including *Lawrence Welk and the Hotsy Totsy Boys*. She's obviously disappointed when nobody in the group cares to spend the time to watch a video documentary of Welk's life. Instead she points out his prolific writing career, in particular his autobiography, *Wunnerful, Wunnerful*. "If you haven't read it, please do," she insists. "He experienced many hardships and I'm sure they have a copy at your local library."

At the homestead, Lawrence Welk has progressed beyond this mortal coil of merely excelling as a famous musician. A plaque emblazoned on the side of the newly built bandstand shows he has indeed achieved the divine, with the words "Dedicated to Him. July 7, 1989." There's a Lawrence Welk Park, a Lawrence Welk Highway, a Lawrence Welk portrait hangs in the state capitol, and Governor Schafer even declared a "Lawrence Welk Week" in 1995.

Interrupting our guide's very thorough tour of the farm implements, Welk's niece Edna shows up wearing a "Wunnerful, Wunnerful" T-shirt and finishes the tour.

"Are you a fan?" she asks someone on the tour.

"My parents were, but I'm not really much of a fan," he responds.

"Well, we are!" both she and Eileen rebut, a little shocked. "And we get him on two channels twice a weekend, so four times total." Welk's TV career began in 1955 and continued for the next twenty-eight years. With cable television, the champagne music is in constant reruns. Eileen still shakes her head sadly, "His parents never lived to see him popular on TV."

→ *Lawrence Welk's Birthplace.* Ludwig and Christina Welk Homestead, 845 Eighty-eighth Street Southeast, (701) 336-7777 or (701) 336-7470. From I-94, take exit 40 and go south fifty miles toward Strasburg (ten miles south of Linton). About a mile north of Strasburg turn right (west) at signs and follow the dirt road for another three miles. Open May 15 to September 15.

WAHPETON

Wahpper
World's Largest Catfish

In the spring of 1997, Wahpeton seemed doomed. The snow was melting and the river was rising. Fields on either side of the Red River of the North had become an enormous lake. Further north, parts of Fargo/Moorhead were submerged, and Grand Forks was flooded and burning.

The water rose in Wahpeton, and people there wondered if they were next. As soon as the waves reached the catfish statue close to the banks, the river crested and the town was saved. No wonder the town declares itself the Catfish Capital of the North and has dubbed the heroic fish "Wahpper" after Wahpeton.

No wonder, then, that North Dakota has protected catfish by outlawing "noodling." Sometimes called "hogging" or "bulldogging," this bizarre technique of fishing for bottom feeders is known legally as "hand fishing" because the person fishing uses their own hands as a sort of bait.

The fisherman, or fish tickler, as they're known, usually takes off his clothes to avoid getting bogged down in the mud. Often the tickler has to be under the murky water for a couple of minutes to make sure he has a good grip on the fish. Catfish like to hide in hollowed-out logs, so a second person is needed to block off the other opening and perhaps pull out the tickler if the fish gets stuck in the log.

"You stick your arm right down there in the mud real slow, and the catfish will slowly 'swallow' your arm," an older man named Rex explained. I assumed he was pulling my leg. "You can't see a thing, but you feel the fish take your whole hand in its mouth, and then you just lift it out of the water. I'm not sure why they call it 'noodling,' but probably because you noodle your hand into its mouth."

As disgusting as this sounds, noodling is real and fraught with danger. Fish ticklers can be surprised when their human bait is bitten by a snapping turtle or beaver. Some catfish can erect spines that sting with a mild venom. If frightened while enveloping the arm, a catfish can grip its sandpaper-like teeth down and halt the

Wahpeton's Wahpper may not dazzle with its beauty, but this *Ictalurus punctatus* catfish is hard to beat for its anatomical accuracy. Even whiskers poke out from the chin—and get snapped off by fishermen in search of a trophy.

tickler from pushing his arm further into the fish. If the fisherman pulls out his arm quickly, he can lose some skin or get scraped up.

Once the arm is sufficiently inside, the fisherman jabs his hand through the gills and raises the fish to the surface. If catfish fight, they'll slap their tails against the log, making a bang known as "thundering." If the catfish is a lunker, the partner pulls the tickler up, and they hope that the hole in the log is big enough to fit.

In the Red River, Wahpper watches over fellow mudcats swimming in the stream and intimidates ticklers who are wary of noodling their arm into such a huge (forty-foot-long) fish. A dainty metal fence has enclosed the five-thousand-pound World's Largest Catfish since a couple of whiskers were broken off, possibly as good luck charms.

Today, people picnic in the shadow of this scale-less beast, and more conventional fishermen drop a line in the muddy Red River in hopes of hooking a mudcat the old-fashioned way.

➡ *World's Largest Catfish.* Take exit 23 east from I-29 nine miles to the 210 bypass. Go for two miles on 210. Turn right on Fourth Street and drive for two blocks. Enter the Kidder Recreation Area by turning left (east) on Danbill Road and drive to the end.

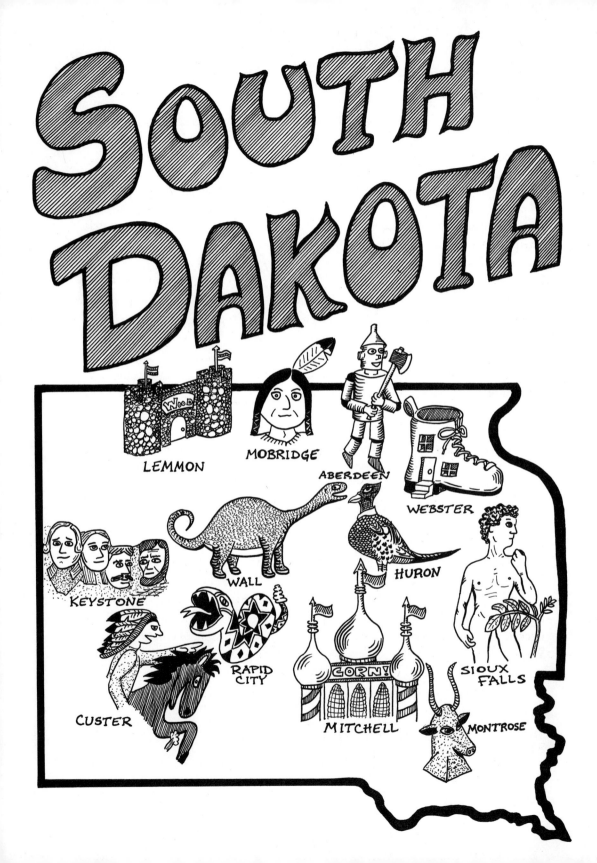

SOUTH DAKOTA

The Black Hills have undergone several transformations: from a sacred Native American site to the Old West with Wild Bill Hickok and Calamity Jane to a tourist destination complete with Flintstones' Bedrock City. Apart from the pristine peaks surrounded by a sea of prairie and thirsty Badlands, the Black Hills offer such oddities as mountain carving (Mount Rushmore and Crazy Horse) and, near Lead, a display of twenty-foot white busts of every president. In stark contrast to this parade of patriotism, Harley riders decked out in black leather converge on Sturgis in August and nearly double the population of the state.

The Black Hills may have the lion's share of South Dakota's roadside attractions, but eccentricities abound in the central and eastern sections of the state. Where else but in the plains can you find the bizarre Petrified Wood Park in Lemmon, the International Vinegar Museum in tiny Roslyn, or the one-and-only Outhouse Museum in Gregory?

South Dakota is still recovering from Kevin Costner's convergence on the state and his ownership of the Midnight Star, the tallest building in Deadwood. Curiously enough, signs in more than one location around the state boast, "*Dances with Wolves* was filmed here!"

Not only can South Dakota brag about Costner as its adopted son, but Cheryl Stoppelmoor was born in the home of the World's Largest Pheasant: Huron. Stoppelmoor changed her mouthful of a name to Cheryl Ladd and acted as Kris Munroe in *Charlie's Angels* and is notorious for her two disco discs, *Cheryl Ladd* and *Dance Fever*.

And yet, South Dakota is known for much more than a knockout supermodel and her boogie hits that were big in Japan. This was the first state to import ring-necked pheasants successfully, and now the Redfield High School teams are known as the tough-sounding Fighting Pheasants. Corn is another recurring theme of the state, and the Mitchell teams are named the Kernels in homage to the cob. In honor of these homegrown symbols, enormous statues of pheasants dot the landscape, and the world-famous Corn Palace is second only to Mount Rushmore—or maybe Wall Drug—as a must-see tourist destination. But these are only the best known of SoDak's impressive attractions . . .

ABERDEEN

Storybook Land
Over the Rainbow

Fed up with the big city, L. Frank Baum abandoned the hustle-bustle of New York and went west. Baum reached the new frontier of the Dakota Territory in 1888 and settled down in Aberdeen, determined to start a new life. He opened a variety store downtown called Baum's Bazaar, which was a dismal failure. He bounded back by buying the local newspaper, *The Aberdeen Saturday Pioneer,* in 1890 and proved himself a first-class writer. Although the paper went belly up the following year, Baum had found his calling.

Over the following years, Baum took up odd jobs such as being a traveling salesman for a porcelain company. The eccentric people he met on the road became fodder for his future writing, most notably *The Wizard of Oz* in 1900, with its whole series of spin-offs.

South Dakota inspired Baum, and he penned the likeness of the locals into his characters but placed Dorothy's black-and-white world somewhere in Kansas to avoid offending his fellow Dakotans. In fact, his niece Matilda Gage was surely the muse behind Dorothy. She lived to be ninety-nine years of age and willed her letters, photos, and other objects to the Alexander Mitchell Library in Aberdeen.

That library also displays an original copy of Baum's newspaper, so visitors can view the political side of this author of children's books. The word "Oz," for instance, is the abbreviation for "ounce," since Baum believed the United States should stick with the gold standard and "Follow the yellow brick road."

Kids don't care about all that political mumbo jumbo, though, and they'd rather play in Aberdeen's Storybook Land with Cinderella, Humpty Dumpty, and

Facing page: Humpty Dumpty sure seemed gay in his pre-fall days. Happiness was the goal of Storybook Land sculptor Leo J. Weber, whose plaque quotes him as saying, "All people are like kids, they never grow old." If only it were true.

More shoelike than the Shoe Museum in Webster, the Shoe House of Storybook Land may not have the old woman who collects shoes, but it does have a nifty slide from the second story.

Jack and Jill. A recreation of Dorothy's "Kansas" farmstead greets guests at the entrance of Wylie Park with her wooden house, a windmill, and an old tractor. A yellow brick road weaves through a little cornfield called Munchkin Land. Luckily, no flying monkeys swoop from the skies to snatch up precocious tots.

→ *Storybook Land,* Wylie Park, (605) 626-7015. Aberdeen is in northeast South Dakota at the junction of Highways 281 and 12. Wylie Park is one mile north of town on Highway 281. Open from April 15 through the end of October.

→ *Alexander Mitchell Library,* 519 South Kline Street, (605) 626-7097. From the intersection of Highways 12 and 281, go six blocks east on Highway 12. If you reach State Street, you've gone two blocks too far. At Kline Street, turn south one block.

The Parade of Fords marks a welcome diversion from its stark surroundings. Painted red with white roofs against the green grass, the LTDs turn heads along Highway 212 as more Fords are added every few years.

CLARK

The Parade
"Conversation Pieces"

Nine poles jut out from the ground at a slant next to a giant slab of limestone; rusty old underground oil drums are sliced with graceful lines and placed upright to break the horizon; and a small fleet of Ford LTDs painted red with white roofs are parked in a procession heading down a ravine.

"I don't really know why I make them things," Ken Bell confesses. "Just sometimes you get some feelings and you go make something. I call them 'conversation pieces.'"

Indeed, these abstract sculptures have sparked conversation around town. "You can't miss 'em," a mechanic tells me. "There's a big old culvert stuck down in the ground and a bunch of identical red Fords lined up. That stuff just leaves a lot of people scratching their heads."

"Those things are a mystery," says the waitress at the Playhouse Restaurant. "Nobody can quite figure out what he's doing out there."

A road worker spraying herbicide at the base of street signs mocks the sculptures from his pickup window: "If you're looking for dumps, I've got one in my yard you can come look at." He laughs and drives away.

With reactions like this, plus ominous religious slogans painted prominently on the sides of buildings and a large sign warning newcomers, "Pheasants and Fur Country: Activists Unwelcome," the town of Clark wouldn't seem like fertile territory for an inspired sculptor to make conceptual art.

"I can't tell you why we do it, most people think it's kind of goofy," Ken tells me modestly. "My son thinks it's the goofiest thing he's ever seen, so he won't help me. My wife won't help me either. It's just something to do out of the ordinary."

Even so, his wife, Sandy Bell, is obviously proud and recognizes the humor in the sculptures too. "Ken doesn't like to talk about them too much. When people ask, he sometimes says, 'Oh, that's some crazy guy downtown who built them!' You should really see his new piece he made just this weekend in front of the shop. He built a deal out of big spools, you know, the kind that they put plastic piping around."

Ken's most unusual sculpture, however, is the huge oil storage tanks cut open on top of the hill. "They look like they're blown up," Sandy explains. "He actually did try to blow them up, but he couldn't, so he cut them open."

"Yeah, I was gonna blow 'em up, I even made my own wick," Ken says. "It'd take me the better part of the afternoon to tell you the story. I'm not done with it yet, though. I want to add something on top, but I've got to have a shooting boom telescopic forklift to get up in the air." These are not ordinary tools for classically trained sculptors.

The "conversation piece" that began Ken Bell's journey into the realm of art is the convoy of two-toned Fords stuck in the field. "We call it 'The Parade,'" Ken explains. "We just paint them by hand; they're nothing fancy, you know. When you get up close to them, you can really tell, but from the road they're really something. It all started when my wife was out checking the cattle and she ran over a rock."

Sandy denies it, though. "He tells everyone that I ran it up on a rock and that's not true. The kids didn't like that car anymore, so he parked it out in the field. See, we used to have the body shop in town and had a lot of old cars, especially '76 Ford LTDs. They're all the same color, that's kind of the eye-catching part. I think there's eight of them now."

Although Sandy may not help build Ken's creations, she does appreciate his work. "It's art," she says, then thinks about it and adds, "No, it's feelings he gets. He likes to do it, and so he does it. Ken's a different breed of cattle."

→ *Ken Bell's Sculptures*, Highway 212. From I-29, take exit 177 west on Highway 212 for thirty-five miles to Clark. The sculptures are a half mile west past town on the north (right) side of Highway 212.

Ken Bell's unfinished oil drum artwork is awaiting its final silver topping. Bell tried opening the tanks with dynamite but opted to cut them open to finish his "conversation piece" of abstract art on the South Dakota prairie.

Flintstones' Bedrock City

A Modern, Stone-Age Community

Soon after Fred Flintstone yelled "Yabba Dabba Doo" for the first time on September 30, 1960, his legacy was carved in stone. The half-hour cartoon launched an animation industry, edging out Howdy-Doody has-beens from children's TV. The cartoon team of Bill Hanna and Joe Barbera struck gold, and soon multimillion-dollar spin-offs of Flintstones' products were marketed to unwitting tots. Spots for vitamins, cereals, and prehistoric dolls competed with the actual show, blurring the lines between entertainment and advertising.

The biggest offshoots of the shows were two Flintstone theme parks dubbed Bedrock Cities—one in Valle, Arizona, near the Grand Canyon, and the other in the Black Hills. Dino the dinosaur stands atop a small cliff at the entrance to show the way back in time as workers dressed as Fred and Barney greet the guests. Inside the thirty-acre Jurassic park of cartoon figures, the entire Flintstone village unfolds with a fire department, a radio station, Mr. Slate's house, and a butcher with a turtle that slips its noggin back in its shell to avoid being beheaded by a cleaver. Near the bubbling volcano ready to erupt stands "Mount Rockmore," with the presidents' faces parodied by Dino, Fred, and Barney. Flintmobiles tool around town and stop for Brontoburgers at the drive-in—don't worry, Dino is a snorkasaurus, not a brontosaurus. The ingredients of the Dino Dogs, on the other hand, are kept secret.

With Stone Age gags parodying 1950s sitcoms, in particular *The Honeymooners*, the Flintstones blurred the lines between the Mesozoic and the Pleistocene, forever frustrating teachers who have to explain that humans and dinosaurs didn't cohab-

Facing page: Dino the dinosaur stands tall on the hill over Bedrock City, probably as a spoof on Rapid City's brontosaurus statue from 1936. Inside the amusement park on Mount Rockmore, Dino, Fred, and Barney parody the presidents.

itate. More than forty years after the Flintstones' debut, Hollywood tried to humanize these two-dimensional drawings with a full-length feature starring John Goodman, Rick Moranis, and the B-52s as the BC-52s. The overly kitsch movie was relegated to the heap of flops of cartoon remakes. One successful show that freely borrows from this Hanna-Barbera creation is *The Simpsons,* in which Homer's bowling technique mimicks that of Fred "Twinkle Toes" Flintstone. The fact that Bedrock City is not a land of the lost but still thrives is a testament to the clever cartoon that is still broadcast in eighty countries.

➡ *Flintstones' Bedrock City,* Highways 16 and 385, (605) 673-4079 or (800) 992-9818. From Rapid City, take Highway 16 south for forty-two miles into Custer. Bedrock City is on the south side of downtown Custer, just southwest of the intersection with Highway 385 on Highway 16. Look for the oversized signs. Open from mid-May to mid-September.

Crazy Horse Memorial
World's Largest Sculpture

Having worked with Gutzon Borglum one summer in 1939 helping to carve Mount Rushmore, Korczak Ziolkowski knew he could make an even bigger sculpture. From Borglum, Ziolkowski learned the fine art of sculpting with jack-hammers and dynamite to blow away excess granite and reveal the faces beneath.

After winning a sculpture contest at the 1939 New York World's Fair, Ziolkowski was invited by Chief Henry Standing Bear to carve Crazy Horse. He served in the military for a few years and landed on Omaha Beach, and then he returned home after refusing to carve war memorials across Europe.

Standing Bear and Ziolkowski chose Thunderhead Mountain in the Black Hills, but Ziolkowski rejected the idea of just carving the top hundred feet. Instead, he declared he'd sculpt the entire six-hundred-foot mountain, making a "sculpture in the round."

On June 3, 1948, five survivors of the Battle of the Little Bighorn appeared for the groundbreaking of the Crazy Horse Memorial. Ziolkowski personally detonated the first blast, which knocked him off his feet and caused him to suffer his first injury. Over the course of the next thirty-four years, Ziolkowski broke his right thumb and wrist, underwent four back operations to remove six disks, endured diabetes and arthritis, suffered two heart attacks, and had quadruple heart bypass surgery. No wonder in 1971 he started sculpting his own tomb near the mountain.

Ziolkowski's determination, however, kept the project afloat in spite of years of debt, near bankruptcy, criticism from environmentalists, and his steadfast refusal to accept millions of dollars in government money. He wasn't even slowed by the "flying cat incident," when one of the bulldozers plunged down a two-hundred-and-fifty-foot cliff. Ziolkowski merely hopped back in the cat with his right foot wrapped in a cast following the surgery on his separated Achilles tendon.

271

Shortly after the seven millionth ton of rock was blown off the mountain, Ziolkowski passed away and was placed in his self-made tomb. His family has vowed to continue the enormous task of sculpting the mountain with the motto "Never forget your dreams." When guides are asked the pesky question of when it'll all be finished, they point to the brochures, which state, "Crazy Horse Memorial is a project that will never end, even after the mountain carving is complete."

→ *Crazy Horse Memorial,* Avenue of the Chiefs, (605) 673-4681. From Rapid City, take Highway 16 south to Highway 244. Go about eight miles past Mount Rushmore and turn south (left) at the junction with Highway 16/385. Follow the sign, and Crazy Horse will be another five miles on the left (east) side of the road. Open all year, dawn till dusk.

The face has finally taken shape: the massive mountain sculpture of Crazy Horse will be 563 feet high and 641 feet long, if the work is ever completed. The official line is: "Due to uncertainties of weather and financing it is not possible to predict when the over-all mountain carving might be completed in the round." Guides at the site are bored by the question and call it a continual work in progress, because watching the explosions is so much fun.

DEADWOOD

Old Style Saloon No. 10
Wild Bill's Demise

Pull open the pistol door handles, shuffle through the sawdust on the wide-board floor, and pull up to the rail at the old tavern where Wild Bill Hickok entered and never left. In a game of five-card draw, Hickok drew the "dead man's hand" of two black eights and two black aces. He never reaped the rewards of his two pair.

A pre-video slot machine postcard shows the kitschy barrel chair tables and down-home, Old West atmosphere of Saloon #10.

Welcome to Deadwood Gulch, a mile-high town founded by miners, mule-skinners, and other fortune hunters who believed they'd found El Dorado. While Ponce De Leon's legendary city of gold may not be Deadwood, nearly any sort of debauchery was permitted in this Wild West town, which had no civil law enforcement because it was a federal Indian reservation.

Amid this chaos, Wild Bill Hickok rode into town in the 1870s in search of fortune. When prospecting didn't bode well for the West's most famous figure, he fell back on his old habit of gambling to strike it rich.

On August 2, 1876, Wild Bill let down his guard. Hickok usually insisted on facing out so he could monitor the action in the saloon, but on this fateful day his back was to the door. In the middle of Wild Bill's poker game, Jack McCall stepped into Old Style Saloon No. 10 and unloaded his six-shooter into Hickok's back.

To relive this momentous occasion, reenactments of the shoot-out and eventual capture of McCall take place daily in the summer at 8 P.M. As part of "The Trial of Jack McCall," this assassin, who killed a lawman as well while trying to escape, is dragged in front of the judge for a hearing in the old Miner's Court.

Nowadays, the good-time girls in lacy slips and hoop dresses have been banished, but their legacy lives on with harlot mannequins peering from the bay windows upstairs in Old Number 10. The cowboys in chaps and spurs and prospectors carrying their tin pans have been replaced by tourists in shorts and sandals. Wild Bill Hickok's poker tables have been replaced by video slot machines. Even so, all of downtown Deadwood has been declared a National Historic Landmark, so the buildings are kept pristine, even if many do sell ice cream and T-shirts.

To preserve the Wild West feel without disrupting business, a smaller version of Deadwood has been built just across Highway 85 with the old tyme shoppes and a boardwalk to boot. Four times daily, cowboy actors stage a reenactment of the shooting of Wild Bill Hickok, often in ninety-five-degree heat. Following the comedic shoot-out, in which all the wrong people drop dead, tourists can pose in a coffin, further victims of the dangerous times in Deadwood.

→ *Old Style Saloon No. 10*, 657 Main Street, (605) 578-3346. From I-90, take exit 30 west (not toward Sturgis). Drive on Highway 14A for eight miles to where it merges with Highway 85 at the beginning of Deadwood. Where the road forks and the highway continues to the left, turn right onto Main Street. Old Style Saloon No. 10 is one block up on the right (west) side.

Daily shoot-outs along Main Street in Deadwood lead to coffins full of tourists. Visitors fake their funeral in this authentic atmosphere—realistic except for their shorts, T-shirts, and the block in the casket to stand on.

Imported from Minnesota, this "Double Johnny" was supposedly built in case blizzards snowed in the first level. Imagine spending the winter stuck in an outhouse! Although two-story outhouses are a running joke, this example (and the one attached with a skyway in Belle Plaine, Minnesota) is proof the gag is true.

GREGORY

Outhouse Museum

A Visit to the White House

"The library," "the ice-house," "Mrs. Murphy," "the john," "the necessary," and "the Roosevelt" are some of the nicknames used in mixed company for the outhouse to avoid embarrassment and garner some chuckles. The Roosevelt, or "the monument," refers to Franklin Delano Roosevelt's decree in 1933 to build a million outhouses as part of the Works Progress Administration (WPA). The South Dakota Outhouse Museum proudly features a WPA outhouse, or the "Presidential Suite," as it's known. A Roosevelt cost five dollars for those who could afford it or was free for those in need.

Richard Papousek, founder and historian of this one-of-a-kind collection, has sought to preserve outhouse lore and arcana. "I do business restorations for a living and outhouses are fast disappearing. They never had sewers in the early days, just outhouses behind every building. We even discovered a four-seater behind the movie theater in the little town of Dixon."

Papousek's pride and joy is the unusual and much-mocked two-story outhouse. A sign posted on the top floor cautions, "Warning: Men Working Below," while a second pleads, "No Dumping Allowed." Another sign tacked on the entrance explains the engineering audacity behind this scatological oddity:

DOUBLE JOHNNY 'Come lately.' Dwell on this . . . 4 feet of snow—an 8 foot drift. How do you open the outhouse door?? Two story Johns were built for stormy weather. Second story holes were located further back than the 1st story holes!! This here 'johnny' was found in Minnesota, dismantled and erected here as you see it today.

As the local historian of the seedy underside of South Dakota, Papousek has preserved the "hideout-house" of Jack Sully, a cattle rustler who "is credited with stealing upward of fifty thousand head of cattle. He was shot <u>DEAD</u> by a pozzee (1904) near Lucas, SD," according to a hand-painted sign on the door of the "Rustlers Refuge" from Iona, South Dakota.

Another squalid tale of criminals hiding in the bowels of an outhouse is told by the sign on the "Gambler$ Hide Out":

> Perhaps one of the most colorful chapters in Gregory County history was the 1904 LAND OPENING. The land was lawlezz. Rabblerousers ruled the town! Legend tells, Bonesteel citizens ran outlaws out of town. 4 gamblers hid in this here outhouse to escape JOHNEY LAW—So goes the BATTLE OF BONESTEEL.

In another privy just a few years later in 1907, the "Jackson Brothers (Graydon, Earnest, Frank) concocted many zhady bizness deals (establishing townz by railroads) in thiz here outhouse." Papousek's version of local legend hardly follows the standard textbook canon as shown in this " '$hady Deal' Privy" from Dallas, South Dakota.

Papousek just records history as he sees it. "Everyone has an outhouse story when they come and visit," he says. "Kids think they're funny, but most adults have bad memories about freezing in an outhouse in the middle of winter."

His colorful storytelling style shines through on the outhouse signs that harken back to cowboy tall tales. A large biffy shielded by a curtain carries the story of a long-gone character of the Old West named "Rattlesnake Pete":

> Pete wuz a Dixon, South Dakota character. He ran a Bath and Barbershop in the bustling prairie town. He was friends with Calamity Jane and is said to have her gold necklace that contained 43 gold nuggets. Pete got his name from his hobby of processing rattlesnake skins. Pete died in 1930. Only then it was learned that Pete was a woman! So goes the true story of Rattlesnake ~~Pete~~ Petunia.

In keeping with the standards of modern museums, the South Dakota Outhouse Museum features special interactive displays. Tourists can pop their heads through a toilet seat for a photo opportunity and special keepsake of their trip. Papousek is quick to point out more of his toilet seat collection: "I have some celebrity seats too. Like Bill Clinton's hot seat in the White House and Dolly Parton's seat called 'Working 9 to 5.'"

Just as Papousek has treasured outhouses and kept them from the dump, archaeologists have found treasures in the dumps of outhouses. Another interactive exhibit shows the remnants of the booty at the bottom of the hole, with a sign that reads:

> Privy digging: America's 'Last' great treasure hunt. Back in the 1960s, many people found antique bottles in dumps behind old farm houses or in farm dumps. Most of the dumps have been dug and the days of 'easy diggin' are gone, or are they?? . . . Look in this privy dig and see the potential. Match the number to the item in this 'privy dig' and see what you find! 1. Chamber pot 2. Patent medicine bottles 3. Ink bottles 4. Silver spoon . . . 12. Shavin' brush 14. False teeth. Many items were dumped for a reason but many were not. Imagine Grandpa's surprise when he looked in the hole and lost his teeth! What a dilemma!

Other oddities include a special doghouse outhouse built for a trained circus dog named King, who could pull the door open with a rope to use the special "custom seat."

Papousek is modest about his life's work, however. "Some people in town like the museum, but others think I'm weird. 'We don't want to be known as the dump of the world!' they tell me. Toilet humor is really big now, though."

With aspirations to appear on VH-1 and *Late Night with David Letterman*, Papousek imagines a much larger collection someday. "There are about seven or eight outhouses now, but I have even more outhouses in reserve just in case I ever need to expand the museum."

→ *South Dakota Outhouse Museum*, behind Naper's Emporium, 520 Main Street, (605) 835-8002. From Highway 18, turn north on Main Street and go about eight blocks. Naper's is on the southwest corner of Sixth Street, across from the old Hipp Theatre and kitty-corner from Stukel's Café.

While in the Area

The turnoff into town is marked by a startled pheasant ready for a noisy takeoff. The fifteen-foot-tall bird was formed by F.A.S.T. of Sparta, Wisconsin, and brightly painted to turn motorists' heads on Highway 18.

A statue of a gorilla, the high school mascot, threatens neighboring teams who venture onto Main Street, and another gorilla leaps from the scoreboard of the football field north of town. The brilliant pheasant seems to upstage the big, black gorilla, just as the town slogan, "The Happening Place," has been overshadowed by the memorable motto, "Ground Zero of Pheasantdom," promising great carnage yet ultimate victory for visiting hunters.

Ten-Thousand-Pound Pheasant
Tinkertown's Trophy

Postwar gas stations along rural highways needed some way to make motorists stop rather than waiting to fill up in the next town. Rather than just better prices at a ho-hum store, visitors wanted an experience they could brag about to the folks back home—and hopefully a photograph to prove it.

With bittersweet nostalgia for the days of the Dust Bowl, Bill Walters built a scrawny old horse out of cement so passersby could take a photo on it as if they were dying of thirst amid miles of dry prairie. "They called it a 'nag' in those days," recalls his wife, Emma. "It was the 'Depression Days Nag.' Everyone was bony in those days, you know, so that's how he made the nag. I never did like that ol' horse too much. 'Why don't you get rid of that?' I'd ask him, but he said that the kids had a lot of fun playing on it. I know a lot of people got a kick out of that old nag."

The current owner, Guy Fish, has kept the nag just as it was in the late 1940s. "This was an old-fashioned convenience store where they sold gas, sandwiches, and beer," remembers Guy. "They called this area 'Tinkertown.'"

"I guess I named it that because my husband, Bill, was always tinkering around. They used to call me 'Mrs. Tinkertown,'" says Emma. "Just like they've got 'Tunerville' on the other side of Watertown because it had a big dancehall with a gas station, we had 'Tinkertown.' I suppose they got their name from that old comic strip *Tunerville Trolley.*"

The art of naming has not been lost in this part of South Dakota. Just as some towns south of Tinkertown carry high-minded names like Naples and Vienna, new businesses in Henry opt for the humorous: "Udder Bar" and "Old Dead Guy's Junk."

The old nag worked to stop tourists on their way to the Black Hills. Soon, Bill Walters dreamed up a bigger project of a South Dakota icon: the pheasant. Emma remembers his technique of using a giant mold. "It was back in about 1948 or 1950.

The ten-thousand-pound pheasant of Tinkertown was made as a two-part mold of solid cement, lifted from the earth with a tow truck, and then bolted together. How did Bill Walters devise this sculpting technique? "I don't know, he probably just dreamed it up," his wife, Emma, speculates. "Girl Scouts painted it, but they didn't get the feathers in quite like Bill did."

He made a great big paper pattern down to the minute detail and then dug it into the ground with a trowel and a spoon and a spade until he got the shape. He did two halves. He poured in the cement and then put the bolts in the wet cement. Once it dried, he got it all loosened up. He hired a tow truck from Watertown to lift up each half and put it together. The bolts were set just perfect. They tightened the two halves together with big bolts.

"The whole pheasant weighs ten thousand pounds because it's solid cement. Once it was together, he painted it with a pink undercoating. A guy driving by slammed on his brakes and nearly had a wreck. He come into Tinkertown and said, 'I heard of pink elephants, but I've never seen a pink pheasant before.'

"After that, Bill painted the feathers in just beautiful! There were pictures of it in magazines like *Life* and *Popular Science*."

The bird's colors have faded over the years, so "Girl Scouts came in the eighties to paint the pheasant as a community project," Guy says. "It needs another coat of paint now, but I'm not talented enough to do it."

To please folks who stopped for a peek, Bill "had a ladder on it with a saddle on the pheasant," Emma remembers. "When he took down the ladder, they always seemed to get up there somehow."

Even today, this little monument is a backdrop for tourists. Guy says, "During hunting season a lot of guys pose next to the pheasant and hold up their dead birds."

Once tourists stopped by regularly, "we changed the gas station to Tinkertown Treasure Shop and Museum," Emma recalls. "Bill started collecting old things he'd find. You know, stuff that museums have, old things for people to look at."

The museum may be gone, but the statues live on. Emma heard that other towns in South Dakota have built pheasants like her husband's. "Did you know that Huron has one too now?" she asked. "That's nothing compared to Bill's, though. Huron spent, I don't know how much, thousands of dollars. Bill did his for about five hundred bucks. Actually, I shouldn't brag, but I think ours looks nicer. Theirs is plastic or something."

➤ *Pheasant and Nag,* northwest corner of Highway 212 and 442nd Avenue. From I-29, take exit 177 in Watertown. Go west on Highway 212 for twenty-three miles. Tinkertown is about four miles past (west of) Henry.

The supposed "healing water" of Hot Springs was revered by Native Americans. Battle Mountain, outside town, marks where two tribes fought for the springs. In the 1890s, the water was considered a cure-all, and trainloads of spa-goers sought treatment for everything from gout to bile buildup. These ladies in their bloomers waited to hop into the warm waters of Evan's Plunge, which even then had a floor covered with pebbles.

Evan's Plunge

Waters to Cure Any Ill

In 1876, Colonel W. J. Thornby wandered into Hot Springs and stumbled across a spring of warm water at the source of a creek. He unsheathed his sword, sliced the bark off a young tree, and scribbled onto the wood: "This is my spring. W. J. Thornby."

The spring was traded a few times, once for a horse, until Fred Evans got his hands on it in 1890. Entrepreneurs opted to change the town name from Minnekahta, the native word for warm waters, to the much more marketable "Hot Springs." Of the many bathhouses established there, Evans Plunge rose to the forefront, boasting mineral baths from sparkling springs to cure whatever ailed you.

In 1876, Dr. John Harvey Kellogg had already popularized spa treatments at his Battle Creek Sanitarium in Michigan, advocating "biologic living" of peanut butter, granola, and, of course, toasted flakes. His treatment went beyond abstinence from smoking, meat, and sex, however, to electrotherapy and hydrotherapy. The latter consisted of an enema machine that pumped fifteen gallons of purifying water through a person's dirty bowel in a few seconds, with claims to cure everything from schizophrenia to acne.

The dozen spas of Hot Springs steered away from these extreme treatments, so when the railroad arrived in 1891, hundreds of visitors opted for this more moderate road to wellville.

With the discovery of penicillin, however, doctors nixed the lengthy stays at spas in favor of scientifically tested antibiotics and other medicines. By the end of World War II, the bathhouses had almost all closed up, except for the huge pool at the famous Evan's Plunge.

With the rising popularity of facials, aromatherapy, and mud baths, spas have returned to Hot Springs after a more than sixty-year hiatus. The Springs Bath

House focuses more on relaxation and rejuvenation, however, than the snake oil curative treatments of the old days.

This valley of healing waters with 177 springs was known to the Lakota as "Wiwilakahta." Now, the oldest spring at Evan's Plunge has been modernized into the world's largest warm-water indoor swimming pool, with a water park boasting bright-colored foam rafts, a wave pool, and enormous fiberglass slides splashing down into this sacred water.

→ *Evan's Plunge,* 1145 North River Street, (605) 745-5165. From Rapid City, take Highway 79 south for fifty-one miles to Highway 385/18. Go right (west) for five miles into Hot Springs. Instead of following Highway 18 onto University Avenue, keep going straight onto Highway 87 (Main Street). Follow it through town, and, at the intersection with Battle Mountain Avenue, turn left (northwest) onto North River Street. Open year-round.

→ *Springs Bath House,* 146 North Garden Street, (605) 745-4424 or (888) 817-1972. Follow Highway 87 into town. Turn right (west) onto University Avenue (Highway 18) and drive for a couple of blocks to Garden Street and turn right (north).

While in the Area

After plunging in the curative waters to pass a gallstone or two, lay down for the night at the elegant Villa Theresa Guest House (801 Almond Street, [605] 745-4633). On the National Register of Historic Places, this old mansion purports to be haunted, but so do many buildings dating back more than a hundred years.

Most likely, the phantoms roaming the halls are those of the avid anticommunist paper baron Frank Osgood Butler and his beloved Fanny, who bought the Villa Theresa in 1924. A Chicago businessman, Butler scorned the parties of which his wife was so fond. To scuttle one such Halloween function, Butler rigged up an elaborate apparatus to mysteriously levitate a dish during dinner. In the age of table-tipping, ectoplasm, and séances, the spooked guests rushed for the door and Butler had his peace.

Drawn to Hot Springs for the curative waters, Butler—like Kellogg— scorned smoking and kept to a strict diet stressing dried fruit and nuts. Mostly, though, Butler bred ponies for polo on his thousand-acre ranch and founded the Hot Springs Polo Club, leaving locals puzzled by his upper-crust city ways.

Butler wasn't fazed by the skeptical cowboys and remained determined to make

This prehistoric mammoth model is ready to squash an insignificant pickup. A whole troop of woolly and Columbian mammoths got stuck in a sinkhole, only to be unearthed twenty-six thousand years later at the Mammoth Site.

Hot Springs the hot spot of South Dakota through his constant philanthropy. While perhaps not exactly what Butler had in mind when trying to lure visitors to the Black Hills, his abode, the Villa Theresa, has since been decked out in different fantasy rooms. Now you can bed down in your choice of luxurious themes such as "Tropical," "Old West," "Royal," "Oriental," "Sportsman," "Indian," or "Music."

The biggest draw to Hot Springs is now the Mammoth Site (1800 Highway 18 Bypass, [605] 745-6017 or [800] 325-6991), where about one hundred woolly and Columbian mammoths lay down to die once they were trapped in a "spring-fed sinkhole." Although this may make squeamish visitors nervous about plunging into the local hot spring–fed pools, no Homo sapiens or other missing links have been unearthed so far. The in situ open dig shows the paleontologists busy dusting off twenty-six-thousand-year-old bones to further uncover these early relatives of the elephant. All of these mammoths were discovered thanks to some suburban tract housing slated to be built here in 1974.

With a pheasant "as big as a car," how could hunters resist Huron for their next trip? Towering above a building on top of a hill, the World's Largest Pheasant greets visitors on the east side of town off Highway 14.

HURON

World's Largest Pheasant
Pose Next to the Ringneck

"There's a pheasant on top of the Dakota Inn that must weigh as much as my car," says the receptionist at the Crossroads Hotel and Convention Center in Huron. Perhaps she's a bit envious of the rival motel across town, since customers usually stop there first for a photo of the bird.

To avert the risk of tourists breaking their necks as they struggle to scale the wall to model next to the pheasant, two little wooden platforms were built on each side of the pheasant. The first platform advises "Pose Here," while the second recommends "Take Photo Here." Unfortunately, the resulting photograph doesn't show how big the bird actually is because the poser is so close to the camera.

Erected in 1959, the thirty-foot-tall pheasant now has the company of a big white bison advertising a car dealer just to the west and an Air Force plane poised to jet off from the VFW supper club over Ravine Park Lake, where kids do cannonballs into the clear water.

Huron hasn't staked a claim as the first city for pheasants, perhaps because Redfield already has a registered copyright next to its motto, "Pheasant Capital of the World®." Instead, Huron opted for the more innocuous motto "It's a brand new day!" and focuses its efforts on the Ringneck Festival in early November. In spite of decreased numbers of pheasants due to excessive mowing at the edge of highways and modern farming methods, tens of thousands of pheasants better beware as the Ringneck Festival boasts an organized hunt for these colorful birds.

→ *World's Largest Pheasant,* Highway 14 at Jersey Avenue Northeast. From I-90, take exit 330 north at Mitchell onto Highway 37. Go fifty-three miles north to Huron. In Huron, Highway 37 turns into Dakota Avenue. Just past downtown and the railroad tracks, turn right (east) on Highway 14 and drive about a quarter mile. The pheasant will be on the right (south) side.

The newest national park is an eighty-foot-deep concrete hole that houses a nuclear missile. When the warheads were still armed, pesky teenagers couldn't pry open the hatch or
the blast-proof doors even with dynamite. Ranger Mark Herberger explains, "If it were
launched, the blast-proof door would go flying fifty yards out there into the field."

Minuteman Missile National Historic Site

Cold War Tourism

Exit 127 off Interstate 90 doesn't seem to go anywhere. There are no towns, no farmhouses, no apparent reasons to build an expensive exit in the middle of the driest section of South Dakota. Upon further inspection, an innocuous vinyl-sided house surrounded by a tall chain-link fence sits in plain view of the highway.

"Here we are!" says park ranger Mark Herberger. "This is Delta-One Launch Control Center, where they controlled ten missile silos." One hundred and fifty-two Minuteman Missile silos were once scattered across the state at the ready to an-nihilate every living being in the U.S.S.R. In case of a Soviet first strike, at least some of South Dakota's missiles might have been spared to attack back.

"Although this looks like just another house out here, if you drove up to the gate, two armed guards would come out to meet you," Mark tells me. "If they no-ticed someone out in the field there, they would hop in this armored vehicle, iron-ically called the 'Peacekeeper,' and see what was going on. Millions of people would drive by every year on the interstate and not realize they were on the front lines of a war zone."

"Here's a volleyball court where they could pass their time, and a horseshoe pitch too." While soldiers were working on their bounce-set-spike, two officers below ground had a hotline to the White House and were plotting coordinates in the Soviet Union to shoot the missiles for maximum damage.

Ranger Mark opens the first door above ground. "We call this the 'Retro Room,' because of all this old exercise equipment and the bumper pool." In this carpeted rec room, soldiers kept in shape thanks to the Ultra Gympac weight-lifting system.

Next to the Retro Room, plush modular furniture fills a lounge with an expan-sive view of an empty skyline. "Everything in here is exactly as the Air Force left it. All the books, magazines, and videos," Mark says. He picks up a copy of *Popular Science* that shows a cover photo of a nuclear weapon and the title "Taking Apart the Bomb." To get in touch with their sensitive side, a dog-eared copy of Shirley MacLaine's *Dance While You Can* supplied much-needed R and R.

"The Launch Control Center had a back-up generator that probably has enough power to supply all of Rapid City, if it had to. It had its own well—three thousand feet deep, not like you have back in Minnesota." Mark points out the helicopter pad and the hardened antenna system to resist attack. "Everything above ground is just to support those two men underground. Even if there was a near miss, it would still knock out everything that's above ground. The capsule underground could still operate for two weeks. Nothing could withstand a direct hit, though."

A chunky old service elevator takes us down three stories and stops with a clunk. Mark opens the lift gate to reveal a large mural of an American missile dramatically piercing a Soviet flag. "Each site had its own artwork that they painted," Mark says. He shows me the photo of another mural of a Domino's Pizza box with the ominous promise, "World Wide Delivery in 30 Minutes or less—Your next one is free."

A big yellow line is painted across the floor and a cryptic message is written on the wall: "No-Lone Zone Two Man Concept Mandatory." Mark explains, "If you crossed this line alone you'd probably be shot. At all times there had to be two people in the capsule." The two of us pass by the five-foot-thick walls enforced by a quarter-inch steel plate. We cross a little gangplank into the "capsule," which looks like a huge bomb suspended by enormous springs to lessen the shock of the impending nuclear blast.

Inside this pod, two red chairs are set up on runners so operators could control a whole string of early computer dials, knobs, and switches. A little cot was set up next to the missile for catnaps and sweet dreams between military tests. A toilet and a microwave oven completed this little bachelor pad deep in the earth. To ensure no silly mistakes, both GIs wore a key around their necks that had to be inserted into different locks ten feet from each other to activate the missile. A red do-not-touch box is prominently mounted on the wall, accessible only by two codes and two keys. "Actually you need more than two people to fire the missiles because the command has to be approved by another Launch Control Center. That is unless the next LCC has been taken out."

The threat of nuclear annihilation was not without its benefits, however. The construction of the silos and military patrols constantly checking on the missiles brought jobs and money to the area. Besides, many people in the Dakotas thought the missiles made them safer instead of making their wheat fields ground zero. "The interstate, jobs, and rural electrification—they were all put in because of the missile fields," Mark says.

Mark pulls aside a Velcro patch in the roof of the pod and tells me, "Here's the escape hatch, but it just opens up onto five feet of dirt, tar, sand, and clay. You'd have to shovel up through all of that. Some guys who manned this LCC called the escape hatch a joke because what would you be going out to? Total destruction and nuclear winter."

"Now, do you want to see a nuclear weapon?" he asks. We drive about ten miles farther down the interstate to another abandoned exit. "See those cement pillars out there?" he says, pointing to stakes fifty yards away. "In the early days, they took measurements for navigation from pillars placed out in the field and by the stars. Once the missile was fired, there was no turning back and no redirecting it or self-destruct mechanism like there is now."

The fenced-in perimeter used to have motion sensors in case pesky teenagers on a dare tried to break in. "The Peacekeeper would have to drive all the way over here to Delta Nine from the Launch Control Center. There's no way anyone could get through the blast-proof doors, though."

This silo, Delta Nine, was controlled remotely, "but they also laid down insulated wire all the way to the Launch Control Center because all electricity goes down immediately after a nuclear blast. There are literally thousands of miles of cable buried across South Dakota to these silos."

We step up on a cement platform and peer down the eighty-foot silo. Poking up through the hole is a gigantic missile that has been ready for the last thirty years to blast off and level Moscow within a half hour. Thankfully, Delta Nine has been disarmed and is the last remaining of the 152 Minuteman II missile silos. All the others were imploded as part of the START treaty, and the resulting holes were left open so Russian satellites could verify their destruction.

"We were planning on getting rid of all the Minuteman II missiles anyway, so the treaty was convenient. There's still five hundred Minuteman III underground at Malmstrom Air Force Base in Minot and Warren Air Force Base in Wyoming."

While the site may feel like a retro trip into the days of the Red Scare, "Peace through superior firepower" obviously is still the credo. Ranger Mark takes it in stride, though, as he plans to make this an interpretive center about nuclear war.

"We've got a lot of work to do. Our job is to spruce up the site a bit and make it spic and span like it was in the '80s. I'd like to set up a conference center, too, where people can debate the Cold War and its effect."

→ *Minuteman Missile National Historic Site,* (605) 433-5552. From I-90, take exit 131 south onto Highway 240. The temporary office is immediately on the right (west) side past the gas station. Call ahead for tours, which are given from Memorial Day to Labor Day.

While in the Area

Just past the Minuteman Missile site office, a fifteen-foot-tall prairie dog beckons tourists to stop and stare at the colony of critters burrowing as far as the eye can see. Perhaps the nuclear radiation from all the buried missiles super-sized this cute rodent, or maybe it was just an advertising scheme to entice drivers to pull over before the Badlands. "This is just a great marketing idea, to have an enormous prairie dog," a mother says to her daughter while posing in front of the beast for her husband, who fiddles hopelessly with his new digital camera. Indeed, who can resist feeding the little fellows popping up in the field, even though a sign warns, "Feed only unsalted food to prairie dogs available in this store." Once inside the Ranch Store Gift Shop with its cow skulls nailed to the eaves, who can resist buying at least a postcard?

Prairie dog colonies provide hours of entertainment for visitors to this dry section of the state. What better way to stop motorists than to give them the opportunity to see an enormous cement prairie dog along the highway?

Sculptor Gutzon Borglum broke artistic ground with his new mountain-carving techniques using dynamite and jackhammers. While Mount Rushmore is now considered perhaps the most blatantly patriotic of monuments, journalists at the time weren't so certain. An East Coast newspaper complained that "Borglum is about to destroy another monument. Thank God it is in South Dakota, where no one will ever see it."

Mount Rushmore
The Bigger the Better

Although Gutzon Borglum was born in Idaho, he studied art in Paris at the Academie Julian. He returned to the United States and succeeded as a painter and sculptor, but he always wanted to leave a legacy. Although in Paris Borglum was impressed by the dynamic sculptures of Auguste Rodin, such as *The Thinker* and *The Kiss,* he didn't want his work to be so puny. Instead, Borglum wanted to create something truly big. Or, as President Calvin Coolidge said of Borglum's biggest work, it's "decidedly American in its conception, magnitude, and meaning. It is altogether worthy of our country."

Borglum had carved some big sculptures already, such as a giant head of Abraham Lincoln in the U.S. Capitol. But he wanted to build the biggest—taller than the Great Pyramid at Giza. Rather than fiddly little chisels and small drills like his hero Rodin used, Borglum would use jackhammers and dynamite. Rather than removing stone from a mountain, he would just transform the whole mountain into his canvas.

Congress was slow to see the importance of such a monument. With Coolidge's prodding, the senators commissioned Mount Rushmore in 1929, two years after Borglum had already begun, but before the stock market crashed. Critics out east blasted the pork barrel project and Borglum's grandiose plan, but they were thankful that at least it was in South Dakota, "where no one will ever see it." Of course those wiseacres never dreamed that two million visitors a year would venture into the Black Hills to see the mugs of Washington, Jefferson, Lincoln, and Teddy Roosevelt carved into a granite cliff.

After all, who can resist at least being curious? George Washington's face alone is as tall as a five-story building and if it had an accompanying body, he would be 465 feet tall and stretch all the way down the mountain.

Although Borglum saw his colossus take shape, he died in 1941 before Mount Rushmore was completed. His son Lincoln continued the blasting to finish the four heads. The work has stopped there, but some politicians have considered adding other faces, in particular Ronald Reagan, to Mount Rushmore.

If visitors want to see the rest of the presidential line-up, the National Presidential Wax Museum boasts all the presidents, "From George W. to George W." Located next to the Holy Terror Mini Golf on the road up to Rushmore, this museum of our governmental figures in wax guarantees you will "Feel the Patriotism." To step into the shoes of the world's most powerful person, guests can bed down behind the imposing white pillars at the White House Resort or the President's View Resort and pretend they wield the power of the West Wing at least for a night.

Most tourists skip these side trips and opt for a view of the four faces. To better present this quintessential vision of America, a new sixty-million-dollar visitors center has been added, and it includes displays of Borglum's studio, complete with huge winches and pneumatic drills. The original model for the monument is a puny one-twelfth the actual size, the size that Rodin might have sculpted, but far too small for America.

→ *Mount Rushmore National Memorial*, 13000 Highway 244, (605) 574-2523. From Rapid City, go twenty-five miles southwest on Highway 16 to Highway 244. Follow the signs. Open all year with a special 9 P.M. closing ceremony held in the summer.

LEAD

Presidents Park
Heads of State

The four heads on Mount Rushmore inevitably spark the debate among visitors: Why only those four? Who else can we add? Then partisan bickering begins. To alleviate the question of whether the next head should be Reagan, FDR, or Clinton, artist David Adickes sculpted all the presidents' heads for his sculpture park outside Lead.

Wander through the beautiful pines of the Black Hills and look up to the twenty-foot-tall statues, appropriately molded in white with each president's state flag mounted next to the Stars and Stripes. In the interest of being complete, Adickes even included President W. H. Harrison, even though he died one month after being sworn in.

Although the exhibit is reverent, special Assassinations and Plots tours are occasionally led through the park. Four presidents were gunned down—Lincoln, Garfield, McKinley, and Kennedy—but only Garfield served for eighty more days from his deathbed while the country waited for Alexander Graham Bell to try to find the bullet with a new electrical device.

All forty-three presidents' big heads can be toured, including Andrew Jackson, lovingly nicknamed "Old Hickory" and known as an Indian fighter for his brutal slaughter of eight hundred Creek Indians at the Battle of Horseshoe Bend. In spite of growing up an orphan, killing a man in one of his many duels, and penning the pamphlet "How to feed a cock before you fight," Jackson helped establish the ten-hour workday, secret ballots in elections, the regulation of banks, and other reforms to help "the rise of the common man."

Adickes hails from Texas, where he erected a sixty-seven-foot-tall statue of Sam Houston in Huntsville, home of the Prison Museum and "Old Sparky," the electric chair. A bust of Sam Houston's head stands at the foot of the colossal statue and proved to be more popular for photographers than the actual statue. Inspired by this bust and, of course, Mount Rushmore, Adickes brought his sculpting craft to South Dakota to enlighten visitors with a presidential history lesson.

→ *Presidents Park,* Highway 85 south of Lead, (605) 584-9925 or (866) 584-9096. From I-90, take exit 30 west (not toward Sturgis). Drive on Highway 14A for eight miles to where it merges with Highway 85 in Deadwood. Continue through town and past Lead as well. Presidents Park is five miles past Lead off Highway 85 just past the Deer Mountain exit.

"Look for the Big Heads!" proclaim advertisements somewhat irreverently. JFK, RWR, and W stand next to Highway 16 as an enticement for tourists to travel to Lead to visit all the big white heads.

LEMMON

Petrified Wood Park
A Depression-Era Vision

Times were tough in the 1930s, especially on the Great Plains. Amateur geologist Ole S. Quammen took it upon himself to help get little Lemmon back on its feet with a big work project to beautify the town.

About 50,000,000 B.C., this whole area was a huge forest, and afterward it was covered with a giant freshwater lake. With the changing climate, the wood in the trees was petrified and lay here for millions of years. That is, until the 1930s. Quammen decided that the world needed to see these wooden stones—only, the world would have to come to Lemmon.

He enrolled a group of unemployed men to lug huge pieces of petrified wood found anywhere within twenty-five miles into the town square. For two years, they hauled these boulders from the fields—some of them twenty feet tall—and stacked them willy-nilly around this one square block in a random pattern known only to Quammen. Some of the rocks were piled into a wishing well, a waterfall, little pyramids, and a little rest area made of petrified wood where one could sit and look at more petrified wood.

As the centerpiece of these stacks stands a South Dakota château made of three hundred tons of petrified wood. Lemmon literature for the site boasts that it's "a fairy-tale-like castle structure whose turrets reach for the sky and whose architecture rivals any existing building in the world."

A thousand people gathered for the inauguration of this new kind of park on June 2, 1932. A little sign at the site attempts to elucidate why all this hard labor was put into these four hundred different petrified wood structures: "THIRTY TO FORTY OTHERWISE UNEMPLOYED MEN RECEIVED SUSTENANCE DURING THIS PERIOD."

The unsettling randomness of these grayish-brown pieces of petrified wood carefully strewn about the park is offset by the Lemmon Pioneer Museum, made entirely of petrified wood. Inside, stuffed jackrabbits play miniature fiddles in

301

The Lemmon museum is housed entirely in a castle of petrified wood. Inside, bizarre dioramas show animals—preserved thanks to the local taxidermist—sporting violins or umbrellas and dressed in dapper doll outfits.

specially made brown pants. Another rabbit holds an umbrella and carries berries next to her friend, who is dressed in a mini-cowboy hat and painting a canvas. The Cherub Model coffin for babies is part of the Lemmon Time Capsule.

The teenager behind the desk at this museum of macabre and peculiar remnants of the early settlers seems very happy that I've stepped inside. "You're only the second person that's come in today," she says when asked what's it like to work here. She adds, "It's kind of creepy. I mean, just imagine working around all these dusty dead animals in a building made of petrified wood that's millions of years old!"

→ *Petrified Wood Park and Museum,* 500 Main Avenue, (605) 374-5716 or (605) 374-5760. Lemmon is at the intersection of Highways 12 and 73 along the North Dakota border in northwest South Dakota. From Highway 12, look for the big sign made of petrified wood. Turn north onto Main Avenue, go four blocks, and the park is on the right (east) side of the road.

With a new design every year, the Mitchell Corn Palace is a town spectacle that lasts only as long as the hungry birds and squirrels can be kept away.

MITCHELL

Corn Palace
World's Biggest Birdfeeder

In 1890, when the wheat harvest produced a bumper crop, the newly settled town of Plankinton erected a "Grain Palace" to honor the wealth of the prairie. To show off the abundance of wheat, residents glued the extra kernels to the building in crop art murals.

Twenty miles to the east, the town of Mitchell upped the ante. Louis Beckwith proposed erecting a towering "Corn Palace" over the fledgling town that had only just been settled in 1879. By 1892, the monument to corn was finished, with a large central tower, smaller turrets surrounding it, and mosaics of corn covering all the sides.

To promote Mitchell to the world, residents called up John Philip Sousa's manager to book him for their Corn Festival. Wary of how this would look on the bandmaster's résumé, the manager bumped up the standard cost of a concert to the hefty sum of seven thousand dollars. Amazingly, Mitchell agreed. Local lore claims that Sousa refused to get off the train when he saw the dirt road that was Main Street until he was paid up front. The festival organizers coughed up the cash and the show went on. Sousa was so fond of Mitchell that he gave an additional concert every day and returned for an encore a few years later.

Mitchell's star was rising, and it was even in the running to be the state capital. New bigger and better Corn Palaces were built to replace the old ones in 1905 and in 1919. Stars such as Lawrence Welk, from the other Dakota, waltzed into the auditorium five times.

Multicolored onion domes were raised above the plains, making this more like czarist Saint Basil's Church rising above Red Square than a monument to corn. Any reference to Mother Russia is conveniently sidestepped, however, by proclaiming the tops of the towers to be "Moorish" domes, or, better yet, calling it "The Taj Mahal of the Great Plains."

Forty thousand dollars a year is invested in redoing the palace for the Corn Palace Festival every September and the 750,000 visitors who stop by every year. Three thousand bushels of multicolored corn, wheat, grain, and grasses cover the concrete walls with crop art themes such as space ships, "ear-chitecture," and the Internet, but most motifs hail the glory of farming.

While Plankinton has long since given up on its Grain Palace, Mitchell keeps up its promotion of corn. The high school sports teams are called the Kernels, and even the call letters of the local radio station are KORN. The biggest advocates for the annual redecorating of the Corn Palace, however, are the birds swooping down for a taste and the squirrels stealing the artwork to stay plump during the frigid South Dakota winter.

→ *Corn Palace,* 601 North Main Street, (605) 996-7311 or (800) 257-CORN. From Sioux Falls, go sixty-five miles west on I-90. Take exit 332 north onto Highway 37. Six blocks past the railroad tracks, turn right (east) on Sixth Avenue. Drive for three blocks and you can't miss it.

Sitting Bull Bust
The Bones of the Medicine Man

Who is buried in Sitting Bull's tomb? This leader of the Hunkpapa band of Teton Sioux was "accidentally" shot near Mobridge when he resisted arrest by Indian policemen under orders from Major General Nelson A. Miles. The U.S. government recognized that his bones represented a symbol of Native American resistance, and both Fort Yates in North Dakota and Mobridge claim his remains.

Tatanka Iyotake, or "Sitting Bull" in English, was born near Mobridge in what is now South Dakota around 1834. His most famous moment—apart from touring in Buffalo Bill's Wild West Show—was as the main medicine man in the preparations for the Battle of the Little Bighorn on June 25, 1876. In the spring before Custer's last stand, Sitting Bull conducted a sun dance and told his fellow warriors that they should no longer show off their bravery in battle but fight to kill.

Following the battle, Sitting Bull and his tribe of Hunkpapa fled to Canada. Upon his return five years later, he was held at Fort Randall for two years and then later moved to Standing Rock Reservation. There, he helped revive the Ghost Dance religion, which promised a return to the old lifestyle: dead ancestors would return to life and the buffalo herds that had been slaughtered by white hunters would return. Dancers wore "ghost shirts" adorned with eagles, stars, and moons, and they believed the garments were impenetrable by bullets or arrows.

Although the Ghost Dance was nonviolent, the U.S. Army feared another Indian war and ordered the arrest of Sitting Bull. When he resisted arrest, Indian police officers shot both Sitting Bull and his son near Mobridge on December 15, 1890. Some of Sitting Bull's followers fled Standing Rock Reservation to join up with another Dakota tribe, but federal troops followed them. They forced the Native Americans to go to their camp at Wounded Knee Creek to disarm them. A shot was fired, and, in the resulting confusion, federal soldiers massacred two to three hundred Indians.

TATANKA IYOTAKE
SITTING BULL
1831 — 1890

SITTING BULL

What happened to Sitting Bull's body afterward is open to speculation. Fort Yates, North Dakota, claims they buried Sitting Bull in quicklime so even his bones would decompose. Nevertheless, residents of Mobridge decided to bring Sitting Bull home to their "oasis on the Oahe" Lake and snuck across the state border to dig up the grave with a backhoe in 1953.

"I don't know if those are his real bones or not," says the receptionist at the Wrangler Inn Motel near the monument when asked about Sitting Bull. "They've already moved him two or three times. First he was buried here, then they dug him up and moved him to Fort Yates, then they took the bones back."

Both towns still claim to have his tomb. Fort Yates poured concrete over their grave to prevent any more tomb raiders. Mobridge hired sculptor Korczak Ziolkowski, who started the Crazy Horse monument near Mount Rushmore, to carve a seven-ton bust of Sitting Bull next to a rather odd monument to Sakakawea in the form of an Egyptian obelisk. A sign at the site of the sculpture on a lofty bluff overlooking the expanse of the Missouri River reads, "April 8, 1953 . . . relatives moved remains to present site and dedicated the memorial burial site April 11, 1953. Tatanka Iyotake Sitting Bull 1834–1890."

→ *Sitting Bull Bust.* Mobridge is in north-central South Dakota. From downtown, take Highway 12 west over the Missouri River (into a different time zone). From the bridge go one and three quarters miles, then turn left (south) just east of Grand River Casino onto SD 1804 and drive for four miles.

Facing page: The sculptor of the Crazy Horse monument in Custer, Korczak Ziolkowski, proved he could indeed carve a beautiful little monument to Sitting Bull, whose bones might or might not be buried underneath.

The enormous hollow bull head is guarded in each direction by tall sentries with curly horned sheep skulls for heads. Sculptor Wayne Porter explains, "See, I used to raise sheep and didn't cut their horns. Basically, I just like sheep with horns." The bull can be entered from the rear, and once inside visitors can climb three stories over spikes, snakes, bats, and farm implement parts. Wayne says, "I welded old tractor seats inside because I needed a place for my brother to sit and keep me company while I worked."

Porter Sculpture Park
"Satanic Pornography"?

Wayne Porter studied politics and history at South Dakota State University, but his hobby of welding thousands of pieces of scrap metal into huge sculptures has taken over his life. "It seems that all art majors I've met never do anything with their degree," Porter says.

Porter, on the other hand, has dedicated his life to his art, especially since he moved his sculpture park from tiny St. Lawrence, South Dakota, to the side of Interstate 90. The postmaster back in St. Lawrence thinks it was a wise move. "Wayne moved down there to get more exposure because hardly anyone comes through here."

"Now I live out of a campground in the summer," Wayne says. "I spend about ten hours a day all summer out here in the sculpture park." The hot days are spent giving tours of his artwork and trying desperately to stop visitors from flicking their cigarette butts into the grass and igniting a wild fire. Meanwhile, Wayne's father rides a mower to keep the paths to the sculptures prim and the wood ticks away.

The tour begins with a trip down Buzzard Row, where sadistic vultures invent new tortures as though each one inhabits another level of Dante's inferno. "These are reincarnated politicians ready to pick the bones of their next constituents," Wayne explains. Obviously he has put his political science degree to work.

One of the largest sculptures is the frame of a giant fishbowl that once doubled as a fountain. Wayne recalls, "Broke my arm on that thing. There used to be water coming down like it was a cracked bowl and the fish was escaping. It's not stainless steel and the metal started getting pitted at the bottom."

Farther on, his colorful dragons welded from old farm implements are a hit with children wandering through the park. "The magic dragon is the first large

Above: The bright yellow hand is ripe with symbolism, but Wayne says the thorn has nothing to do with the stigmata. He reveals his intended meaning: "Pain and joy can coexist, but neither stays forever. Butterflies fly away, thorns are pulled."

Facing page: While this statue that stayed in St. Lawrence may appear like a cross with a woman's naked body, Wayne argues it's a knife hilt on the Venus de Milo, making the statue a sort of femme fatale. Fellow residents of St. Lawrence don't agree. Wayne exclaims, "I've been called a 'satanic pornographer.' They have some petition against me, but I'm not worried."

sculpture I did. Named because people would get engaged under it. One of my friends even met his wife under it."

The reason most visitors stop at the Porter Sculpture Park, however, is the sixty-foot-tall head of a bull with graceful horns curving into the prairie sky. "It's as high as the heads at Mount Rushmore, and the eyes are copies of Michelangelo's *David*," Wayne is quick to point out. He describes how dangerous it was to piece the metal sculpture together with his acetylene torch. "When you're hanging on with one hand for dear life and trying to weld with the other, the welds don't turn out so smooth. It took me three years to build, and there are twenty-five tons of metal in it."

Unlike Mount Rushmore, however, Porter's Bull can be entered from the rear. "Please don't frighten the bats, and look out for snakes," he teases as he climbs up inside the sculpture. Two stories up, Wayne hung a love seat dangling from chains. He swings and sings on the chair and encourages others to clamber up through the maze of metal spikes and metal creatures, including a crucified demon.

In spite of Wayne's devilish side, he's obviously at home among the wildflowers as he points out the purple prairie clover as much as the meaning of his art. Nevertheless, his clever wit and irreverent politics get him in trouble when some don't appreciate his symbolism. A sculpture of what appears to be a cross, with the vertical beam in the form of a woman's body, remains in Porter's hometown of St. Lawrence. When asked about this possibly sexualized crucifix, Porter replies, "Oh, good grief, that one gets me in a lot of trouble. I've been called a 'satanic pornographer.' They have some petition against me, but I'm not worried. If I hadn't been born in St. Lawrence, I'm sure they would have run me out of town by now. It's actually a knife handle and Venus figure. What you call the cross is actually the hilt. Artists live in their own head, you know. I didn't move it down here, because I'd rather be stoned by two hundred people than lynched by everyone that passes on the interstate."

Not everyone in St. Lawrence is so damning of their famous sculptor. The postmaster raves, "His sculptures are really something special. Of course, I'm biased because I'm a local."

→ *Porter Sculpture Park*, Interstate 90 at exit 374, winter: (605) 853-2266; summer: (605) 870-0079. From Sioux Falls, take I-90 west for twenty-three miles. Take exit 374 at Montrose, but go south (not toward town). Take the first left onto a dirt road and follow it to the sculpture park. Open Memorial Day through Labor Day.

Chapel in the Hills

Ole and Lena's Home

When Vikings realized the error in their ways of razing towns, burning monasteries, and plundering booty, they became born-again and partook in the body of Christ. Saint Olaf gave his wayward Norsemen little choice but to join the legions of Jesus or else he'd have their heads.

Viking master shipbuilders were left jobless when the need for single-masted long ships plummeted as the berserkers stayed home to pray. Taking advantage of Norway's recent conversion to Christianity, these woodworkers made ends meet by harnessing their skills to construct intricate wooden stave churches with nary a nail in sight. The layered walls, wooden pegs, and slate roofs bear a striking resemblance to inverted clinker-built Viking ships. On some of these holy sites, the carpenters couldn't resist their overpowering nostalgia for the good ol' days of plundering, so they tacked dragon heads from Viking ships onto the eaves.

Usually these nailless churches were perched at the bottom of a rocky mountain next to a fjord. Rapid City's stave church, however, is at the end of a long suburban development and on the edge of the pristine forests of the Black Hills. This "Chapel in the Hills" is based on the Borgund Church in Lærdal, one of the most famous *stavkirker* along the Sognefjord in western Norway. The builders of South Dakota's church skipped slapping on the layers of overpowering pungent tar that their Norwegian counterparts used, and opted instead for the modern touch of a continuous tape loop of Lutheran hymns for nonstop piety.

Also on the grounds is a Norwegian Log Cabin Museum holding artifacts of the early immigrants. Chainsaw sculptures of Ole and Lena, archetypal slow Scandinavians, guard the door, proving that Norskies aren't too stiff to appreciate good self-deprecating humor.

A gift shop in a grass-roofed *stabbur* imported from Norway contains all things Norwegian, including translations of common expressions such as "Uff Da:

Arriving at a lutefisk dinner and getting served minced ham instead." To complete the scene, a guide will sometimes don a *bunad,* the Norwegian national costume, in front of the striking stave church with its Viking and Christian imagery.

→ *Stavkirke:* Chapel in the Hills, Route 11, (605) 342-8281 or (605) 343-9426. From I-90, take exit 57 south onto West Boulevard (Highway 190). Turn right (west) on Main Street. Turn left (southwest) on Jackson Boulevard (Highway 44) and drive for five miles. Turn left at Chapel Lane (Route 11) and follow the signs to the church at the end of the road. Open May through September.

Above: Thanks to the miracle of a chainsaw, old stumps were transformed into Ole and Lena, the butt of Scandinavian jokes. Inside the Norwegian Log Cabin Museum, learn about how early immigrants survived due to the wonders of *rømmegrøt,* sour cream porridge. *Facing page:* The Chapel in the Hills is a Norwegian-style stave church of overlapping wooden boards. The eaves of this sacred site sport dragon heads inspired by Viking ships to push the Christian soldiers onward.

While in the Area

Along Jackson Boulevard from Rapid City out to the Stavkirke lies every tot's dream: a free theme park, this one boasting 142 fairytale sets covering almost seven acres. Characters from Snow White to Seuss's *Cat in the Hat* are frozen as statues, and the rest is left up to the imagination as kids wander through their favorite stories. Storybook Island (1301 Sheridan Lake Road, [605] 342-6357) is the sister park to Storybook Land in Aberdeen, and they have some of the same sets of enchanted creatures. All is gratis.

Storybook Island in Rapid City has Humpty Dumpty midfall, ready to make an omelet for all the king's men.

Dinosaur Park

T. Rex vs. Triceratops

During the Great Depression, President Franklin Delano Roosevelt didn't want to send out welfare checks to the needy who sat back and twiddled their thumbs. As part of his New Deal, he initiated the Works Progress Administration (WPA) for the unemployed to build bridges, swimming pools, runways, parks, fairgrounds, and so forth. The wages were low, but the workers improved the country's infrastructure while they lived on the government dole of this quasi-socialist program.

Conservative critics assailed many projects of the WPA, later called the Works Project Administration, as unnecessary and expensive, especially the arts and literature aspects. In hindsight, we see these opponents of the arts were short-sighted. While some of the buildings, roads, and bridges have disappeared, WPA-commissioned murals in Iowa post offices, for example, have been lovingly preserved as the pride of their town.

In 1936, FDR's WPA commissioned South Dakotans to construct giant prehistoric lizards to watch over Rapid City. Enormous dinosaurs may seem extravagant and hardly essential, but these beasts have remained a symbol of Rapid City and provided a mountaintop playground for toddlers for generations. Tyrannosaurus rex squares off with triceratops (South Dakota's official fossil); a duck-billed anatotitian and spiny stegosaurus quietly graze on ferns; and apatosaurus, a.k.a. brontosaurus, towers above the whole scene.

While Roosevelt's Depression-era amusement park at the beginning of the Black Hills may have seemed like another pork-barrel project, at least Rapid City can now boast a Jurassic jungle gym that appears on the National Register of Historic Places.

Since 1936, Tyrannosaurus rex has squared off with triceratops at Dinosaur Park. Recent findings note that perhaps T. rex wasn't such a slow dinosaur after all and even could have been brightly colored, as opposed to the usual drab green depicted on screen. The herbivore triceratops, the official state fossil from the late Cretaceous period, might have been a multicolored lizard—and hardly an easy catch with that big bony head.

→ *Dinosaur Park*, 940 Skyline Drive, (605) 343-8687. From I-90, take exit 57 south onto 190. Cross the creek and the railroad tracks, and then a few blocks later turn right (west) on Quincy Street. Take it up to the top of the hill and Skyline Drive. The parking lot is on the left opposite the steps to the dinosaurs.

The Road to the Hills

From Singing Cowboys to Yogi Bear

The main route from Rapid City to the Black Hills is flush with roadside gems. Highway 16 passes mind-numbing signage, innumerable hotels, and chain restaurants, but be sure to stop for a *chimichanga* and *sopapillas* at the Casa del Rey (1902 Mount Rushmore Road [Highway 16], [605] 348-5679). Enter the windowless hacienda along the strip and bathe in the light of the little fountain with its colored lightbulbs that tint the splashing water and stucco walls. Casa del Rey, with its Mexican lounge mystique, has been a Rapid City landmark for more than thirty years—plenty of time to come up with cheeky drink names like "Three wise amigos," "Red-haired señorita," and "Between two señoritas." Wrought-iron guitars, plush Naugahyde booths, and black velvet matadors provide the décor while you munch the heart-stopping but miraculous fried ice cream. "It sounds crazy, but they figured out how to fry ice cream!" our waitress exclaims.

Farther along the highway toward Mount Rushmore, the first site to grab drivers' attention is the Black Hills Maze (three miles south of Rapid City on Highway 16, [605] 343-5439). While it may appear to be a feedlot corral full of confused tourists, this thirty-seven-thousand-square-foot maze has two stories of trails around the walls of the labyrinth. True explorers, however, find their way, sans compass, in the dark through the 1.2 miles of paths on Flashlight Friday. No word on whether search committees venture through to find lost souls before closing time.

Continuing along Highway 16, the first roadside attraction has statues of the "smarter than average bear" in front of the picnic pavilion at a mini Jellystone Park (five miles south of Rapid City, [605] 341-8554 or [800] 579-7053). Boo Boo's Caboose makes the rounds around Yogi's campsite a few times a day to convince the little ones that camping is fun.

Yogi Bear greets visitors to his park, "where you camp with friends." Sleep in a tent and risk those pesky bears, or rent a barn-shaped log cabin with a swinging chair on the front stoop. In the evening, take a spin on Boo Boo's Caboose.

This dapper prospector stands outside a gold and jewelry shop and looks more like Clark Gable in a polo shirt than an old-time miner.

About five miles southwest of Rapid City on the west side of Highway 16 and just a bit past Yogi stand two oversized gold diggers. A giant miner, nicknamed "Stamper" after the store he advertises, wields a mighty pickax to get the gold out of those hills. Stamper the miner is a biker at heart, with a huge Harley-Davidson belt buckle and a Harley red polo shirt—products coincidentally sold in the store in all sizes.

Just up the hill from Stamper, a not-so-lucky prospector pans for gold with a forlorn gaze on his bearded face. Perhaps you can be more fortunate when panning for gold at Dakota Designs Direct, behind the prospector. Although you probably won't recoup the $1.50 cover charge, at least it'll keep the kids busy for a couple of hours.

Apart from the dinosaurs along Skyline Drive, one of the oldest tourist sites in Rapid City is the Reptile Gardens (five miles south of Rapid City on Highway 16, [605] 342-5873 or [800] 335-0275). "How do you handle an angry alligator or a cranky crocodile? Very carefully! Let the experts show you how it's done," warn the brochures, in case brave audience members want to try it at home. With the world's largest collection of reptiles and amphibians, the Reptile Gardens are not for the squeamish. Lush flower gardens, however, are planted especially for parents who haul their begging little ones to see all the predators, from vipers and cobras to owls and hawks.

Right next door to the Reptile Gardens is a window into our nostalgic view of the old West. Put on the feedbag at Flying T Chuckwagon Supper and Show ([605] 342-1905) for barbecued grub on a tin plate. Cowboys "sing for your supper" in the old barn and stage a comic western act with sing-alongs to help you digest the vittles.

Past Old McDonald's Farm (ten miles south of Rapid City on Highway 16, [605] 737-4815), with its goat bridge and potbelly pig races, stands one of the most inexplicable South Dakota attractions: Cosmos Mystery Area (sixteen miles south of Rapid City on Highway 16). Perplexing scientists for ages, the laws of gravity don't seem to hold up in this tilted house. The biggest baffler of all, though, is that the probability that a mystery spot will be discovered is directly proportional to the number of tourists in the area.

Facing page: Let's hope you'll be luckier than this poor prospector with sad bags under his eyes. Plunk down a buck and a half and take your chances panning for gold.

Not only does Roslyn have the International Vinegar Museum, but everyone comes out in force for the annual Vinegar Festival. The receptionist at the museum explains, "You know, every small town needs its festival, and this one is kind of quirky. There's Miss Vinaigrette, Miss Sour, and the other vinegar royalty."

International Vinegar Museum
Taste the Sour Power

Someday we could be driving in vinegar cars, wearing vinegar clothes, and even using vinegar for rocket casings when we shoot astronauts to Mars. Or at least that's what displays at the Vinegar Museum claim. All of these wonders are thanks to microbial cellulose, which is a fancy way of saying "vinegar paper." Regular paper is made from cellulose—trees, plants, grasses—but microorganisms in vinegar can make any shape or thickness desired, given the right surroundings.

Who would have expected a small town in South Dakota to house probably the largest collection of vinegars in the world? The Vinegar Museum is less about these miracle products that will someday propel us into a brave new world of vinegar and more about the tart taste that raises food to a new level. Shelves are stocked with everything from British malt vinegar to handmade Japanese rice vinegars to hundred-dollar bottles of forty-year-old balsamic vinegar from Modena, Italy.

Lawrence Diggs, a.k.a. the Vinegar Man, dreamed up the International Vinegar Museum and the organization Vinegar Connoisseurs International, which "brings together people who are interested in vinegar and want to share their excitement with others." Moreover, the International Vinegar Research Institute was established to further the cause of vinegar studies around the world.

Diggs will gladly let you sample some of the more unusual vinegars in his collection. If asked, he'll surely expound on all the possibilities for vinegar paper, from camping with disposable tents to bank notes for legal tender. Did you know that someday this microbial cellulose could be molded into artificial arteries and skin? With vinegar, the possibilities are endless.

→ *International Vinegar Museum,* 104 West Carlton Avenue, (605) 486-0075. Roslyn is in northeastern South Dakota. From I-29, take exit 207 west onto Highway 12 for twenty-two miles into Webster. Turn right (north) onto Highway 25 for twelve miles. From Highway 25 (Bryant Avenue) turn south on Main Street. The museum is three blocks south at Carlton Avenue. Open June through October.

U.S.S. *South Dakota* Memorial

"Battleship X"

I n the Pacific theater, the battleship U.S.S. *South Dakota* protected the enormous aircraft carrier *Enterprise* at Guadalcanal and other battles. Twice, the Japanese sank the *South Dakota*, or so they thought. The Navy nicknamed this phoenix "*Battleship X*," perhaps so it could mysteriously appear in battle and take the

The U.S.S. *South Dakota* looks sunken in a sea of green grass as nearby softballers pop home runs onto its deck/lawn.

enemy by surprise. Sixty-four Japanese Zero planes were gunned down as this supposedly nonexistent boat kept chugging along.

When *Battleship X* fought in the Battle of Santa Cruz, however, a Japanese dive bomber put the boat in its sights and successfully lobbed a five-hundred-pound aerial bomb onto the battery turret. The thick metal shields of the ship were scraped, but they saved the boat from sinking. The shrapnel, on the other hand, downed Captain Gatch, who was rushed into the sick bay.

Not one to mince words, the valorous Captain Gatch announced when he recovered that he wasn't scared of a measly Japanese plane. As literature at the memorial of the U.S.S. *South Dakota* declares, "When asked why he had not hit the deck when he saw the plane coming, Gatch answered, 'I considered it beneath the dignity of a captain of an American battleship to flop for a Japanese bomb.'"

Gatch survived to be reinstated as captain of his ship and soon was promoted to admiral for his risky heroism. The *South Dakota* survived until 1962, when it was scheduled to be scrapped. As the story behind this mythical boat goes, years later when the ship was moored in a harbor waiting to be mothballed, a Japanese merchant ship trolled by the old battleship. The wake from the moving boat bounced the *South Dakota* up so high that the ropes came off the mooring posts. The Japanese ship unwittingly liberated the *South Dakota* and subsequently saved it from just drifting out to sea as a ghost ship, *Battleship X*.

A group of South Dakotans sought to save the ship from the crusher, but realized that sailing it to landlocked Sioux Falls would be a bit difficult. Instead, the gun turrets, propeller, thirteen-ton anchor, projectiles, sixteen-inch-diameter gun barrels, and tower were sent to the memorial site. This matériel was set up inside a big concrete outline of the *South Dakota,* an appropriate memorial to the missing *Battleship X.* The boat seems to be sinking in a sea of green grass now, as girls' softball teams knock foul balls onto the deck of this monumental ship in absentia.

→ *U.S.S.* South Dakota *Memorial,* Kiwanis Avenue and West 12th Street (Highway 42), (605) 367-7060. From I-29, take exit 79 east onto Highway 42 (West 12 Street) for about half a mile. The ship's outline is on the southwest corner of the intersection with Kiwanis Avenue. The museum is open summer only.

While in the Area

Continuing in downtown Sioux Falls to Fawick Park along the river (between 10th and 11th Streets on 2nd Avenue), a striking brass version of Michelangelo's *David* watches over the walkway. After inventor Thomas Fawick made a boatload of

Bronze replicas of Michelangelo's *Moses* and *David* were given to Sioux Falls, but some folks in town didn't share the sculptor's Renaissance love of the perfect human figure.

money on his designs, he donated *David* and a copy of the Italian sculptor's *Moses* (at Augustana College) to the city of Sioux Falls. Supposedly passing motorists didn't appreciate this sort of public nudity. Rather than stitching a pair of oversized boxer shorts, protests were quelled by simply turning Michelangelo's masterpiece away from traffic and avoiding any subsequent accidents by distracted drivers. His brass behind is shrouded by newly planted trees and shrubs.

On the east side of town, an enormous muffler man stands guard over the intersection of Cliff Avenue and 12th Street. "Mr. Bendo" clasps a huge tailpipe that he can bend to fit any car for Buck's Muffler (400 South Cliff Avenue). Usually this blue-and-white-dressed man wears his spiffy mechanic's uniform, but he has been spotted sporting sunglasses and sideburns like an oversized Elvis and a plaid shirt and axe, as yet another Paul Bunyan.

Facing page: Mr. Bendo wants to change your muffler, and he's got the muscles to subjugate any measly pipe to his will for your convenience.

Wall Drug
From Jackalopes to Ice Water

Wall Drug is proof that advertising works. Signs for Wall Drug were erected in each state and everywhere from London to the Taj Mahal to the North Pole indicating how many miles to this once-unknown little pharmacy on the Dakota plains. Mottos such as "Where the Hell is Wall Drug?" "Wall I'll be Drugged!" and "Have you Dug Wall Drug?" were painted on wooden signs and later silk-screened onto free bumper stickers to spread the word.

Of course this type of hyperbole was inherent to the Great Plains, where tall tales of fantastic newly discovered creatures were told around the campfire. A new species dubbed the "Camelce," a crossbreed between elks and camels, was announced in the New York *Herald* after journalist R. B. Davenport was duped during the Newton-Jenney expedition to the Black Hills in 1875. The jackalope, an extraordinary mixture of jackrabbit, antelope, and sometimes pheasant, used to mock singing cowboys by mimicking them like a parrot in the distance. These intelligent "attack rabbits" with horns could only be duped with the sweet smell of whiskey, or at least that's what the tenderfeet believed. Appropriately, Wall Drug sells stuffed jackalopes and even erected a six-foot-tall jackalope statue in the back garden.

The success of Wall Drug is the result of more than smoke and mirrors, however. When Ted Hustead came up from Nebraska in 1931 to open the only drug store for five hundred miles, he needed to trump up more business during the

Facing page: The first reported sighting of a jackalope came in 1829 from Douglas, Wyoming (now the Jackalope Capital of America). Jackalope hunting licenses can be bought for a small fee, but catching these "warrior rabbits" with antlers requires luring them with a bottle of whiskey to slow them down. This rideable jackalope sits in the Wall Drug backyard along with a mini brontosaurus, Mount Rushmore, and a musical quartet of animals.

Depression. Travelers escaping the Hoovervilles of the city made it across South Dakota during a drought that lasted seven years. During this time, Hustead's wife, Dorothy, had the simple idea of offering these thirsty travelers a glass of ice water.

Free ice water began an empire. Wall Drug became a must-stop along the desolate "wall" of the bone-dry badlands to have a sip of water and break up the monotony of the trip. Ice water is still on the house, and a cup of coffee is only a nickel.

During the years of the Dust Bowl, Ted Hustead offered free ice water at his drugstore to travelers. Soon signs for Wall Drug spread across South Dakota and every state of the Union. What was once just a drugstore has become the biggest employer in town and takes up most of Main Street.

All signs led to Wall, and the town's self-deprecating humor extended to its pronouncement that it was "the geographical center of nowhere" in retaliation for Rugby, North Dakota's, claim of being the center of North America, and Castle Rock, South Dakota's, claim of being the geographic center of the United States.

To avoid visitors being disappointed after all the advertising, Wall Drug soon grew to be a mini museum, with Native American artifacts, cowboy photos, six hundred different cattle brands seared into the walls, and knickknacks for the whole family. Soon, a mechanical cowboy band dubbed the "Chuck Wagon Four" was rigged up for some entertainment. For a mere quarter plopped in a machine, a tattered gorilla would tickle the ivories of an old player piano to produce "Pop Goes the Weasel."

Even a Pharmacy Museum is displayed to wax nostalgic about the early days of Wall Drug and some of the snake oil remedies ground up by the apothecary. Farther on, the mythical prairie jackalope stands next to a mini version of Mount Rushmore, spoiling the surprise of the wonders that lie ahead in the Black Hills.

A traveler's chapel that is a replica of an 1850s Trappist monastery was set up so church-deprived tourists could pray to Saint Christopher to keep their campers from overheating. Never mind obeying the order of these self-denying Cistercian monks who lived in almost complete silence and abstained from meat. Instead, head to Wall Drug's restaurants for huge cowboy portions of hearty beef. The dining rooms now seat 520 diners—impressive considering the population of Wall is only 542.

In fact, a third of the residents of Wall now work for the drug store, making it the largest employer in town. The ever-expanding store supposedly serves a million visitors a year, or perhaps this is more Dakotan exaggeration.

While Wall Drug signs may have originally been tongue in cheek for this tiny town with an even tinier drugstore, the promise of these billboards has now been fulfilled. Wall Drug is indeed one of the most beautifully kitsch spots in America.

➡ *Wall Drug,* 510 Main Street, (605) 279-2175. Wall is sixty miles east of Rapid City. From I-90, look for the eighty-foot-long brontosaurus on the hill and take exit 110 north into town.

Shoe House

There Was an Old Woman . . .

Mildred O'Neil has a shoe fetish. When she was a teenager in the 1970s she began collecting shoes of all different shapes and sizes. When word of her collection spread, people from around the world began sending her special shoes. Even Imelda Marcos would turn green if she heard of O'Neil's closet, blossoming with more than seven thousand shoes.

When she wanted to share her passion with the world, the town of Webster built her a two-story house in the shape of a shoe next to the Wildlife, Industry, and Science Museum. Since Webster's population is only two thousand, O'Neil's collection of more than nine thousand shoes could provide more than two pairs of shoes per person. Now, not only does Webster have the requisite pioneer village with an old blacksmith, general store, railroad depot, and post office, but the town can also boast one of the world's largest shoe displays in a shoe.

Since O'Neil is an ex-librarian, her collection is organized with the precision of the Dewey decimal system, complete with a little card catalog entry for each shoe. A printed card adorns each pair of footwear to illuminate its history. Shoes are separated into twenty-two classifications, including babies', children's, cowboy boots, straw, sport, jewelry, clown, and so forth.

As a taste of the Old West, a shoemaking workshop is decorated with an old cobbler's sign in the shape of a boot. It even has a bullet hole, perhaps from an unsatisfied cowboy doing target practice.

On special occasions, O'Neil dons a fairy tale costume to tease the tots into believing she is truly the old woman who lived in a shoe.

To get to the shoe, you walk by a stuffed giraffe, a dead wildebeest, gazelles, and other exotic African animals. Only slightly shoe-shaped, Webster's Shoe House has practical vinyl siding but clever black piping for laces, black tar paper for a sole, and wildflowers popping up around its footprint.

→ *Shoe House, Museum of Wildlife, Industry, and Science,* 760 West Highway 12, (605) 345-4751. Webster is in northeastern South Dakota. From I-29, take exit 207 west and go twenty-two miles west on Highway 12 into town. Drive past the junction with Highway 25, and the shoe house is at the intersection with Seventh Street West. Open May through October.

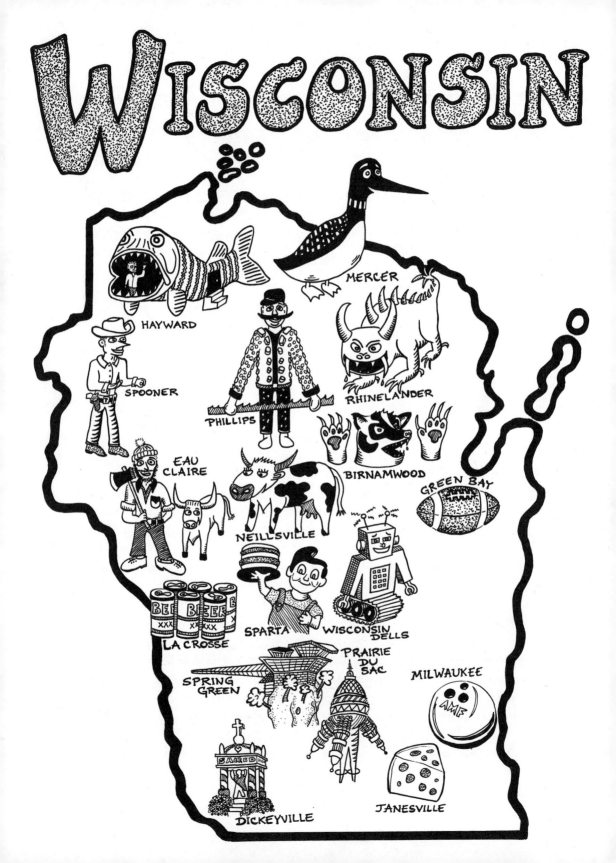

WISCONSIN

Rather than cower from criticism of "cheeseheads" or "cheddarheads," Wisconsinites have embraced the moniker and even produced giant foam cheesehead hats to show their pride at Green Bay Packers' games. This speaks well for a population not afraid to poke fun at itself and ready to turn an insult into a compliment. And when one man's head was protected by his cheesehead hat in a helicopter crash, the state received vindication that cheese is indeed a savior. As far as roadside attractions are concerned, this cheese worship translates into giant mice munching wedges of Swiss and oversized talking cows extolling the virtues of dairy.

Wisconsinites are so proud of their bovine bounty that they were the first to send one of their cattle into flight, as an elaborate "cow jumped over the moon" joke. In February 1930 at the St. Louis International Air Exposition, the Elm Farm Ollie Fan Club launched Ollie the Cow in an airplane, milked her in the air, and dropped bottles of her milk via parachute to the crowd.

Such crazy shenanigans are respected in Wisconsin—like the pranks of Eugene Shepard in Rhinelander when he found a live specimen of a mythical beast (part buzzard, part bull). This extraordinary ingenuity is seen in rival Wisconsin architects Alex Jordan and Frank Lloyd Wright. Jordan's House on the Rock stands as one of the most indescribably bizarre, almost macabre, attractions in the Midwest. Wright's Taliesin is the much-copied epitome of Prairie School modernism, even though he was born the same year as Laura Ingalls Wilder, who later lived in a sodhouse.

Wisconsin is filled with people who defy the norm, including the folks at F.A.S.T., who built a 145-foot fish in Hayward, or Tom Every, who is busy making his Victorian-era rocket ship to the stars. Milwaukee bandleader Bob Kames wrote "Dance Little Bird" in 1982, and polka dancers across the state were not the least bit embarrassed to flap their wings in time to this "chicken dance." Only these lush green valleys could breed the likes of the disparate eccentric entertainers Orson Welles, Harry Houdini, and Liberace.

Obviously, the good folks in Wisconsin do not settle for mundane entertainment. Many places have go-cart tracks, but how many have one that spirals into the intestines of a sixty-foot-tall Trojan Horse? Even when tipping back a cold one for fun, locals from La Crosse can rest assured that they indeed have a year's supply of suds safely stored in their World's Largest Six Pack. Wisconsin is full of people following their vision for literal greatness—and then able to laugh at the result. Wisconsin is a state of superlatives.

Behn's Game Farm
World's Oldest Lion Tamer

"**W**ilbert! Wilbert!" his wife yells at the top of her lungs toward the makeshift house behind the llama cage at Behn's Game Farm in the tiny town of Aniwa in northern Wisconsin. "He's hard of hearing," she explains. With a slight limp, Wilbert slowly walks out of the plywood building as though just awakened from a nap.

At more than eighty years old, Wilbert Behn is the oldest lion and tiger tamer in the world, as well as being a fire eater and chainsaw sculptor in his free time. His white hair is frazzled, perhaps from his snooze, and his ratty jeans and soiled shirt carry a ripe smell that shows he knows animals. As he walks by the tiger cage, the fierce Bengali and Siberian cats eye him nervously. Obviously, they know who their master is.

How does one become a lion tamer? "One day I just jumped in the ring and tried it out," Wilbert remembers. "I've been doing shows ever since for the last forty-nine years. You should try it! You never know if you're a natural until you get in the cage," he tells me, and I can't tell if he is joking. I refrain from pointing out that if I find out I'm not a natural, I'll be dead.

I ask his wife what they usually feed these big cats, who eye us hungrily. "Oh, fresh meat. Usually beef or veal. We don't get as many horses anymore because people sell them for dog food." Wilbert interrupts that even this can be dangerous, though. "Once when I was feeding the lion, I got bit through both of my legs and I got clobbered. I stepped over the trough and he just figured I was meat. I was real hung up for a while until someone came to help me. If it wasn't for rubber boots, I wouldn't be around anymore."

Nevertheless, Wilbert retains his cool composure around the cats. "I always look them in the eye; if you don't, that's when they get you. I use two objects since

Wilbert Behn—lion tamer, fire eater, and chainsaw sculptor—shows me the arena where he tames his tigers. He tells me, "If you want, I could bring the cats into the ring and give you a show now!"

the cats can't concentrate on two things at a time. You know if I didn't want to get hurt by the cats, though, the only thing I could really do against them would be to stay the heck out of the ring!"

The danger isn't only to the tamer, however. "I've had up to six cats in the ring at the same time, and once I did a show and the lioness went after the tiger. She bit the tiger right through the shoulder blade and blood was everywhere. I finally was able to get them separated by distracting them so they didn't kill each other. I looked [through the bars] into the stands and noticed that the audience had run away.

"See, most cats are declawed to make them less dangerous, but I never declaw or neuter them. If they're neutered or declawed, I wouldn't even have them on a plate! Even if they neuter and declaw them, they're still dangerous. A woman just got maimed down in Busch Gardens, Florida. A cat got her and chewed off her arm at the elbow."

Wilbert seems to love the danger of training lions and tigers, however, and lifts up his shirt to show me scars from tiger bites across his body. Most lion tamers aren't as lucky to get mere scratches, though; he tells the gruesome story of his friend Dwayne who started another circus in northern Wisconsin. "The first show he did, a cat got a hold of him. The lion dragged him around the ring in front of two hundred schoolkids and their parents. He was dead by then, though." Wilbert shakes his head sadly, "Now, every time I do a show, I can still see him standing there in the ring with me."

Wilbert views this incident as reason to continue on with his work. He points out his plywood auditorium with the large "NOT RESPONSIBLE FOR INJURIES" sign above the door and says, "If you want, I could bring the cats into the ring and give you a show now!"

→ *Behn's Game Farm*, Route 52, (715) 449-2971. From I-29, go north fourteen miles on Highway 45. Turn left (west) on Highway 52, and Behn's is almost immediately on the left (south) side of 52. Admission charged. Summer only.

While in the Area

The World's Largest Badger has fallen on hard times. The owner of Badger Country Gas Station in Birnamwood built the badger on top of a huge log garage where motorists would enter the stump to fuel up. To save his skin, this symbol of Wisconsin has been relegated to luring lusty lumbermen into the Badger Country Exotic Dancers Club (N11004 Rte. 45, two miles south of Behn's and north of the intersection with Route ZZ). The pumps are gone, and banners exclaiming "Hot Girls, Cold Beer" have been strung up. The badger's former lair may have been overrun with naked women, but what's left of the critter has been creatively displayed with his claws and head jutting out from the ground. The earth serves to clothe the rest of his body.

The gas station that built the badger and put pumps inside the huge log under the squirrel has been bought out by an exotic-dance nightclub. The badger used to sit atop the log, but now this Wisconsin state symbol is ready to leap from its lair.

BARABOO

Dr. Evermor's Forevertron
A Transemporal Spaceship

"If it could be, why not make it be?" Dr. Evermor asks me. We're walking around the enormous electromagnetic space station he's building to propel himself to the heavens. If the blueprints for his Forevertron masterpiece are ever completed, his life's work would make it the largest scrap metal sculpture in the world.

Before the big tour, Dr. Evermor, a.k.a. Tom Every, invites me into his camper for a chat. On the side of the now wheelless bus is painted "Tommy Bartlett's Thrill Show" in sixties-era writing. How did Dr. Evermor get his hands on a Tommy Bartlett classic? "Oh, I just got it. They were throwing it away."

This is the first clue to who this mysterious man is. "You have to understand that there's something within all of us. A passion to do something," he says. "I was an industrial wrecker. I would tear down breweries." From the wreckage, he would create new worlds.

Tom designed the carousel at House on the Rock. "I was there from 1964 to 1982. I went to Michigan to pick up the carousel and brought it back to make it the world's largest. I also built many of the fantasy rooms," he remembers. "I was always a friend of Alex Jordan, then a horse went through his windshield."

"I started working on the Forevertron in 1983, and by God you do something until you drop over dead! It now weighs four hundred tons, and all the things on it come from the American Industrial Revolution. It's from around the 1890s, so it has a Victorian aura to it." In fact, Dr. Evermor's creation is derived partly from the mentality of a turn-of-the-century explorer and partly that of a mad scientist, like Captain Nemo meets Nikola Tesla. "If you like Jules Verne, you'll love talking to me about the possibility of what could be."

Outside under the six-story-tall Forevertron, the eccentric Tom Every explains his experimental machine. He points to what look like two telescopes and says, "Two people can sit there in the Celestial Listening Ears and listen for alien voices

347

"See that?" Tom Every asks. "That's the Gravitron, where the good doctor will de-water himself to reduce his weight before blast off." This is the Forevertron, a Victorian-era spaceship that will propel Dr. Evermore to the heavens.

from the heavens and beyond. Information will then be relayed to the Overlord Master Control Center.

"See that? That's the Gravitron, where the good doctor"—he often refers to his alter ego in the third person—"will de-water himself to reduce his weight before blast off. Almost all of human weight is water, so this will make the blast off easier."

The podlike Gravitron has electrical gizmos—from transformers to dynamos built by Thomas Edison—sticking out in every direction. "Then the doctor will walk down that spiral staircase, go over the bridge, and step into the copper egg inside the glass ball before being shot into space," he tells me as though it all makes sense.

Then Tom chuckles at the elaborate farce and recalls, "A graduate from UW in electrical engineering called and wanted to get it all wired up. I just told him, 'Hmmm, that's nice. . . .' I've done a good job fooling him. There's some P. T. Barnum in all of us, I suppose. I just wonder what the hell they taught him in college!"

Underneath the Gravitron, the Big Bird Band is ready for the countdown to begin playing their scrap metal violins and junked tools for clarinets. Giant peacocks with metal violins and trombone tails await the word from the doctor to begin the send-off song.

Tom inspects a new shipment of laser pet cookies that he'll weld as scales onto an enormous monster. "They're intergalactic dragons!" he yells. Then he hands a young girl a hammer to bang on the beasts' scales, which form a melodic pun because they are tuned to play a chromatic scale.

"I get it! You're trying to make something musical," says little Megan from Minneapolis.

"Exactly! They'll play forever for the Forevertron!" replies Tom.

The last stop is a new shipment of enormous I-beams that have just been delivered next to a section of NASA's Apollo decontamination chambers that he scrapped. "Next summer, I'm going to finish up the Overlord Master Control, which will be the biggest section so far, and connect over to the Juicer Bug to give us extra juice."

Dr. Evermor then describes the scene of the much-anticipated day. "A hum buzzes through the air, all the lightning rises, and the doctor climbs into his pod. The lights go from red to amber to green. They pull all the switches. The good doctor in his transtemporal copper egg chamber shoots out on his magnetic lightning force beam. All the nonbelievers and doubting Thomases are drinking tea. It's a very happy day, and everyone in the band begins playing. Everything is built for that great day."

→ *Dr. Evermor's Forevertron*, (608) 393-9377. From I-94/I-90 go south at exit 92 onto Highway 12. Go through Baraboo and drive another seven miles south. If you get to County Highway C, you've gone too far. The art park is on the right (west) side behind Delaney's Surplus and across the road from the Badger Ammunitions Plant. Open daily until 5 P.M.

While in the Area

Rather than waiting for the Ringling Bros. Circus to come to town, go to Circus World Museum, which is open all summer just east of Baraboo on Highway 113. More than 170 circus wagons are filled with memorabilia, such as the balancing chair of the Flying Wallendas, the cannon for human cannonball Frank "Fearless" Gregg, and mini circus scenes. Reminiscent of the shock-and-awe days of the circus, freak show tents feature replicas of the Cardiff Giant, Jo-Jo the Dog-Faced Boy, Chang and Eng the Siamese twins, and the bearded lady. This winter home of the Ringling Bros. Circus from 1884 to 1918 is now run by the Wisconsin Historical Society and stretches for fifty acres of three-ring spectacles. Circus World is located at 426 Water Street in Baraboo; call (608) 356-8341 or (608) 356-0800.

A bit farther down the interstate toward Madison at DeForest lie a couple more enormous roadside sculptures. To the west of the exit on County Road V outside the Citgo gas station stands a pink elephant with oversized Buddy Holly glasses, like the waterskiing pachyderm in Marquette, Iowa.

On the east side of the exit toward DeForest is another former World's Largest Cow. Sissy the Cow comes from the same mother mold as Chatty Belle in Neillsville and has an identical speaker mounted in its mouth. The poor Holstein hasn't had the care that a talking cow deserves.

Inside Ehlenbach's Cheese Chalet at County Road V and I-90/94, the cheese clerks aren't too interested in Sissy. "I heard they put it there to advertise cheese or something. I'm not really sure." Then an argument ensues about whether it's a cow or a bull because "cows don't have horns."

"It used to talk, but I can't even remember what she said," one clerk remembers.

"I think it's out," says the other. "Yeah, that cow used to talk a lot, maybe too much."

Facing page: Texans taking snapshots in DeForest of Sissy the Cow can't resist pulling on her udders. "We're gonna send 'em home this photo and show that they really grow 'em big up here!" "Yup, they honor their cows, all right!" the wife responds.

The entrance to the Dickeyville Grotto looks like an enormous mouth ready to swallow up true believers and transport them to Paradise.

DICKEYVILLE

Holy Ghost Grotto

A Vision from God

Thanks to the wonderful adhesive power of concrete, Father Mathias Wernerus could glue crystals, coal, copper ore, coral, quartz, iron ore, jewelry, petrified wood, moss, mirrors, shells, starfish, pottery, gems, glass, fossils, and anything else that was bright and colorful all over a little chapel in Dickeyville. The results are dazzling, and his Holy Ghost Grotto, usually called simply the Dickeyville Grotto, is one of the most beautiful, but bizarre, attractions in the Midwest.

Father Mathias Wernerus was born in Germany and noted the lack of religious artifacts and shrines in the United States. He had a vision to make his grotto in Dickeyville the biggest pilgrimage site in the country.

At the same time, however, he scorned the tacky world he sometimes saw in America and abhorred the idea that his shrine would turn into a tourist site "with ice cream parlors and God knows what." In accordance with his wishes, the local parish runs the site, so they haven't cashed in on the commercial value. In spite of Wernerus's lofty wishes, sixty thousand tourists a year have passed through for more than seventy-five years, some of whom admire his work while perhaps enjoying an ice cream cone.

Wernerus set to work in his free time from his priestly duties and joined stone to mortar between 1925 and 1931. In the spirit of a "grotto," Wernerus dug a fake cave with the ambiguous word "Religion" written next to it across a large cross. Standing next to the Holy Ghost Catholic Church, this is the primary structure of the site, dubbed the "Grotto of the Blessed Virgin," and it contains a Eucharistic Altar with the Stations of the Cross nearby.

Also nearby is the bold word denoting the other main theme of the grotto: "Patriotism." A bald eagle proudly stands next to a statue of Columbus and pictures of Lincoln and Washington. You've heard of separation of church and state, but what about state and church? Vatican City's flag made of glass and stone is on the left, juxtaposed with the American flag on the right without any real explanation. Dickeyville Grotto's inspired idiosyncrasies of nationalism stirred up with religion are what confuse the spectator just enough to make this the perfect early roadside attraction.

The artistic Father Wernerus died in 1931. His followers helped finish the main grotto, but then work stopped for a spell. In 1963, however, motivated parishioners added another section of the impressive Stations of the Cross to honor Wernerus and his successful pilgrimage site.

The Holy Ghost Grotto is one of the best examples of the rock garden/grotto craze that swept across the Midwest from the 1910s to the 1930s, and little by little the religious aspect was downplayed in Dickeyville copycats. Yellow buses of schoolkids on field trips would regularly visit these sites, and the call to worship was probably not nearly as interesting as all the colorful rocks, crystals, shells, and other shiny devices affixed to the wall. Unfortunately, some irreverent tourists have pried such bric-a-brac loose, so the main part of the grotto is covered with Plexiglas. Perhaps this was the type of sacrilegious riffraff Wernerus warned us about.

➡ *Dickeyville Grotto,* Holy Ghost Catholic Church, 305 West Main Street, (608) 568-7519. From Dubuque, go north on Highway 151 for about twelve miles to Dickeyville. The grotto is at the intersection of West Main Street and Route 151 (just one block west of the intersection of 151 and Highway 61). Open May through October.

While in the Area

About forty-five miles northwest of Dickeyville along the Mississippi lies another Wisconsin marvel at the Fort Crawford Medical Museum in Prairie du Chien (717 South Beaumont Road; call [608] 326-6950). Two see-through women bare all their organs for schoolchildren eager to learn about what's inside. The Transparent Twins glow in the ark while a somber woman's voice dictates the function of each gland, intestine, and organ. Sex ed loses its giggles as these seventies-era mannequins state, "An egg cell is fertilized by one of thousands of sperm cells from my husband, and then nine months later I have a baby." Don't miss the dioramas of leg amputation from the 1933 World's Fair or the true story of the man with a hole in his stomach!

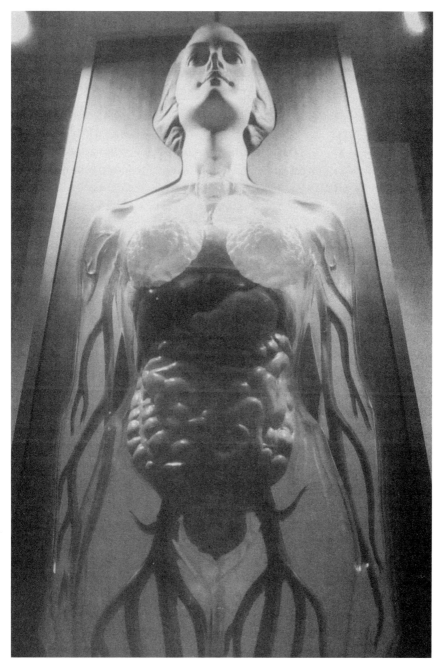

One woman is blessed with all the organs, while the other has the skeleton and the nervous system. Together they form the Transparent Twins, a medical marvel of the Fort Crawford Medical Museum in Prairie du Chien.

Carl Schel was awed by the wonderful world of burls. Displays of burls at his museum advise, "What it took one man a lifetime to collect, you can view at your leisure."

Carl's Wood Art Museum

Wonderful World of Burls

Carl Schel emigrated from Bavaria in the 1920s and settled in Eagle River as a logger and a trapper. His whole life he loved all the different kinds of wood and especially the bizarre world of burls, which are the twisted configurations of knots sometimes found in older trees. Displays of "fascinating burls" show that

The world's largest wooden chain doubles as a railing for the porch of Carl's Wood Art Museum. Inside, Carl sculpted himself out of a stump and inserted a tape loop so he could live forever in wood.

"what it took one man a lifetime collect, you can view at your leisure." If you're not impressed, the clincher is a photo of the Largest Burl in the World, measuring 118 feet around and 30 feet high with a weight of approximately a million pounds.

Carl's collection of lumber oddities are exhibited throughout the museum. There's the "toothache tree," with bumps called "warts," that the Native Americans would chew on as "natural Novocain." Another tree ensnarled a tricycle in its trunk as it grew up. After you tour the museum, venture into the dark Translucent Room, where a bright light shines through more than a hundred veneers of wood to illuminate the grain.

All the wood scourges—from termites to woodpeckers, ants to porcupines—show their handiwork, which often can be as beautiful as it was destructive. Carl found a dead tree with another tree growing in it and wrote this sign: "I was a fair size Norway [pine]. In my crotch is a small dead tree. A porcupine got a hold of me." Mostly, though, these pests are just menaces, as Carl shows in another display: "Some primal termite knocked on wood and tasted it and found it good. And that is why your cousin Mattie fell through the parlor floor today."

To keep the tots happy in any museum, there must be games. Rather than high-tech gizmos, Carl carved "Paul Bunyan-size games." Games of skill made of wood fill each room. Test your hooking skills with Josh's Jammer, and see how the lumberjacks passed the time with Paul Bunyan's Pinball Machine. Carl also hollowed out huge logs to make Flintstones-style cars for prehistoric photo ops.

Carl was helped by his son Ken, who has taken over the daunting task of operating the museum. As a chainsaw artist, his accomplishments include the World's Largest Wooden Chain, measuring twenty-five feet long, and a five-thousand-pound grizzly bear sculpture that towers fourteen feet into the air.

Carl died in 1996 at the age of ninety, but he lives on via a statue in the museum. Punch a button and a tape recording of Carl's voice comes to life in a thick German accent to welcome you to his museum: "I'm old man Carl Schel. I'm eighty-eight years old. . . ." In the background of the recording a chainsaw is fired up, and the sound cuts out.

→ *Carl's Wood Art Museum,* 1230 Sundstein Road, (715) 479-1883. From Rhinelander, go north for twenty-one miles on Highway 17. Turn right (east) at the intersection with Highway 70 and go across the channel bridge. Look for the huge sign on the right (south) side of the road. Open Memorial Day to mid-October.

While in the Area

Twenty-five miles to the west of Eagle River in the small town of Woodruff stands another World's Largest, this time oversized counterfeit coinage.

Dr. Kate Pelham, a.k.a. the "Angel on Snowshoes," dreamed of a hospital for the Lakeland Area in the 1950s. Dr. Kate appeared on TV to help the cause, begging

The World's Largest Penny is not made of a ton of copper from melted coins. Instead the money from the Million Penny Parade was invested to build a hospital.

kids to help her raise a million pennies. Construction began when the goal was reached, and now a Million Penny Parade honors the feat every year.

For posterity's sake, the World's Largest Penny was erected in front of the Penny Senior Housing (Hemlock Place and Third Avenue, one block west of Highway 51). Rather than melting those million pennies to make bona fide legal tender, bronze paint was splashed on a mock-up made of less precious cement.

Rock in the House

Living Dangerously

When a fifty-five-ton stone smashed through the ceiling of Maxine and Dwight Anderson's little house on April 24, 1995, they realized it might be time to move.

People in Fountain City are thankful for each day they survive in the shadow of

The radio is on, the door is open, c'mon in! This house is normal except for a wheel-like stone that broke off the cliff high above and crushed the back room. Not an easy sell to new tenants, the Rock in the House has become a magnet for curiosity seekers. You can even buy a rock for a buck!

the beautiful but dangerous four-hundred-foot cliff next to some houses. Why worry about the infinitesimal possibility that an asteroid will crash into the earth or that a terrorist will spread anthrax with a crop duster when odds are much higher that a chunk of rock could plop through the roof?

Like Sisyphus, the Andersons realized the futility of rolling the rock out of their house and instead sold out to real-estate agent John Burt, who recognized a tourist attraction when he saw it. With a twist of a phrase, he piggybacked on publicity of the world-famous House on the Rock, turning it into the Rock in the House.

No receptionist guards the site, and the reason is soon apparent. Newspaper clippings tacked on the wall tell of other natural disasters in Fountain City. In fact, Mrs. Dubler, next door, wasn't quite so lucky as the Andersons when another rock from above decided her fate.

Instead of paying a guide, just plop a buck in the bucket for a peek. If you don't, beware of divine retribution from the cliff above.

→ *Rock in the House,* 440 North Shore Drive, (608) 687-6106. Fountain City is forty miles north of La Crosse on Highway 35. The Rock in the House is about a quarter mile north of downtown on the right (east) side of Highway 35, across from the railroad tracks and the Mississippi River.

While in the Area

About eight miles north of Fountain City and just south of Cochrane on Highway 35 lies a fabulously preserved rock garden of cement and broken glass. Prairie Moon Museum and Garden has a fresh coat of paint slapped on Herman Rusch's Moorish designs of flowing archways, a two-story castle turret, and a mini Orthodox-style church. Inside the museum is the Depression-era rock art of Fred "Fritz" Schlosstein, who modeled his buildings after those in tiny Cochrane. Up in the cliffs above town, Fritz placed little trolls in the nooks and crannies of the rocks to scare hikers and turn youngsters into believers.

Facing page: These graceful cement arches guard the entrance to the Prairie Moon Museum and Garden just south of Cochrane.

Among the Sea of Fishes at Freshwater Fishing Hall of Fame, the Walk-Thru Muskie is king of the school. Twenty people can stand in the mouth of this freshwater whale, which is why some diehard fishing fans opt to tie the knot here.

Freshwater Fishing Hall of Fame
Into the Mouth of the Muskie

Just like Jonah or Geppetto, you're swallowed whole—only this time you have electricity so you can admire the stuffed World's Largest Nightcrawler hung on the wall. You have just entered the ultimate colossus of the deep, mounted on the grounds of the Freshwater Fishing Hall of Fame.

The world's largest muskie was gutted to make a half-block-long museum in its innards. Weighing in at five hundred tons and measuring 145 feet long, she's obviously a keeper.

Outside the belly of this whale is the Sea of Fishes, with a whole stringer of underwater creatures vying for attention. Any of the other fish statues—a fiberglass walleye, Coho salmon, bluegill, perch, smallmouth bass, rainbow trout—would make any other Midwestern town proud, but in the shadow of the Walk-Thru Muskie, they appear to be just bait for the beast.

In 1979, Creative Displays, which later became Fiberglass Animals, Statues, and Trademarks (F.A.S.T. Corp.), of Sparta, Wisconsin, built this half-block long masterpiece. It was a great time for giant fiberglass monuments, as Jerry Vettrus of F.A.S.T. recalls, "That was a boomer year. We did both the Jolly Green Giant [in Blue Earth, Minnesota] and the muskie, which took us nine months! The fish never would have fit on one truck, so we had to ship it up to Hayward in parts and assemble it there. I don't think we'll ever do anything like that again, and I'm sure nobody could afford it nowadays!"

Hayward's fish is the largest fiberglass structure in the world—the mouth alone will hold twenty people. Coupling a love of fishing with holy matrimony, six inspired couples have even tied the knot in the muskie's mouth.

If that's not enough, another building (that isn't remotely fish-shaped) houses more than 350 classic outboard motors, six thousand lures, and many rods and reels. The walls are decked with grip-and-grin photos of record-setting freshwater fishermen from around the world holding up their trophy fish.

→ *Walk-Thru Muskie, Freshwater Fishing Hall of Fame,* 1 Hall of Fame Drive, (715) 634-4440. From Highway 53, go east on Highway 63 at Trego for twenty-one miles to Hayward. Turn right (southeast) onto Highway 27. Cross the river and look for the muskie on the left side of the road at the intersection with Route B (and across from the enormous windmill). Open Mid-April through October.

While in the Area

Who ever heard of Native American barbecue from northern Wisconsin? Local boy Dave Anderson proclaimed himself "famous," grilled up some of the best ribs in the Midwest, and soon shares of DAVE were traded on the New York Stock Exchange.

East of Hayward about seven miles lies the original Famous Dave's restaurant (12359 West Richardson Bay Road, off County Road B). While the menu may be the same barbecue fare found at the chains, the location certainly isn't. This gorgeous whole-log lodge overlooks beautiful Round Lake, which allows boaters to dock in the summer and cross-country skiers to skate across in the winter to enjoy the cozy stone fireplace inside the roadhouse. The Americana antiques covering the walls somehow seem to make more sense here than in a suburban strip mall.

HAYWARD

Moccasin Bar
Taxidermists Gone Wild

At first sight, the Moccasin seems like just another northern Wisconsin bar with a stuffed fish on the wall. Upon further inspection, however, this is far from the norm.

Apart from the stuffed fawns, grouse, fox, and many kinds of pheasants, the Moccasin boasts an extinct passenger pigeon, walrus tusks, and a whole slew of albino critters—including skunk, mink, pheasant, squirrel, raccoon, and peacock—all properly placed behind glass. "I bought the bar in 1978, and the animals were here, oh, about twenty years before that," explains bar owner Bernie Tworek.

All of these impressive beasts are overshadowed by the comical, but somehow morbid, little animals acting out various dramatic situations. For example, a couple of raccoons box, one of them KOed while the referee (a beaver) hails the victor, "The Winnah!" The raccoon's gloved hand is held high, and a skunk cries outside the ring over the bloody loser.

Another theatrical moment is played out with Perry Mason–style melodrama in a mock courtroom scene with Judge Wolf presiding. Bobcat the Sheriff nabbed Bucky Badger for poaching, and the Big Bad Wolf is throwing the book at him.

"Nah, I don't make 'em or come up with these scenes," Bernie says. "The taxidermists do all that and I buy 'em. I can't really tell them what to do, so they come up with the ideas."

The last two of the four dioramas pay homage to what the Moccasin is really all about: beer. A poker game features a bear cub puffing on a pipe and secretly trading a carrot to a white rabbit for an ace, while his rival bear accepts a nice tall beer from a stuffed otter. And finally, little chipmunks dressed in mini lederhosen raise high their beer steins in a rock garden in a toast to suds.

Even though the odd animal scenes are the highlight of the Moccasin Bar, the

In the Northwoods Kangaroo Court, the violator badger got nabbed for blasting a wood-cock out of season. Note the World Record Fisherman mounted on the wall, a spoof of the Moccasin Bar's largest muskie caught with a lure rather than a revolver.

requisite mounted fish is here, and how! Bernie points out that his Wildlife Museum on the other side of town has the World's Largest Muskie, found dead in Chippewa Flowage. The nearby Freshwater Fishing Hall of Fame may have its 145-foot-long Walk-Through Muskie, but the Moccasin Bar has Cal Johnson's world record muskie mounted on the wall, stretching more than sixty inches and weighing in at more than sixty-seven pounds. "Yeah, this is still the largest muskie in existence," Bernie tells me. "They caught another one sometime in the fifties,

During the long cold winters in northern Wisconsin, inspired taxidermists get creative with their work. Besides, who wants to see just another stuffed rodent? At least make the poor, dead critters drink Hamm's beer and cheat at cards.

but when they got it near the boat, they shot it. I don't think that really counts as angling."

→ *Moccasin Bar*, 124 First Street, (715) 634-4211. From Highway 53, go east on Highway 63 at Trego for twenty-one miles to Hayward. The bar is downtown at the junction of Highway 63 and Highway 27. Open year-round until 2 A.M., when you have to go home.

While in the Area

Thirty miles southwest of Hayward, a roadside giant challenges passing drivers to take a spin on some speedy souped-up four-wheelers at Bulik's Amusement Center (N5651 Highway 63, Spooner, [715] 635-7111). The blue-and-white cowboy holds out his hands as though he should be clutching a branding iron, but many of these statues were born into the world holding mufflers to advertise mechanic garages. This lone cowhand, named "Mel" from his previous life at Mel's 66 south of Spooner, now just needs a steed as he stands alone in a field on the west side of Highway 63, a bit north of Spooner.

Facing page: Cowboy Mel used to stand near Spooner at a service station, but the wrangler now has been relegated to Bulik's Amusement Center to convince motorists to take a break from driving and drive a go-cart instead.

Nick Engelbert's house is covered in shards of glass and other shiny objects similar to the nearby Dickeyville Grotto. Visitors on their way back to the parking lot pass an organ grinder clasping his squeeze box, and he and his monkey thank you for coming to this "historical backyard."

Grandview
A Historical Backyard

Engelbert Kolethick was born in Slovenia in 1881, settled west of Hollandale with his wife, Katherine, in 1922, and thought it was great. "If a man can't be happy in a small farm in Wisconsin, he hasn't the makings of happiness in his soul," he said.

Once settled in the beautiful rolling hills of southwestern Wisconsin, Kolethick changed his name to the more "American-sounding" Nick Engelbert. He and his wife probably traveled to the famous Holy Ghost Grotto in Dickeyville and returned home inspired. Rather than meddling with building a church on their plot of land, however, the Engelberts covered their entire two-story house with glass, ceramic shards, and colorful stones, all attached with cement.

Their work did not stop there, however, as Nick wanted to show his patriotism and gratefulness for his new country. According to the signs at the Grandview site, Nick once said, "You can't really appreciate the United States unless you have actually lived in other countries. It is because of my deep appreciation for what the United States has given me that I am constantly working on this historical backyard."

Nick's gift back to his adopted country was stretching wire mesh over cardboard boxes, slapping down a thick coat of concrete, and affixing a mosaic of shells, stone, glass, and beads to give life to forty sculptures. Most of these statues are truly of historical events or important places. For example, there's a miniature Hapsburg castle with a double-headed eagle for the Austro-Hungarian Empire that dominated his country of Slovenia. There's a Viking in Norway standing on a little boat, a Blarney Castle, and the three founding Swiss fathers (now diminished to two due to the ever-present danger to roadside sculpture by artistically challenged vandals with baseball bats). The Swiss guards are in honor of Nick's wife, who emigrated from Switzerland, and the other sculptures are in homage to Norwegian and Irish friends.

The religious theme of the Dickeyville grotto, however, is notably vacant from Grandview. A drunk man guzzles a bottle of hooch while cement monkeys play on a concrete tree above his head; an elephant and a donkey pay respect to Republicans and Democrats and the open political system Nick found in the United States; and an organ grinder and his monkey welcome visitors to the yard. The oddest juxtaposition of all is Snow White and Her Seven Dwarves and Paul Bunyan, with the fair maiden matching the giant in height and the number of dwarves diminished to five.

Nick already had a job operating the Grandview Dairy, so the purpose of his garden had nothing to do with profit. He seemed to simply want to share his fortune and art with others by making a low-tech amusement park and the perfect picnic spot with a fantastic view.

After Nick grew tired and weak from slapping cement on sculptures, he took to painting until he died in 1962. Just as with his statues, he was prolific in spite of having no formal training, and he produced nearly two hundred paintings, many of which are inside the house. Once again, his artwork is a recognition and testament to the happiness he found on a hill in rural Wisconsin.

→ *Grandview*, 7351 Highway 39, (608) 967-2151. From Hollandale, go about two miles west on Highway 39. It's visible from the road (on the south side), but call for an appointment to tour the house. Open Tuesday through Sunday, Memorial Day to Labor Day.

LA CROSSE

World's Largest Six Pack
Beer Is Back!

Whet the Old Style brewery shut its doors, La Crosse seemed ready to hand in its brewing crown to Milwaukee and St. Louis. The famous World's Largest Six Pack, painted like enormous Old Style cans, was whitewashed, and the town mourned.

The World's Largest Six Pack does hold beer—688,200 gallons, to be precise. In 1969, the La Crosse brewery had the brilliant brainstorm of painting six silos after its flagship beer, Old Style. In 1999, Stroh's sold the brewery, and this town symbol disappeared. In 2003, locally owned City Brewery repainted the World's Largest Six Pack after its flagship brew, La Crosse Lager.

Following public outcry demanding the return of the town symbol, the city council finally brought back the beer. With a fresh coat of paint, the six silos are packed with enough suds for 22,200 barrels of beer, or 7,340,796 cans. A sign at the base of the monument claims this "would provide one person a six pack a day for 3,351 years. Placed end to end these cans would run 565 miles." These are facts to ponder while sipping a cold one in a town with one of the highest densities of bars per person.

Opposite the dazzling six pack stands a statue of the fifth-century Duke Gambrinus, known as "The King of Beer," who wielded his power to aid farmers in raising hops for harvest. Gambrinus raises his overflowing stein high to toast the six pack and the return of beer to La Crosse.

→ *World's Largest Six Pack,* 1111 South Third Street. From I-90, take Highway 53 south into town (about five miles). Highway 53 becomes Third Street/Highway 61. Keep going straight for about six blocks (past Highway 16, which goes over the river). The six pack is on the left (east) side of the road at Mississippi Street.

While in the Area

In Riverside Park, next to a cannon aimed across the river at Minnesota, stands a twenty-five-foot tall, twenty-five-ton statue of Hiawatha. La Crosse Queen paddleboat sightseeing cruises dock at the base of the Indian with crossed arms, who welcomes visitors to Wisconsin (just west of downtown on State Street at the far end of the loop along the Mississippi).

The story of this Iroquois leader was made world famous through Henry Wadsworth Longfellow's poem "The Song of Hiawatha" in 1855, but unfortunately the verse carries some glaring mistakes. Although the poem with the tom-tom rhythm spurred interest in Indian history, Hiawatha probably never set foot in the Midwest, and Longfellow mixed him up with the Ojibwe hero Nanabajo.

Apart from those bloopers, Hiawatha loved lacrosse, so the 1962 statue by Anthony D. Zimmerman and his sons is especially appropriate. According to legend, the chief called for games to be played to raise his spirits after his daughters had been cursed by witchcraft and he'd fallen into a nasty cannibalistic spell. Thanks to the prophet Deganawida, Hiawatha formed the precursor of the Iroquois Confederacy, whose constitution became one of the models for the United States'.

Hiawatha probably never set foot in Wisconsin, but he was known to have liked playing lacrosse.

Just ten miles east of La Crosse along Highway 33 lies the little town of St. Joseph and another beautiful Wisconsin grotto. The Grotto of the Holy Family is by Father Paul Dobberstein, famous for the Grotto of the Redemption in West Bend, Iowa.

Frank Daughterman knew something was wrong with his house because he kept falling over. He begged a geologist to test the unusual gravitational pull in the area. The scientist blamed the bizarre gravity not on liquor or Daughterman's lousy carpentry skills but on the dicey-sounding "igneous rock."

Wonder Spot

The Laws of Nature Repealed

The advertising successes of Burma Shave and Wall Drug, billboards for Ride the Ducks and Tommy Bartlett's Thrill Show on Water dotted the roads in the 1950s within a hundred miles of Wisconsin Dells. More and more tourists flocked to the area, at least until Lady Bird Johnson tried to rid our nation's freeways of pesky signage. Soon inventive entrepreneurs thought of new ways for tourists to happily separate themselves from their cash.

Frank Daughterman built a house near the town of Wisconsin Dells in 1948 and "discovered" that the Dells not only are an unusual geological formation, but they also, he claimed, contain an extreme magnetic pull that makes for unexplained phenomena. A little tourist shack now sells tickets for just five bucks to one of nature's conundrums.

The teenage guides led our group down a series of rickety wooden steps into a heavily wooded dell to a large sign that offers this caveat:

There are places in this area in which you neither see correctly, stand erectly or feel quite normal. In fact, on the cabin site the laws of nature seem to be repealed. Discovered June 16, 1948.

Hidden behind a tall wooden fence is a silly-looking tilted house built on a treacherous slant. Frank Daughterman was either a terrible carpenter or a sly businessman, or else he had a soft spot for the sauce. The legend goes that Frank fled the area in 1948 claiming mysterious forces had caused his balance to go haywire.

Inside the house, water and balls roll what appears to be uphill. Dining room chairs must be nailed to the floor to keep them from falling over; otherwise they can be balanced on two legs. The terrific tilt of the house skews one's orientation without any fancy machines, slides, or other gadgets used at the other Wisconsin

Dells tourist traps. Volunteers step up for a sobriety test and fall victim to the same curse that plagued Frank Daughterman. No one can put one foot in front of the other.

The guides explain with pseudoscience that Daughterman thought the unusual geological formation of the Dells caused an extreme magnetic pull that distorted reality. The guides also tell us otherwise: "Modern scientists think it's caused by the high concentration of igneous rock," as if this fairly ordinary rock were somehow dangerous. "It's not magnetic as much as gravitational pull."

In spite of attempts to explain this "unsolved" phenomenon, everyone leaves the Wonder Spot dizzy but happy. This mysterious spot is a bit of marketing genius, in that five hundred people a day have each plunked down the present-day equivalent of five dollars since the fifties. The small wooden house is merely built skewed into the hill and does indeed give the feeling of vertigo and challenges one's perception. Incidentally, ten other such places in the United States have been discovered with a similar phenomenon and coincidentally also happen to have enormous "Wonder Spot" signs.

➜ *Wonder Spot,* 100 Scott Drive, (608) 254-4224. From I-94/I-90, turn north off exit 92 onto Highway 12 (Wisconsin Dells Boulevard). Go past Camelot and look for R Place Restaurant on the left and Fischer's Supper Club on the right. Turn left at the enormous billboard and drive downhill to the parking lot. Summer only.

While in the Area

Dinner time in Wisconsin means supper clubs, and Lake Delton has two classics. The first was designed by a student of Frank Lloyd Wright, architect James Dresser, who "cherished exposure to this great individual's philosophy of life, work, and play," which means it's a classy place to munch on a steak. The Del-Bar, named for its location halfway between Lake Delton and Baraboo, was once upon a time a little log cabin with six tables, but it was soon converted to a swank roadhouse. This prairie-style supper club (800 Wisconsin Dells Parkway/Highway 12 [608] 253-1861) actually has a dress code stating that "Men must wear shirts with sleeves," and the restaurant will provide a "clean, laundered shirt" if need be.

Across the street is the equally classy Wally's House of Embers (935 Wisconsin Dells Parkway, [608] 253-6411), with three fireplaces, stained-glass lamps, and papier-mâché birds hanging from the ceiling for that tropical feel.

Marshfield

Jurustic Park
Swamp Monsters

On the edge of the dense, muggy McMillian Marsh north of Marshfield, sparks fly from an acetylene welding torch inside a wooden workshop. Country music blares out through the cracks in the door, as Wisconsin's Dr. Frankenstein pieces together body parts to create new monsters to inhabit his world.

Having retired from his law practice, Clyde Wynia found his true calling in sculpting swamp monsters, or, as he likes to say, devoting "his efforts to paleontology." Now he creates everything from a Whirly-saurus ("the largest known airborne marsh critter") to a gallery of lynched Bad Critters.

Visitors pull up to the parking lot across the street and then venture over a little bridge into the land of the lost sculptures. Oxide, "a merciless attack dog," guards the gate. Once newcomers are safely past this vicious canine's rusted-out teeth, Clyde's wife and fellow artist, Nancy, greets the group.

She shows some metal frogs playing golf and bending clubs over their knees in a fit of frustration. "They like to play, but they're not very good," she explains. These amphibians' gaze jumps to life. "We use *millefiori* glass from Murano, Italy, that we heat and attach for the eyes," she says.

Clyde also made a troupe of these frogs tooting horns in an orchestra for Tom Every's Forevertron south of Baraboo. The ones that didn't make it out of the bog risk being chomped up by another monster, the aptly named Frog Eater. Life isn't so bad being food, however, as the sign on the base of these captured beasts explains: "Due to slow metabolism of these marsh inhabitants, it takes years to digest their prey. The frog can lead a long, comfortable existence inside its captor."

Just as much time is spent imagining the nature of these beasts as doing the creative welding work. A Marsh Mouse has a cutting torch for a nose because its teeth are too soft. A sign elaborates, "They can pump their bodies full of swamp gas . . .

this causes a lot of fires in the marsh and resulted in major flatulence problems." An Octanoggin is a bird with eight heads, "created on the theory that if two heads are better than one, then eight heads are better than none." A Turtle-Shelled Bulldog is "an example of interspecies cross breeding [in which] a turtle was molested by a wild dog the same night a large ostrich-like marsh bird had his way with her. . . . Unfortunately, it is sterile; there will be no more."

As more and more beasts are unearthed in the workshop at Jurustic Park, the only limit seems to be Clyde's outrageous imagination for the creatures from the swamp.

→ *Jurustic Park,* M222 Sugarbush Lane, (715) 387-1653. From Marshfield, go north three miles on County Road E. Turn left (west) on Sugar Bush Lane, which is a loop and has two entrances off County Road E. Jurustic Park is about halfway around on the inside of the loop.

Facing page: Weird genetic mutations that have been seen only in Clyde and Nancy Wynia's garden spring from McMillian Marsh. Cross a footbridge into Jurustic Park, and the first monster to frighten guests is this club-wielding dragon with rusting metal scales.

World's Largest Loon
The Battle for the Bird

Loon statues rival large fiberglass fish for prominence in the northwoods. In Minnesota, International Falls and Bemidji have loon statues at their fairgrounds, and Vergas has a huge cement bird overlooking Loon Lake.

Mercer, Wisconsin, decided to up the ante by hiring the Creative Displays in Sparta (later F.A.S.T.) to make the largest loon in the world. The Mercer Chamber of Commerce raised ten thousand dollars in contributions, and, in 1981, the two-thousand-pound bird was erected on a bed of cement. Standing sixteen feet tall, a thick coating of black-and-white fiberglass covers the entire sixteen-foot-tall solid foam body.

Now the town is even more loon crazy than ever. The local inn is the Loon's Nest Motel; the dry goods store is Loonatic Clothing; and Tom's Country Café has a loon as its logo. On the first Wednesday in August, nearly ten thousand people gather for "Loon Day," with a special loon-calling contest.

A sign by the loon declares that Mercer is the Loon Capital, so I venture into the Mercer Chamber of Commerce to investigate what it's the capital of. The woman at the tourist desk tells me, "We had to register with the Wisconsin Board of Tourism. Originally we wanted to be the 'Loon Capital of the World,' but some town in Minnesota had already registered for it." In fact, Nisswa holds that claim and is home to the North American Loon-Calling Competition.

When probed about this national register for towns claiming to be the capital of something, the receptionist explains, "There must be because they wouldn't let us do it. Otherwise, anybody could say they're the 'Loon Capital of the World.'"

Facing page: The town of Mercer downplays the fact that Al Capone's brother, Ralph "Bottles" Capone, lived here until he died at eighty-one years of age at a local nursing home. Instead, Mercer calls itself the Loon Capital and displays this sixteen-foot-tall statue. The two-thousand-pound bird diverts attention from the gangster past.

The year after Mercer built its loon, Virginia, Minnesota, threw down the gauntlet with a twenty-foot-long, ten-foot-high loon built by Bill Martin in 1982 that floats on Silver Lake in the summer.

I prod the receptionist at the tourist desk, stating that there might be a larger loon over the border. She looks a little embarrassed and annoyed. "That could be. I'm really not sure."

→ *World's Largest Loon,* Mercer Chamber of Commerce, 5150 North U.S. Highway 51, (877) 551-2204. Mercer is fifty-five miles northwest of Rhinelander and twenty-five miles south of Ironwood, Michigan. The loon is on the south edge of town on Highway 51.

Mustard Museum
Welcome, Alumni of Poupon U

"I started collecting the morning after the Red Sox lost to the New York Mets in 1986," Barry Levenson explains about his unusual obsession. "I went to the all-night grocery to try to forget. It was ridiculous. Here I was practically crying over this baseball game, so I decided I had to get a hobby. I saw some jars of mustard and thought 'If you collect us, they will come.' "

Barry left his occupation as a lawyer and together with his wife, Patti, began collecting all sorts of mustard memorabilia from around the world for his little Mustard Museum. Old advertising posters adorn the walls where there is space amid shelf upon shelf of jars, some of which are the very first samples of certain brands. "We even have the first and only bottle of mustard ever to appear in the Supreme Court," Barry boasts.

A glass display of fancy ceramic Prussian pots stands as the centerpiece under lock and key. Visitors are more interested in some of the off-brands, however, such as Highlife Mustard, with a label that looks suspiciously like the Champagne of Beers'. Perhaps a lawsuit is imminent, but Barry explains that "Miller doesn't know anything about it."

Now the collection has blossomed to more than four thousand kinds of mustard besides the original ones Barry bought at the supermarket that fateful night. Although he claims the museum has achieved a mention in the *Guinness Book of World Records* as the largest collection of mustard in the world, he hasn't rested on his laurels but has instead continued to enhance the collection. A small screen is set up to show *Mustardpiece Theater,* a film about the museum and the history of mustard in general narrated by James Earl Jones. "We want to do more exhibits with better lighting," he envisions and points out that both French's and Plochman's are now corporate sponsors, "even though they say I'm not serious enough sometimes."

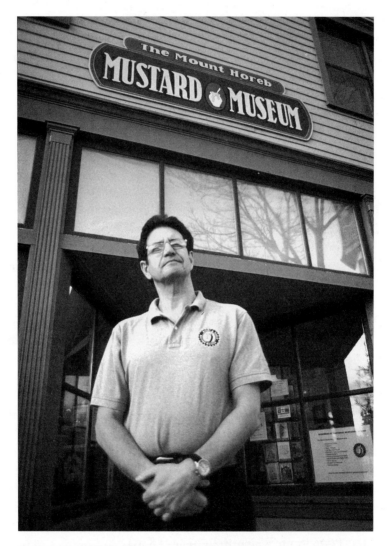

Fresh from his recent stint in a nun's habit for *The Sound of Mustard*, Barry Levenson stands proud in front of his museum of mustard. Where else can you see a historical collection of mustard pots or splurge your senses by buying mustard herbal baths?

Barry has moved on to chutneys, hot sauces, salsas, jams, vinegars, and curds, but these are mostly to stock the shelves of the store and fill his catalog with more than five hundred mustards and other condiments. Partially to sell his sauces—but mostly just for fun—mock ads for musicals fill the catalog, such as *The Sound of*

Mustard, with Barry frolicking in a nun's habit. Apart from his roles in off-off-Broadway performances, Barry has assumed the professor's podium by printing shirts and pennants for Poupon U, spoofing nearby UW.

What do people in town think of all his shenanigans? "I think they just tolerate me because I bring people into town," Barry reasons. He's just returned from a speaking engagement at a museum in Napa Valley: "I'll go around the country and talk to people about mustard, if they'll listen to me." And they do. In fact, the Mustard Museum has been featured on *Oprah* and in the *Chicago Tribune,* and it has the coveted position of being an answer to a *Trivial Pursuit* question.

Barry is busy preparing for National Mustard Day, held at the museum the first Saturday in August. I ask him if all the Norwegian troll statues that line Main Street have anything to do with it. He rolls his eyes and says, "No, I don't think the town is even that Norwegian. I think the Chamber of Commerce just needed a marketing ploy."

➜ *Mustard Museum,* 100 West Main Street, (608) 437-3986 or (800) GET-MUST. From Madison, take exit 142 from I-90/I-39 west onto Highway 12/18. Stay on Highway 18 as it joins Highway 151 and drive for seventeen miles to Mount Horeb. The museum is on the north side of Main.

While in the Area

While Barry may mock the Norwegians in the area, southeastern Wisconsin had one of the largest settlements of Norskies in the country. Just west of Mount Horeb a couple of miles off Route ID is an 1856 farmstead built by Norwegian settlers and boasting a small *stavkirke* (stave church) built in Trondheim, Norway, for the 1893 World's Columbian Exposition in Chicago. To prove they haven't forgotten about the Old Country, guides don *bunader,* folk costumes from the fjords, to add some authenticity as they lead visitors through the grass-roofed *stabbur* homesteads of Little Norway (3576 Route JG North, [608] 437-8211).

Chatty Belle has similar sister cows in DeForest and Janesville, but she has stolen the limelight as the World's Largest Talking Cow. Her voice, however, has been co-opted by WCCN to push the radio station rather than educate the public on the wonders of milk.

Chatty Belle
World's Largest Talking Cow

To show the world the milk-making capacity of the cheese state, Wisconsin sent an enormous twenty-foot-tall cow to the 1964 New York World's Fair. Push the button on the base and hear Chatty Belle expound on the merits of producing 270 pounds of milk per day and how much cheese could be made from this cream. The Largest Talking Cow in the World, along with her baby, Bullet, who hadn't learned to speak yet, made up the Wisconsin Pavilion and proudly showed the world that Wisconsin means cheese.

Following the fair, Chatty Belle was moved to some prime farmland on the edge of Neillsville. Inscribed near her hooves are the words: "Made by Sculptured Advertising, Sparta WI. Serial no. 109." Could there really be another 108 similar talking cows?

She stands next to the building that helped shoot her to stardom, the Wisconsin's World Fair Pavilion, now the WCCN radio station. The fantastically modern structure seems to shoot its angular lines into the Wisconsin sky, or, as a native from Neillsville described it to me, "It's just a weird-looking building from some old fair."

Plop a quarter into the slot and hear Chatty Belle chat. Alas, no longer does she elucidate the finer points of dairy production, because she's been forced to be an advertising shill. "Thanks for stopping at the WCCN Radio headquarters, which is housed in that building right over there," Chatty says to kids who already want their twenty-five cents back.

The WCCN receptionist inside admits it's kind of a rip-off, but the original tape got old. "It's only a twenty-second recording now," says the receptionist, a little embarrassed.

The more important question is, Where is Chatty's little heifer? This time the receptionist is less apologetic. "What happened to Bullet? After its eyes were poked out, its tail broken, and it was moved around by the Pepsi machine you mean? Each time it cost six hundred dollars' worth of fiberglass to fix, so my boss just threw Bullet in the trash. A lot of little kids were very unhappy. We thought about filling Bullet full of cement or putting an electrical fence around him, but that kind of would spoil the fun." I don't dare suggest that tossing him in the garbage was worse.

If Chatty isn't enough to convince drivers to pull over for a peek, the Cheesemobile refrigerated truck trailer stands along the highway. Sixteen thousand cows (or the equivalent of twelve hundred Chatty Belles) donated their milk to produce the Largest Cheese in the History of Mankind, which was carted off to the New York World's Fair along with Chatty and Bullet. This specially designed Cheesemobile had glass sides so the famous cheese could tour the country. After the same cheese went back to the world's fair for an encore the next year, it was ripe and ready. The Wisconsin Dairymen and Cheesemakers Association met in 1965 and ate the seventeen-and-one-quarter-ton piece of choice cheddar.

The display trailer holds faded photos from 1964 of the "actual photo history." The refrigeration has been turned off, and in place of the real cheese is a huge box of yellow plywood dubbed the World's Largest Replica Cheese.

→ *Chatty Belle,* 1201 Division Street. From I-94, go east on Highway 10 at Osseo for thirty-two miles until Neillsville. Follow Highway 10 (Division Street) through town, and the cow is about a half mile east of town on the north (left) side of the road.

While in the Area

At the turnoff from the interstate to see Chatty Belle, load up on pie at the Norske Nook in Osseo (13807 West Seventh Street, [715] 597-3069). Waitresses wear Norwegian outfits with little hats as they serve up Nor-Mex specialties like cod *lefse* wraps. The sharpest and best-endowed customers sign up for the Norske Nook Pie Club, which promises a free pie after you consume seven.

Another half hour southeast on the interstate at Black River Falls, motorists are distracted by a mouse in a sailor suit and two bright orange moose, perhaps a ruse to keep hunters from pumping them full of pellets. The Orange Moose Restaurant in the Arrowhead Lodge Best Western (600 Oasis Road, [715] 284-9471) looks out on these fiberglass critters along with a gigantic fiberglass deer grazing next to a bucolic man-made pond.

To top these relatively small roadside attractions, Black River Falls drew up plans to create the World's Largest Beer Stein, towering an astounding 138 feet into

Purple cows, green eggs and ham—but who has heard of an orange moose? The Oasis rest stop along Interstate 94 in Black River Falls is the perfect place for a stroll among fiberglass deer, blaze orange moose, and a mutant mouse eating Swiss cheese.

the air. Blueprints for the ten-story mug included an old-fashioned beer hall and shops inside with a pair of glass elevators shooting up the handles. When I ask the cashier at the Black River Crossing Oasis if the beer stein was completed, he responds, "Oh yeah, I remember hearing about that. No, they never finished. I think they ran out of money because it was kind of a bone-headed idea." Unfortunately, these skeptics won the battle.

Fred Smith was a former logger, bar owner, farmer, and musician, but he will always be remembered in Phillips as the concrete sculptor of "outsider art."

Fred Smith's Concrete Park

"For All the American People"

Fred Smith had too many beer bottles. After working as a logger and a farmer, he ran a tavern in Phillips, Wisconsin. In 1950, he retired at age sixty-five and got to work. He smashed the colored bottles and carefully placed the shards onto hundreds of concrete statues he created. He used his logging skills to construct a wooden scarecrowlike frame, then he covered the beams with "mink wire" followed by layer upon layer of cement. Curious friends stopped by to peek and began to bring their old glass bottles and any other objects they thought he could incorporate into his sculptures.

Fred's new world of people mushroomed to two hundred figures, with everyone from Sacajawea to Abe Lincoln living side by side. Animals, such as an anatomically correct moose, mixed with mythical characters, all composed of the same rigid frame covered by a colorful mosaic of glass and ceramic that sparkles in the sunshine. Some of the sculptures were so cumbersome—such as Ben Hur and his chariot—that they had to be constructed in sections and reassembled in his garden.

Paul Bunyan, of course, makes a cameo—Fred was a logger, after all. Since he couldn't read or write, the sculptor "narrated his thoughts to a typist," who wrote about "THE GLOB [sic] OF PAUL BUNYAN . . . the greatest logger in the state of Wisconsin, and his three oldest lumberjacks. And I thank you."

Fred's fifteen years of sculpting were his gift "for all the American people." He worked until 1964, when he suffered a stroke and gave up his artistic endeavor. After he died in 1976, his statues fell into disrepair.

One day, a thunderstorm swept through his concrete park and bowled over three quarters of the sculptures. Luckily, the Kohler Foundation stepped in to restore the statues, as it has with so many other rock gardens in Wisconsin.

While the name "Wisconsin Concrete Park" conjures up visions of a concrete jungle cityscape, Fred scattered his statues across his three and a half acres of land so that visitors would have to stroll through the forest to see a new set of sculptures. To maintain the Kit Carson, the Statue of Liberty, and others, almost all of the artwork has since been moved next to the parking lot near Fred's house, which has been turned into a gift shop for visitors. Just south of the concrete park on Highway 13 stands Fred Smith's Rock Garden Tavern—now named Stoney Pub—which has many old beer bottles just waiting for another sculptor.

→ *Fred Smith's Concrete Park,* 8236 Highway 13 south, (715) 339-4505. The town of Phillips is on Highway 13 in the middle of northern Wisconsin. From downtown, take Highway 13 about a mile south of town. Just past County Road D on the left (east) side will be the statues at the top of the hill. Open year-round.

Fred Smith received inspiration from Paul Bunyan, Abraham Lincoln, the Budweiser horses, and the movie *Ben Hur*. Although not as dramatic as Charlton Heston's chariot scene, Smith's sculpture certainly shines in the sun.

The Hodag
Beware the Bovine Spiritualis!

Eugene Shepard was a prankster. In the 1890s, he traveled extensively through-out northern Wisconsin and Minnesota and became rich as a land cruiser. Undoubtedly, he heard the tall tales of Paul Bunyan being born, and he probably added some of his own embellishments to these legends. Later, he spun his own yarn of a whole new species, and a gullible world took his bait.

Around Rhinelander, Shepard became known for his discovery of a new species of "scented moss" that he was kind enough to sell to the curious for twenty-five cents. Together with the local women's organization he sold his new find—that only he seemed able to find—to believers in Milwaukee and Chicago. At least until someone recognized the smell of the cheap perfume that he used to douse piles of moss.

With the money he made from his schemes, Shepard helped tout nearby Ballard Lake as the "Greatest Muskellunge Fishing of the World." To convince skeptical fishermen, he rigged a system of wires out in the lake to make mechanical muskies leap from the waves.

Although Shepard became appreciated locally as the "P. T. Barnum of Northern Wisconsin," he would go on notorious drunken escapades through town. As part of a holiday parade, he somehow trained a pair of moose from northern Minnesota to pull his carriage. Even though Rhinelander was a dry town, Shepard kept drinking and drove his carriage on the sidewalks, frightening the pedestrians. To make him sleep off his booze, his family once put him in his bed without his clothes and locked the door. Not to be cooped up, Shepard stripped the bed, wound the sheets into an escape rope, and fled out the window. The next morning, he was found sleeping naked on a couch in the shop window of a Main Street furniture store. "I wanted to let the people know that I hadn't made a New Year's pledge to swear off

Hodags were the cursed souls of lumberjacks' oxen come back for revenge, or at least that's the claim of Eugene Shepard, the P. T. Barnum of northern Wisconsin. A waitress sums up the story: "Some guy planted a big monster out in the woods and had everyone believing it. They even got some guy from the Smithsonian to come and check it out. Only in Rhinelander!"

drinking," he declared, according to the book *Long Live the Hodag*. The down side of his drinking sprees was the bitter breakup of two marriages.

That didn't stop him from expounding his invented northwoods legends, especially the one about what happened to the poor oxen used by lumberjacks when they died. These beasts of burden lived only about five or six years until they fell over dead from the exertion of lugging logs through the forests. Lumberjacks swore and cursed at these poor animals so much that their bodies needed to be burned for seven years to cleanse their souls of all the profanity. Just like a phoenix, an awful monster in search of revenge arose from the ashes. The lumbermen named this scourge the "hodag" (horse meets dog), or referred to it by its Latin name *bovine spiritualis.*

The hodag smelled like a mix between a buzzard and a skunk and had the head of a bull with a demonic grin. Usually black, but sometimes red or green, the hodag scurried along on thick stubby legs and dragged a long tail riddled with deadly spikes. By merely opening its grinning mouth, a hodag could kill a man with the noxious gases of its deadly halitosis.

Shepard's account of the hodag changed with each telling. From his bully pulpit at the *New North* newspaper, he wrote that the hodag has "the strength of an ox, the ferocity of a bear, the cunning of a fox, and the sagacity of a hindoo [*sic*] snake."

With much of the American wilderness unknown, the idea of new species was very possible. In 1893, Shepard wrote that he had noticed a pestilential odor near the source of Rice Creek in Oneida County and recognized that it must be a hodag. With some of his men, Shepard tried to snare it, but their weapons were worthless against it. After the hodag devoured their dogs, they lobbed sticks of dynamite at the monster. For nine more hours, the hodag thrashed around before it finally died. Shepard and his comrades dragged what was left of the beast into town and showed off the assortment of bones.

Then, in 1896, Shepard managed to photograph a hodag in the wild, and the photo was reprinted as front-page news across the country. With a group of men, Shepard set out to capture this dangerous devil of the northwoods. In his next column in the *New North,* Shepard wrote that he changed his tactic this time. A rag was doused with chloroform and held on a long pole to put the beast to sleep. Along with his lumberjacks, Shepard hauled the seven-foot-long prehistoric creature to the fairgrounds to a dimly lit cave behind a thin curtain.

The first hodag caught "alive" was actually a large piece of carved wood wiggled with wire by Shepard's sons hidden in the hay—a trick that had worked before with his mechanical muskies. Others remembered the captured hodag as a dog covered in a horse hide. In any case, people paid a dime to see the jailed hodag at the Oneida County Fair and to hear Shepard embellish his story to sometimes include trailing the animal for days and digging a tiger trap.

The next year, Shepard brought his hodag to the Wisconsin State Fair, where he advertised it as "the transmigrated soul of an ox used by Paul Bunyan." In spite of relating his creature to myth, newspapers continued to run stories about the hodag as "the long-sought missing link between the ichthyosaurus and the mylodoan" of the Ice Age.

Shepard's original hodag went up in flames—and some say it burned his house down on Ballard Lake—so he hired some taxidermists to piece together another hodag suitable for the next year's state fair.

By this time, the Smithsonian got wind of his incredible discovery and sent a representative to examine the hodag. In spite of Shepard's warnings, the museum curator insisted on getting near the beast. The ruse was up, but strangely enough it didn't seem to matter. Even though the hodag was proven to be a hoax, fairgoers still demanded to see this mysterious beast.

The hodag became a cottage industry in Rhinelander. Postcards filled the racks of hunting parties killing enormous hodags out in the woods; books on the beast stocked the shelves of local bookshops; a ballad about Shepard's heroic capture was written; and a play about the hodag even toured Europe.

More than a hundred years later, the hodag is alive and well. A huge smirking statue of the hodag greets visitors to town, the local athletic teams proudly sport the hodag emblem, and even the cop cars carry a little hodag emblazoned on their doors. Gene Shepard would be proud that his little prank survived the centuries to become the symbol of his beloved town.

→ *Hodag statue,* Rhinelander Chamber of Commerce, 450 West Kemp Street, (800) 236-4386. From Wausau, go north on Highway 51 for forty-five miles. Go right (east) on Highway 8 for seventeen miles into Rhinelander. The statue is in front of the Chamber of Commerce at the intersection with Highway 47.

F.A.S.T.: Fiberglass Animals, Shapes, and Trademarks

The Graveyard of Roadside Attractions

"Look! A giant cheeseburger!" exclaims Jerry Vettrus as he shows visitors around "the graveyard," a field of enormous fiberglass figures and molds for everything from giant cows to King Kong. As we pass the statue of a well-endowed kid in overalls holding up an oversized hamburger, he says, "A guy called me asking for a couple of Big Boys for his yard. He didn't want them painted, he just wanted to look at them."

F.A.S.T. (Fiberglass Animals, Shapes, and Trademarks) is a factory of roadside Americana. Its roots stretch back to a small company called Sculptured Advertising from Minneapolis, which went out of business in 1974. The phoenix rising from its ashes was called Creative Displays, and then finally F.A.S.T. in 1983. Jerry bought out his partner, Norb Anderson. "As part of the agreement, I have to make him a thirteen-foot dairy cow," Jerry says matter-of-factly.

Many of F.A.S.T.'s fiberglass behemoths once inhabited a mini-putt golf course run by Norb Anderson next to the Minnesota State Fairgrounds on Como Avenue. Alas! No more putting golf balls through the legs of enormous moose and cows; the state fair needed a larger parking lot.

Creative Display/F.A.S.T.'s most original work was done in their early years: the forty-five-foot Jolly Green Giant in Blue Earth and the breathtaking 145-foot, walk-through muskie in Hayward, Wisconsin. Now F.A.S.T. statues are headed all over the world—slides to Cyprus, dog fountains to Brazil, and an aquasplash to Italy—but most of their business still comes from the Wisconsin Dells and small-town Minnesota.

Moira Harris, in her book *Monumental Minnesota,* writes that in 1990 "guidelines for 'Celebrate Minnesota' had suggested that towns seek ways to celebrate their history and welcome former residents home." Many Minnesota towns agreed

The "graveyard" of fiberglass statues is next to the artist's atelier of all things big. Some of the undead statues are just duplicates; others are molds, in case someone wants to order, say, another King Kong for the backyard.

WELCOME TO SPARTA, WISCONSIN

As a gift to the town of Sparta, Fiberglass Animals, Shapes, and Trademarks (F.A.S.T.) built the World's Largest Bicyclist along Highway 16 as a tribute to the cycling trails that weave through the valleys.

the best way to "celebrate" their heritage was to erect an enormous animal sculpture. Nothing lures tourists off the interstate like a huge fiberglass fish.

Jerry says his technique requires "a fiberglass gun and lots of foam to make the mold. It takes a thousand dollars' worth of foam to make a twenty-two-foot-high pirate. I've already sent three pirates to Hong Kong, but they wanted one even bigger." Apparently, buying bulk statues pays off. "The first A&W Bear I made cost twelve thousand dollars. Since I then had the mold, the second one was only eight thousand!"

F.A.S.T. has a five-page price list of already-made molds ready to form a sculpture costing anywhere from seven hundred dollars up. Hmmm, wouldn't the Joneses turn green seeing a fourteen-foot Spartan in our suburban plot?

Jerry prefers designing original sculptures. "Appleton needed a heart slide," he says, "but it had to be anatomically correct. We consulted with a doctor, and now children can climb right through the aorta."

Even though their huge fiberglass sculptures scream out to be noticed, F.A.S.T. is a relatively well-kept secret. Jerry doesn't mind, though, and keeps a zenlike attitude. "People fifty miles from here don't even know we exist! But that's okay, because we know we exist."

➡ *F.A.S.T.,* 14205 Highway 21 east, (608) 269-7110. Once in Sparta, Wisconsin, look for the World's Largest Bicyclist, then turn north on Highway 21 for about three miles. Look for F.A.S.T.'s latest sculptures—from UFOs to moose—on the left side of the road. No organized tours.

While in the Area

While F.A.S.T. and company toil away making fiberglass wonders for small towns across the Midwest, just a few miles north lies one of the early roadside attractions in Wisconsin: the Paul and Matilda Wegner Grotto.

Once the Wegners retired in 1929, they set to work constructing a sculpture garden on their property a few miles south of Cataract and didn't stop until 1936. The present owners of the property hypothesize that the couple was inspired after having traveled the hundred miles to tour the Holy Ghost Grotto in Dickeyville, although no one knows for sure.

The locals refer to the Wegners's garden as "the glass church" because of the tiny one-room chapel covered with shards of broken bottles. Strangely, the couple didn't attach the glass like a smooth mosaic, so sharp edges protrude, turning the

The glass chapel at the Paul and Matilda Wegner Grotto near Cataract is at once inviting for its colorful mosaics and perilous for the sharp shards of glass protruding from this religious shrine.

small building into a big porcupine. Perhaps only the true God-fearing believers were bold enough to pray in this beautiful but dangerous little church.

The Wegners' art went beyond the glass chapel, however, and they used their newfound technique of cement and colored glass to create a whole series of garden statues. With no formal art training, the Wegners built their mosaic-covered sculptures for themselves (apart from the glass church). A cement cake honors their fiftieth anniversary, and a small ocean liner called *The Bremen* that sailed in the 1930s was perhaps the ship where they spent their honeymoon or perhaps it took them to America. Even the glass-and-cement American flag could be in lieu of hauling Old Glory up and down the flagpole every day.

The Wegners' creations were homemade lawn ornaments from an era before mass-produced flamingoes and ladies bending over with bloomers were sold in lots on the wayside. Of course, the "bigger is better" mentality soon took over lawn ornaments, as tourist sites and shops discovered the value of enormous sculptures to impress drivers to pull over for a peek. Who knows? Perhaps the folks at F.A.S.T. were inspired by this nearby little glass church and sculpture garden to beautify small towns with enormous roadside Americana.

House on the Rock

The Ultimate Bachelor Pad

Alex Jordan was an eternal bachelor. He lived around Spring Green, Wisconsin, near where Frank Lloyd Wright was born and raised. When Jordan heard about Wright's building projects at Taliesin and other Prairie School projects in the area, Jordan tried to get hired by the up-and-coming architect. The legend goes that Wright hated Jordan's architectural ideas and wouldn't hear of working with him. Wright supposedly pouted, "I wouldn't hire you to design a cheese crate or chicken coop!"

Jordan didn't need Wright's bigheaded ideas and decided to create his own masterpiece, a sort of Prairie School perch gone awry. While Wright was off in search of international fame building his masterpieces in New York, Tokyo, and Chicago, Jordan was a cab driver and never left the area around Madison.

Instead, Jordan found a nice spot for a picnic on the top of a protruding boulder called Deer Shelter Rock. The farmer who owned the land caught him sunbathing one day on the sixty-foot-tall rock and asked what he was doing there. Eventually, Jordan worked out a deal with the farmer to lease the rock, and he started building on the spot. Jordan supposedly carried the materials in baskets on his back up the sixty-foot chimney rock to complete the fourteen-room house. Perhaps as a parody of Wright's ideas, he built a "Japanese House" with very low ceilings that have since been padded for tall tourists.

Alex Jordan's search for an inaccessible place in the Wisconsin hills to be alone with his creativity achieved just the opposite result. By the time Jordan and his son Alex Jr. finished the House on the Rock in 1946, word had trickled out about this bizarre attraction and how he supposedly lugged building materials up to the rock by baskets dangling from ropes. In an attempt to shoo away the gawkers, Jordan began charging people four bits to climb up a precarious rope ladder to see his

One of the hundreds of scenes at House on the Rock has an armored knight preparing his lance to impale a long-tongued dragon, while a dusty damsel looks on in awe.

Halfway through the House on the Rock tour, semi-nude angels hover overhead next to the World's Largest Carousel.

masterpiece in 1959. Once again, the effect only increased his fame. Today, the House on the Rock stands as the most expensive museum in Wisconsin.

Eventually, a precarious 350-foot Flying Bridge through the treetops made the site somewhat more accessible. Chinese-style serpents along with dragon heads guard the entrance. Inside, Indonesian teak blinds, Tiffany-style lamps, and staircases to nowhere make up the décor. Carpeting runs up the walls and covers the parts of the ceiling where there is no enormous fake fireplace and no tree jutting up through the roof. Mechanical bands provide the mood music with the "Love

Theme from *The Godfather*" and "Bolero," offering the ultimate bachelor pad experience amid low lighting and sectional couches.

Jordan didn't rest on his laurels, however; he tacked on the bizarre Infinity Room, a cantilevered walkway jutting out 218 feet precariously over the Wyoming Valley. The pierlike structure with 3,264 windows ends in a point to give the optical illusion of infinity. Feel the floor quiver with each step as you peer straight down through a window near the end of the room. For further vertigo, Jordan supposedly perilously placed an E-Z Boy chair on the absolute end of the room over a drop of a hundred feet, the perfect expression of the sublime mix of danger and beauty where only the very brave would relax for a sit.

Once Jordan had finished his House on the Rock, he began collecting in earnest with the new influx of cash from visitors. With an estimated value in the millions —the World's Largest Carousel alone cost $4.5 million to build—Jordan's museum is the envy of collectors the world over. Jordan didn't hide away any of the money for himself, though, but took all the profits and reinvested them in his projects for the museum. This in turn brought in even more tourists, more money, and therefore more items on display.

Soon, vendors around the world knew they could sell out their own beloved collections—as hard as that may be—to the eccentric Jordan. Areas of Jordan's collection at House on the Rock seem strangely unrelated, but somehow it doesn't make any difference after the second hour of the surreal tour through the claustrophobic psychedelia. "I don't remember much, just being kind of scared," recalls Madison resident Adam Jablonski after being led through by his parents.

The mind tires of asking "Why?" and just accepts the hundreds of elaborate dollhouses near the pyramid of life-sized elephants and not far from the limo with the heart-shaped hot tub. Soon, the awe is perpetual as you gape at the World's Largest Fireplace, the World's Largest Steam Tractor, the World's Largest Chandelier, the World's Largest Theater Organ, the World's Largest Cannon, and the World's Largest Perpetual Motion Clock.

The first building on the tour after the actual House on the Rock is the Streets of Yesterday, in which Jordan recreated an entire town built about half the normal size. This Lilliputian village makes the tourist the powerful giant from the future in this stagnant, but quaint, past. This is a literal trip down memory lane, without any of the inconveniences of pesky inhabitants getting in the way. The Streets of Yesterday contains a miniature barbershop, an apothecary, a sheriff's office, and more.

Perhaps Jordan just wanted to be secluded in his own perfect little nostalgic world, but he was probably too busy collecting to lollygag in the past.

Throughout the lengthy tour, very few signs or cards explain what the objects are. This is not a museum to further one's knowledge of Americana or anything else in his collection. The tour of House on the Rock takes at least four hours—five if it's crowded—and time spent reading cards would easily double the time and make the trip excruciating. These objects are meant to be appreciated at face value for amusement and awe.

The authentic is often indistinguishable from the imitation at House on the Rock. Red lights flash amid gory displays of nonexistent knights in empty armor protecting the Crown Jewels and royal gems from around the world. Only later did I realize that this jewelry, which is shown as "authentic," would probably be more valuable than the entire collection combined. The guide replies to my query, "The gems are imitations and there's a little sign on the case that explains this." I returned for another peek and discovered an insignificant card noting "not authentic" that was easily lost within the blinking lights. Real or replica doesn't matter as throngs ogle at the diamonds, or, rather, search for a way out after four hours of walking through the labyrinth.

Another outstanding display is the Blue Room's eighty-piece mechanical orchestra with wax dummies dressed as celebrities—from Lincoln to Leno—playing everything from tubas to pianos thanks to twenty-one hundred pneumatic motors pumping away. "There's Sonny Bono on piano! Cher's on the other side of the orchestra, but they were separated by then anyway," jokes the guide. I asked her how on earth all the violins stay tuned all day long. "You must be a musician; the musicians always ask that," she responds. Then she lowers her voice so others won't hear. "Actually, the strings aren't really playing because it would be impossible to continually tune all the strings many times a day. There's a CD playing the music in the background, and the only instruments that are actually performing are the percussion."

Jordan's final opus was the Heritage of the Sea. He purchased an entire museum of model ships—from a Spanish armada to paddleboats to Soviet subs—and placed them in a new warehouse with a spiral walkway winding up to the top (a reference to Wright's design for the Guggenheim in New York?). In the center, Jordan built his largest piece so far: a two-hundred-foot "part white whale, part killer whale" with a chewed-up boat in its mouth battling a giant squid. Unfortunately,

Jordan died at seventy-five years of age in 1989, a year before the work's completion. If he had lived, however, this surely wouldn't have been the end of his days of obsessive collecting.

→ *House on the Rock*, 5754 Highway 23, (608) 935-3639. From I-90/I-39 in Madison, take exit 142 and follow Highway 18 west (it will merge with Highway 151) until Dodgeville. Take Highway 23 north and look for the signs.

While in the Area

To top off the dreamlike day at the House on the Rock, turn south on Highway 23 and look for the giant plane parked on the west side of the road. Welcome to the Don Q Inn, "Unique in all the World" (3656 State Highway 23 North, Dodgeville, [608] 935-2321 or [800] 666-7848). Stay in one of twenty Fantasuite Rooms, from Up, Up & Away in a mock hot-air balloon to Caesar's Court with Roman orange shag carpeting to the Medieval Room, complete with novelty manacles. Lounge in the lobby around a huge fireplace surrounded by swiveling barber chairs.

A three-hundred-foot cavelike passage delves underground to the restaurant in a refurbished barn from 1914. Businessmen toting Bloody Marys love the Don Q Inn for meetings at their breakfast banquet. The cozy décor boasts a stone fireplace, and stained-glass windows light up the hanging wagon wheels, decorated saws, and the bar made of old copper bourbon barrels.

SPRING GREEN

Taliesin
Frank Lloyd Wright's Utopian Oasis

The gentle rolling hills around Frank Lloyd Wright's bucolic workshop and houses south of Spring Green hide the turbulent past that nearly undid America's first celebrity architect. Murders, mistresses, FBI surveillance, and groundbreaking architecture were all part of the local gossip during Wright's Wisconsin days.

Born in nearby Richland Center, Wright designed Hillside Home School in 1901 as one of his first projects and as a favor to his two aunts. They taught youngsters the then radical concept of "hands-on learning," a concept that Wright continued later with his apprentices at his Taliesin West school in Scottsdale, Arizona.

He also worked under the famous architect Louis Sullivan in Chicago. Always in search of the spotlight, Wright was fired for taking his own commissions, which went against his agreement with Sullivan.

Never quite satisfied with the status quo, Wright moved to Europe in 1909 with his mistress, a client named Mamah Borthwick (Cheney), leaving his family and kids in the process. He finally settled with her in Spring Green, perhaps in hope of letting the scandals subside for the moment. Here, he built his studio and home in 1911, naming it Taliesin for the mythical Celtic poet who was destined to die and be reborn. Even today, the distinctive layers of horizontal lines of Taliesin leave modern architecture struggling to match its simple elegance and harmony with the surroundings.

This apparent tranquility, however, hides the gruesome slaughter behind those Prairie School doors. While Wright was away in 1914, his mistress and six others, including her children, were axe murdered during dinner, and the house was set ablaze.

Wright was devastated, and for the next twenty years his roller-coaster life consisted of another fire at Taliesin, bankruptcy, arrest, a couple more love affairs,

Frank Lloyd Wright's home for the last fifty years of his life was Taliesin, meaning "shining brow" in Welsh (because it is on the brow of a hill). Called his "autobiography in wood and stone," the beautiful building saw its share of tragedy during Wright's turbulent life.

marriage, and many lawsuits. While many had written Wright off as an arrogant has-been architect, he didn't begin his most prolific work until 1935.

With success, Wright's ideas became even bolder. In 1956, he unveiled his plan for a mile-high building with a twenty-six-foot-tall model. Towering four times the height of the present-day Sears Tower, Wright's behemoth would be serviced by atomic-powered elevators that would shoot residents to the top. Fifteen thousand parking spots would fill the base of the building, while 150 helicopter landing pads would jut out from the roof. All puny buildings on the ground around this structure would be leveled for parks. He demonstrated to skeptics how the building wouldn't sway in spite of Chicago's famous winds, and he conveniently avoided mentioning any fire hazard. As part of his Mile-High Illinois plan, building just ten of these skyscrapers would supply as much office space as in all of New York City. With a hundred-million-dollar price tag at the time, Wright admitted, "No one could afford to build it now, but in the future no one can afford not to build it."

The same year, Wright contradicted himself by proposing to build the Arizona capitol as a single-story building that would stretch over many acres. "Vertical is vertigo, in human life," he wrote. "The horizontal line is the life-line of humanity."

Wright never did receive a government contract, probably due to his progressive pacifism. His Taliesin Fellowship signed a petition against the United States' entrance into World War II and labeled the draft immoral and futile. This didn't endear Wright to J. Edgar Hoover, who put Wright under surveillance and tried twice to bring sedition charges against him that were denied by the attorney general. Wright's condemnation of the treatment of Japanese civilians in the United States and his support of socialism caused further suspicion at the FBI and probably hindered many of his architectural projects from getting off the ground.

Wright persisted, however. From 1945 until his death in 1959, Wright wrote, built, and campaigned tirelessly for his "deurbanization" scheme—which might be called "suburbanization" today. Of his more than eight hundred blueprints—he even designed a doghouse—half were built, and Taliesin stands as one of the most beautiful.

→ *Taliesin*, Frank Lloyd Wright Visitors Center, 5607 County Highway C, (608) 588-7900. From Madison, go west on Highway 14 for about thirty miles to Spring Green. Turn left (south) on Highway 23 and go two miles past town. After crossing the Wisconsin River, the visitors center is on the left (east) side at County Highway C. Following 23 will take you to Wright's Taliesin, as well as his Midway, Hillside (both on the right side of the road), and Unity Chapel, on the left at County Road T. May through October.

While in the Area

To sleep in Frank Lloyd Wright style, bed down at the Usonian Motel along Highway 14 at the intersection with Highway 23 or call (877) USONIAN. The first house built in this Prairie School style was for Herbert Jacobs, a journalist for the *Madi-*

son Capital Times, in 1935. Jacobs was an admirer of Wright but didn't have the cash for a fancy Taliesin-style house. Wright drew up his first "Usonian" house and built it for a mere $5,500. No one is certain how he came up with the term "Usonian," but perhaps during his travels to Europe he had overheard the United States referred to as "Usona" (United States of North America) to differentiate it from the Union of South Africa.

Wright made the unusual proclamation that his Usonian houses were meant not to last forever, but merely for the lives of the present owners, much like the Japanese houses that influenced his designs. Regardless, costly remodeling is keeping the Usonians alive, such as the Gordon House in Oregon that was recently moved for $1.2 million and cost a mere $10,000 to build.

To sleep in a little more luxury, rather than a knockoff of a working-class abode, book a night at the Frank Lloyd Wright–inspired Spring Valley Inn (6279 County Highway C, [608] 588-7828). Although built in 1990, the inn shows how Wright's influence could—and should—influence modern construction.

VALTON

The Painted Forest

"I Am Death!"

"Ernest Hüpedon would paint just about anything for food, wine, or whiskey," guide Gordon Johnson recounts. "When he was painting the inside of the hall, someone brought him a bucket of beer each noon; perhaps that was his payment." Hüpedon had led a rough life before immigrating to southeastern Wisconsin.

This detail of Hüpedon's Painted Forest shows the antics that the Modern Woodmen of America would inflict on new initiates to scare the pants off them before they could sell life insurance.

He was born in Germany and thrown in the clink for embezzlement from a bank where he worked. With too much free time in jail, he took to painting to pass the hours. When a coworker on his deathbed confessed to the crime, Hüpedon was freed. To escape further such mix-ups, he hopped a boat for the United States in 1878.

He arrived in Wisconsin and kept painting to earn his keep. Everything from barns to plates were painted with his self-taught art, and usually in exchange for food, lodging, and a stiff drink. "He even did a triptych of cattle poisoning alongside the road," explains Gordon.

Hüpedon's masterpiece, however, is the Painted Forest in the tiny town of Valton, which isn't even on Wisconsin maps because it's so small. "All the county roads on the official state map are incorrect. We've been trying to get Valton back on the map, and they've promised us that the next state map will have us on it."

One of the only buildings in town that isn't a house is the camp hall of the Modern Woodmen of America, a fraternal group that pushed (and still pushes) life insurance.

From the outside, this white wood structure appears to be nothing special. Passing through the old wooden doors is like entering a dense jungle, with huge trees painted on the walls extending up to the ceiling, where puffy clouds float through a crystal blue sky.

Besides the forest, Hüpedon painted scenes of the Woodmen's bizarre hazing rituals for new members. One scene depicts the Woodmen dragging poor newcomers to be burned at the stake—all in good fun, of course.

The favorite ritual in this secretive life insurance club, however, was the old goat joke. The recruit was usually blindfolded and placed on a wooden goat on wheels. He was then wheeled around the hall as mayhem ensued. Once the blindfold came off, an insurance agent in a death costume appeared from out of nowhere (the closet actually) and announced:

I am Death! Relentless and unsparing! I visit the cradle and take the smallest of humanity, leaving the mother to wail and mourn. The strongest of men are crushed beneath my hand. Fortune has no exemption from my mandate, nor does fame stay my coming. I strike where I like, when I please, and whom I desire. I have remained here that I might turn you [pointing to candidate] into lifeless clay. I have but to breathe upon you, and all that you are,

The Modern Woodmen of America building may seem bland from the outside, but the main hall is covered floor to ceiling with paintings of dense woods. To finish their lodge, the woodmen/insurance agents commissioned Ernest Hüpedon to create the Painted Forest and promised him food, lodging, and probably some hooch (even though Valton was a dry town).

or all that you hope to be, shall be gone. The work you have done must go unfinished and those whom you love shall hold you only as a memory.

If that doesn't convince you to buy life insurance, what will? If the Woodmen were satisfied that their pranks had sufficiently scared the initiate, he would be permitted to pester his neighbors to buy insurance as well. Gordon the docent is happy to show the goat and the death costume and explain the other bizarre rituals of the Woodmen in rural Wisconsin.

Although Hüpedon probably wasn't a member of the Modern Woodmen of America, he was commissioned to paint their Sistine Chapel in Valton and only got room and board in exchange. "Valton was a dry town," Gordon says, "but somebody said there was a speakeasy in town, which is where he got his fill." Around the turn of the century, Hüpedon was found dead in a snowdrift in nearby Hillsboro. He had no insurance policy, and only a handful of his paintings have ever been found.

➙ *The Painted Forest,* Sixth Street and Painted Forest Drive, (608) 983-2352. From I-94/I-90, take Highway 80 south at New Lisbon. Follow it for about thirty miles (through Hillsboro) and turn left on County Road EE into Valton. At Sixth Street, turn left (north) one block to Painted Forest Drive and look for the large white building with an MWA sign on the front. Open Saturdays, summer only, 1:00 to 3:30 P.M.

WISCONSIN DELLS

The Ducks
Thrills, Spills, and Splashes

The Wisconsin Dells are spectacular rock formations along the Wisconsin River that lured tourists to the area as early as the 1880s. Photographer H. H. Bennett snapped the first stop-action photo of someone jumping to Stand Rock in the Dells in 1886. This shot, as well as his photos of lumberjacks and Ho Chunk Indians,

The Wisconsin Dells Ducks were decommissioned army surplus amphibious vehicles that can travel on land and water. What was once a tranquil boat trip on the river through the beautiful cliffs now is a thrills and spills adventure.

helped to publicize the area for its natural splendor. Downtown Wisconsin Dells even boasts a museum dedicated to the photographer on 215 Broadway.

Naturalist Aldo Leopold, author of *Sand County Almanac,* lived near the Dells and warned about keeping the environment and its delicate relationship with humans intact. Ironically, the area has now become a homespun Disneyland, but nature is no longer the biggest draw to the area.

Little steamboats full of tourists used to chug along the Wisconsin River to see the famous rock formations with evocative names like Cow in the Milk Bottle (this is Wisconsin, after all), Beehive, Devil's Elbow, and Baby Grand Piano. The boat rides would land at Stand Rock, where the finale of the trip was an Indian powwow hosted by the Winnebagos.

The Dells began to change after World War II, when decommissioned army surplus amphibious vehicles were brought to the Dells. Known as the "Ducks," these mighty boats could drive fifty miles per hour on land and cruise right back into the water with a spine-wrenching splash. This big entrance into the water became one of the highlights of the river trip, and interest waned in the short amount of time actually spent cruising the river.

In the fast-changing Wisconsin Dells world of thrills and spills, the Ducks are now one of the classic rides and one of the few to actually venture out into the natural wonder of the area. The ride comes with a hefty price tag, however. When I ask for two tickets for the hour-long trip on the Original Wisconsin Dells Ducks. The cashier nonchalantly replies, "That'll be thirty-five dollars and fifty cents."

The bus driver to the Ducks commiserates, saying she can't afford to eat or go out in the Dells: "It's cheaper to go to Las Vegas!"

Instead of a simple hike along the river trails, the boat rides along the Wisconsin River are a relaxing way to see the layered cliff formations made famous by H. H. Bennett before the area gets even more built up and Aldo Leopold's warning comes true.

→ *Original Wisconsin Ducks,* 1890 Wisconsin Dells Parkway, (608) 254-8751. From I-94/I-90 take exit 87. Go east on Highway 13. Turn right (south) on Highway 12 (Wisconsin Dells Parkway). The Ducks are just past Route A on the left. Open April through October.

→ *Dells Duck Tours,* 1550 Wisconsin Dells Parkway, (608) 254-6080. From I-94/I-90 take exit 87. Go east on Highway 13. Turn right (south) on Highway 12

Monster truck rides are the ultimate in stomach-churning thrills, but the temperamental hemi motors often send the beasts to the repair shop. For owner Tim Sanders, the monster truck is a labor of love; as he says, "Like all-star wrestling, you make all your money selling T-shirts."

(Wisconsin Dells Parkway). At the junction with Route 23, turn left (east) to stay on Highway 12. The Dells Ducks are just east of this intersection. Open summer only.

While in the Area

Tim Sanders is very proud of his monster truck ride concession. "My truck used to be on the circuit. . . . It was a really popular truck." In his scratchy John Travolta voice, Tim explains all the recent improvements, even though I understand little of the tech talk: "I've got air suspension in it. I put in a 429 this year . . . top of the line . . . extra shocks . . . I've got three shocks on each wheel . . . twice the power that I had last year. The master cylinders were shot, and I won't drive without good brakes!"

It is 10 A.M. on Memorial Day weekend—far too early for monster truck fans. "I tried to figure out why my customers always come so late," Tim wonders. "I've asked them over the years. Most of them are in their hot tub in the morning, probably trying to recover from the night before." These are serious pleasure seekers.

"We go down through this creeklike thing," he explains. "I do a skit between each section, do a donut in the valley. Then I drive over eighteen cars. The whole thing takes about twelve minutes."

He points down to the road where he drives his gargantuan pickup. "The track down there took two and a half months of dump trucks working full time. That's a lot of dirt," he says proudly.

Tim then explains how he likes to scare any complainers on the ride. "When kids brag that this ride is boring, I have them sit in the back of the truck. Then we go up 'Killer Hill' and hit a 'roller.' Imagine a schoolbus hitting railroad tracks at sixty miles per hour. These kids that think they're so cool are no longer so tough. It's pretty funny."

If you dare, you can hop in the back of his enormous pickup, parked across from the Original Wisconsin Ducks and behind Olde Kilbourn at 633 Wisconsin Dells Parkway.

Tommy Bartlett's Robot World

"Caution: High Radiation Area"

Any trip to the area wouldn't be complete without paying homage to Tommy Bartlett, the man who more than anyone else made the Wisconsin Dells what it is today through his waterskiing shows. Bartlett was a visionary who prophesied that in the future, robots would be doing the dishes, cleaning our toilets, and just being our friends. Except for, of course, the evil robots bent on world domination. After all, what's the fun of an exhibit of robots if there isn't some urgent danger? This lesson wasn't lost on Bartlett.

It's time for the countdown as I am led into Emergency Hatch 7, an elevator turned "shuttle" that blasts by constellations visible outside the glass hatch. Upon my landing on this alien planet, known as the second floor, a series of robots are hard at work with lots of colored plastic, wires, and flashing lights, while beeping sound effects like Moog keyboards fill the air. Signs warning "Danger High Voltage" and "Caution: High Radiation Area" flash overhead.

Sirens blare and a mechanical voice repeatedly shouts, "Radiation Alert!" Robots looking suspiciously like C3PO from *Star Wars* scramble about and speak in stiff, formal accents: "Security Alert! Levels are excessive. Radiation detected in an anti-matter area." (Why do robots so often have perfectly stilted English accents?)

All hope to avoid radiation poisoning lies with a frantic robot scurrying about yelling in a Scottish accent (a dead ringer for Scotty from *Star Trek*), "Two minutes to melt down! Move along before the whole place goes up like a Roman candle!" In other words, Keep moving along, folks! Bartlett knew that while little glitches may annoy us, huge catastrophes thrill us.

Just when things look safe, we enter the video arcade and are greeted by a robot who challenges us to a laser duel to the death: "I am Rob-a-Tron from the planet Zircon. My order is to seek out inferior humans. You have three chances to disarm me. . . . Good luck, humans!"

Outside Tommy Bartlett's Robot World, this red robot with
a beating heart greets guests with a dazed expression from
his dreams of electric sheep.

Bartlett must have studied Baudrillard, who wrote in *The System of Object*, "The robot is a slave, then, but let us not forget that the theme of slavery is always bound up—even in the legend of the sorcerer's apprentice—with the theme of *revolt*." In other words, robots could be the dangerous, yet entertaining, nemeses and perfect for the Dells.

The friendly robots, however, are just as nefarious as the evil rebels, as Zord Robovend exclaims, "Hi kids! My name is ZORD. I want to be your friend. I have a special surprise I picked just for you!" First, however, you must feed it a quarter. Apparently Bartlett's utopian vision of a free society with robots attending to our every need isn't on the house.

Perhaps disgruntled that no one shared his leisurely 1970s vision of the future, Bartlett scrapped part of Robot World to make room for a Science Exploratory, with updated views of a futurist myopia. He bought part of the Mir space station from the Russians and hung some of the pod in a hangar with a slight tilt—a nod to the marketing genius of the Wonder Spot—to simulate the nausea of weightlessness. As with everything in the Dells, the goal is to get dizzy, whether through waterslides, virtual reality, or optical illusions. After all, if it isn't somewhat disorienting through speed, balance, or other tricks, it would be normal. Vacation is pointless if things are the same as at home.

I ask one of the guides if this Mir module had been in space. "No, this was actually one of three built that never went up," is the response, even though a sign declares it is the "Original Core Module of the Russian Mir Space Station." No one seems to mind, but I didn't see anyone actually take the time to read the sign explaining, "There are two Mir Space Stations. One in Russia and the other one you are about to enter."

Sputnik is also on display, once again as a replica. After running on double A batteries, this not-so-menacing satellite burned up on reentry to earth after ninety-six days of transmitting its terrifying beep from space. Otherwise Bartlett would have surely bought the original.

Nearly the whole area is dedicated to cosmonaut memorabilia because Bartlett couldn't get his hands on old NASA gear. In case anyone gets suspicious of his loyalties, plenty of American flags are plastered around his Russian acquisitions.

After you view the impressive Mir capsule, the SR2 Simulator tempts you with a sign promising a "roller coaster in space" for just three more bucks. Visitors exiting this pod look nauseous but happy as they try to get their land legs. A sign next to the SR2 warns that time in space makes "the body become weak from lack of use," a motto that could be applied to the entire Wisconsin Dells.

At the end of the Robot World tour, a teenage guide is asked what happened to the body of Tommy Bartlett, the futurist visionary who died at eighty-four after his quest for eternal fame. The irreverent youngster responds, "I think they burned him and spread his ashes in a few different places: Milwaukee, Lake Denton, and I don't remember where else."

→ *Tommy Bartlett's Robot World*, 560 Wisconsin Dells Parkway, (608) 254-2525. From I-94/I-90, take exit 89 east on Route 23. Turn left (north) onto Highway 12 (Wisconsin Dells Parkway), and Robot World is on the right side. Open year-round.

An outlaw with a pistol and a rope hearkens back to the old days in the Dells when it was called Kilbourn City, with the rough part of town known as Bloody Run.

Driving Tour of the Dells

From Vinland Vikings to a Trojan Horse

The Gear Daddies sang about their "Dream Vacation in the Dells" and all the thrills, spills, and robots promised in this water-filled wonderland. Where else can you blast a go-kart through the insides of a sixty-foot Trojan horse, drop fifty feet on a slide to be slammed into a wall of water, and get a bellyache from world-famous fudge all in the same day?

Wading through the plethora of attractions can be grueling, but just driving through the Dells and all the oversized statues is sometimes better than having your pocketbook lightened by actually spending the night. If you're driving between Minneapolis and Madison on the interstate, simply take a quick detour—assuming no summertime traffic jam—to see this gold mine of roadside kitsch.

Beginning from exit 87 off Interstate I-94/90, drive east on Highway 13. A cowboy on the right (south) side threatens drivers to stop for gas and a blue slushee at the Mobil Snack Shop or else he'll blast you with his pistol and hang you high with his lasso.

Across the street lies the sad remnants of the Paul Bunyan Mini Golf with moss overgrowing the once-manicured greens. The parking lot may be full, but tourists seem far more interested in the Paul Bunyan Shanty with its all-you-can-eat breakfast buffet. A walk through the putt-putt course, however, reveals such gems as a fiberglass statue of a moose, a bison, and a Vinland Viking in a sort of tan dress with matching high boots. All the once-brisk business has moved to the Pirate's Cove putt-putt course, which has five eighteen-hole courses (for a total of ninety holes!) around seventeen waterfalls and a bursting volcano.

Rather than continuing downtown to see the UFO museum, the haunted mansion, and all that fudge, turn right (south) on Highway 12 (Wisconsin Dells Parkway). Over the crest of the hill stands the most impressive site in the Dells: a

This Vinland Viking was one of the golfing hazards at the
ruins of the Paul Bunyan mini golf course along Highway 13.

sixty-foot Trojan horse with a go-cart track through its belly. Big Chief Go-Kart
used to have an Indian chieftain holding a hamburger to signal the way, but no
more. Either due to newfound sensitivity to the Native Americans in the area or
the simple shift in theme to all things Aegean, the chief had a facelift to make him
a skirted Trojan clutching a go-cart.

A bit farther along the Wisconsin Dells Parkway on the left side is the Hotel Atlantis mini theme park, its mythical Greek gods towering over colossal waterslides and fountains. Mighty Poseidon, however, seems more like a little water sprite holding a pitchfork than the God of the Sea.

Down the hill from Atlantis is the Storybook Gardens, featuring Little Miss Muffet, Simple Simon, Humpty Dumpty, and the whole gang. The sister attraction, the Biblical Gardens, has gone the way of Xanadu: the Foam House of

Circle up the spiral of wooden track inside the sixty-foot-tall Trojan in a two-stroke go-cart, as the historical-themed Big Chief Go-Kart explains why one should never trust a Greek bearing gifts, especially a gift horse.

Tomorrow and other old Dells attractions. Biblical Gardens was dismantled in lieu of Storybook Gardens; apparently religious reenactments don't lure tourists as well as Little Bo Peep.

Continuing on the Wisconsin Dells Parkway leads to a giant mouse in blue

Mighty Poseidon guards his waterslide in front of Hotel Atlantis. What the brochures portray as a fantastic life-threatening slide not for use by those with heart problems turns out to be a glorified kiddie pool, with the alluring siren of the sea bearing a striking resemblance to Disney's Little Mermaid.

Even though the Dells is vacation never-never land, this is still Wisconsin, so an oversized mouse with an enormous wedge of cheese is perfectly appropriate.

jeans munching on a chunk of cheddar. When I pull out my camera to shoot a picture of this fiberglass rodent, a couple of tourists stop and ask me, "Are you here to repair the mouse?"

The other interrupts, "Is it a mouse, or is it a rat? Look at that tail! I think it's a rat."

The first person rebuts, "Oh come on! Who's ever heard of a rat eating cheese? Besides, why would they put a rat in front of their restaurant?"

The restaurant next door is Mr. Pancake. Amid the ubiquitous all-you-can-eat buffets, the only way for a restaurant to survive in the Dells is with a shtick. Housed in a steamboat-themed building with whitewashed dowels, Mr. Pancake is plastered with flowery wallpaper and has a tin ceiling, decorations that lack only a Dixieland band to complete the nostalgic scene. The menu bursts with dozens of types of pancakes: Swedish, potato, cherry, buckwheat, buttermilk, chocolate, Iowa corn, pigs in a blanket, peanut butter, blintzes (with sour cream), dollar-sized, banana, Hawaiian, and so forth.

Farther down the strip toward Lake Delton, a string of out-of-this-world hotels has been built up with not only the requisite swimming pools, but entire aquatic entertainment complexes. The carousel is a bit on the modest side, with a Candyland theme that would make Willy Wonka proud. Tots in their swimsuits can enter the bulbous pink (cotton candy?) cave with candy canes popping out the top and slide through the sugary scene into the cold water.

The list of new megahotels in the Dells is staggering, boasting themes from Polynesia to the Kalahari. One of the most remarkable is Camelot, complete with turrets and battlements. Rather than the castle at Glastonbury, however, the coats of arms adorning the towers bear names like Krosno, Gdansk, and Wroclaw, leading one to wonder about Anglo-Polish collusion around the Arthurian round table.

The tour of these ever-changing roadside attractions comes to an end as the parkway joins up the interstate once again.

BIBLIOGRAPHY

Arany, Lynne, and Archie Hobson. *Little Museums.* New York: Henry Holt, 1998.

Baudrillard, Jean. *The System of Objects.* London: Verso, 1996.

Bergheim, Laura. *An American Festival of "World's Capitals": Over Three Hundred World Capitals of Arts, Crafts, Food, Culture, and Sport.* New York: John Wiley and Sons, Inc., 1997.

Blashfield, Jean F. *Awesome Almanac Minnesota.* Fontana, Wisc.: B & B Publishing, 1993.

Boese, Alex. *The Museum of Hoaxes.* New York: Dutton, 2002.

Breining, Greg. *Minnesota.* Oakland, Calif.: Compass American Guides, Fodor's Travel Publications, Inc., 1997.

Cantor, George. *Historic Festivals: A Traveler's Guide.* Detroit: Visible Ink, 1996.

Davies, Anne, ed. *Fodor's Road Guide USA: Illinois, Iowa, Missouri, Wisconsin.* New York: Fodor's LLC, 2001.

DeGennaro, Denise, ed. *Fodor's Road Guide USA: Minnesota, Nebraska, North Dakota, South Dakota.* New York: Fodor's LLC, 2001.

DeGroot, Barbara, and Jack El-Hai. *The Insiders' Guide to the Twin Cities.* Manteo, N.C.: Insiders' Guides, 1995.

Des Garennes, Christine. *Great Little Museums of the Midwest.* Black Earth, Wisc.: Trails Books, 2002.

Dickson, Paul, and Robert Skole. *The Volvo Guide to Halls of Fame: The Traveler's Handbook of North America's Most Inspiring and Entertaining Attractions.* Washington, D.C.: Living Planet Press, 1995.

Dierckings, Tony, and Kerry Elliot. *True North.* Duluth, Minn.: X-communication, 2001.

Dregni, Eric. *Minnesota Marvels: Roadside Attractions in the Land of Lakes.* Minneapolis: University of Minnesota Press, 2001.

Dregni, Michael, ed. *Minnesota Days: Our Heritage in Stories, Art, and Photos.* Stillwater, Minn.: Voyageur Press, 1999.

Erickson, Lori, and Tracy Stuhr. *Iowa off the Beaten Path.* Guilford, Conn.: Globe Pequot Press, 2001.

Feldman, Michael, and Diana Cook. *Wisconsin Curiosities.* Guilford, Conn.: Globe Pequot Press, 2000.

Friedman, Jan. *Eccentric America*. Bucks, England: Bradt Travel Guides, 2001.

Frost, Robert. *The Poems of Robert Frost*. New York: Random House, 1946.

Gauper, Beth. *Midwest Weekends: Memorable Getaways in the Upper Midwest*. Kansas City: Andrews & McMeel, 1996.

Griffith, T. D. *South Dakota*. Oakland, Calif.: Fodor's Travel Publications, 1998.

Gurvis, Sandra. *America's Strangest Museums: A Traveler's Guide*. Toronto: Citadel Press, 1998.

Harris, Moira. *Monumental Minnesota*. Pogo Press, 1992.

Hauck, Dennis William. *National Directory of Haunted Places*. New York: Penguin, 1996.

Hintz, Martin, and Daniel Hintz. *Wisconsin off the Beaten Path*. Guilford, Conn.: Globe Pequot Press, 2000.

Hintz, Michael, and Stephen V. Hintz. *Wisconsin Family Adventure Guide*. Old Saybrook, Conn.: Globe Pequot Press, 1995.

Jensen, Jamie. *Roadside USA: Cross Country Adventures on America's Two-Lane Highways*. Emeryville, Calif.: Avalon Travel Publishing, 2002.

Keillor, Garrison. *In Search of Lake Wobegon*. New York: Viking Studio, 2001.

———. *Lake Wobegon Days*. New York: Viking Penguin, 1985.

Kirchner, Paul. *Forgotten Fads and Fabulous Flops*. Santa Monica, Calif.: Rhino Records, 1995.

Kortenhof, Kurt Daniel. *Long Live the Hodag: The Life and Legacy of Eugene Simeon Shepard, 1854–1923*. Rhinelander, Wisc.: Hodag Press, 1996.

Laabs, James. *The Wisconsin Dells: A Completely Unauthorized Guide*. Madison: Prairie Oak Press, 1999.

Lesy, Michael. *Wisconsin Death Trip*. New York: Anchor Books, 1991.

MacDougall, Curtis D. *Hoaxes*. New York: Dover, 1958.

Margolies, John. *Fun along the Road: American Tourist Attractions*. Boston: Bulfinch Press, 1998.

Marling, Karal Ann. *Colossus of Roads: Myth and Symbol along the American Highway*. Minneapolis: University of Minnesota Press, 1984.

McMacken, Robin. *The Dakotas off the Beaten Path*. Guilford, Conn.: Globe Pequot Press, 2002.

Munson, Kyle. *Iowa Nebraska Travel Smart*. Emeryville, Calif.: John Muir Publications, 2000.

Naylor, Cliff, and Monica Hannan. *Dakota Day Trips*. Bismarck: North Dakota Department of Commerce, 1999.

―――. *More Dakota Day Trips*. Bismarck: North Dakota Department of Commerce, 2001.

Norman, Scott, and Michael Norman. *Haunted Heartland*. New York: Warner Books, 1985.

O'Reilly, Jane H. *Quick Escapes: Minneapolis/St. Paul*. Old Saybrook, Conn.: Globe Pequot Press, 1998.

Pohlen, Jerome. *Oddball Minnesota: A Guide to Some Really Strange Places*. Chicago: Chicago Review Press, 2003.

―――. *Oddball Wisconsin: A Guide to Some Really Strange Places*. Chicago: Chicago Review Press, 2001.

Rabinow, Paul, ed. *The Foucault Reader*. London: Penguin, 1984.

Rath, Jay. *The M-Files: True Reports of Minnesota's Unexplained Phenomena*. Madison: Wisconsin Trails, 1998.

―――. *The W-Files: True Reports of Wisconsin's Unexplained Phenomena*. Madison: Wisconsin Trails, 1997.

Reiersgord, Thomas E. *The Kensington Rune Stone: Its Place in History*. St. Paul: Pogo Press, 2001.

Ringsak, Russell, and Denise Remicks. *Minnesota Curiosities*. Guilford, Conn.: Globe Pequot Press, 2002.

Rubin, Saul. *Offbeat Museums: The Collections and Curators of America's Most Unusual Museums*. Santa Monica, Calif.: Santa Monica Press, 1997.

Rustad, Mark, Curtis Johnson, and Mark Utter. *Brainerd Bound: Landmarks to the Lakes*. Minneapolis: Landmark Publishing Inc., 2004.

St. Clair, Jeffrey. "Usonian Utopias: Frank Lloyd Wright, Working Class Housing, and the FBI." *CounterPunch*, 13 August 2002.

Sayre, Robert F. *Take This Exit: Rediscovering the Iowa Landscape*. Ames: Iowa State University Press, 1989.

Shepard, John. *Minnesota off the Beaten Path*. Chester, Conn.: Globe Pequot Press, 1989.

Stein, Gordon, and Marie MacNee. *Hoaxes: Dupes, Dodges, and Other Dastardly Deceptions*. Detroit: Visible Ink, 1995.

Stelling, Lucille Johnsen. *Frommer's Guide to Minneapolis and St. Paul*. New York: Simon and Schuster, 1988.

Wilkins, Mike, Ken Smith, and Doug Kirby. *The New Roadside America*. New York: Simon and Schuster, 1992.

Will, Tracy. *Wisconsin*. Oakland, Calif.: Compass Travel Guides, 1997.

Born in the shadow of the World's Largest Six Pack in La Crosse, Wisconsin, **ERIC DREGNI** is a freelance writer for the *Rake* and the *Minneapolis Star Tribune*. He is the author of several books, including *Minnesota Marvels: Roadside Attractions in the Land of Lakes* (Minnesota, 2001), *The Scooter Bible, Ads That Put America on Wheels,* and *Let's Go Bowling!* He lives in Minneapolis.